ECONOMICS OF DISTANCE AND ONLINE LEARNING: THEORY, PRACTICE, AND RESEARCH

This book provides a comprehensive overview of the organizational models of distance and online learning from an international perspective and from the point of view of economic planning, costing and management decision-making. The book points to directions for further research and development in this area, and will promote further understanding and critical reflection on the part of administrators, practitioners and researchers of distance education and training. The experiences and perspectives in distance education in the United States are balanced with those in other areas of the world.

The strength of this book lies in its all-encompassing coverage of the field of economics of distance education into one complete volume. Topics include:

- The analysis of various applications of distance learning
- The examination of key organizational and economic issues of distance learning
- The use of distance learning in diverse settings
- The effectiveness of varied economic models for calculating costs and financial decision-making within distance learning

Dr William J. Bramble is a Professor in the Department of Educational Leadership and Organizational Learning at the University of New Mexico (UNM) College of Education, Albuquerque, USA.

Dr Santosh Panda is a Professor of Distance Education and Director, Staff Training and Research Institute of Distance Education, Indira Gandhi National Open University (IGNOU), New Delhi, India.

ECONOMICS OF DISTANCE AND ONLINE LEARNING: THEORY, PRACTICE, AND RESEARCH

Edited by

William J. Bramble
University of New Mexico

and

Santosh Panda
Indira Gandhi National Open University

Routledge
Taylor & Francis Group

NEW YORK AND LONDON

First published 2008
by Routledge
270 Madison Ave, New York, NY 10016

Simultaneously published in the UK
by Routledge
2 Park Square, Milton Park, Abingdon, Oxon OX14 4RN

Routledge is an imprint of the Taylor & Francis Group, an informa business

© 2008 Taylor & Francis

Typeset in Minion and Optima by EvS Communication Networx, Inc.
Printed and bound in the United States of America on acid-free paper by Sheridan Books, Inc.

Library of Congress Cataloging in Publication Data

Economics of distance and online learning : theory, practice, and research / William J. Bramble and Santosh Panda, editors. — 1st ed.
p. cm.
Includes index.
ISBN 978-0-415-96388-6 (hardback : alk. paper) — ISBN 978-0-415-96389-3 (pbk. : alk. paper)
1. Distance education—Costs. 2. Computer-assisted instruction—Costs. I. Bramble, William J. II. Panda, Santosh K. (Santosh Kumar), 1959-
LC5800.E28 2008
378.1'758—dc22
2007037876

ISBN 10: 0-415-96388-5 (hbk)
ISBN 10: 0-415-96389-3 (pbk)
ISBN 10: 0-203-89298-4 (ebk)

ISBN 13: 978-0-415-96388-6 (hbk)
ISBN 13: 978-0-415-96389-3 (pbk)
ISBN 13: 978-0-203-89298-5 (ebk)

CONTENTS

CONTRIBUTORS

William J. Bramble (Ed.)
University of New Mexico, USA

Santosh Panda (Ed.)
Indira Gandhi National Open
University, India

Zane Berge
University of Maryland Baltimore
County, USA

Thomas Clark
TA Consulting, Illinois, USA

Chris Curran
Dublin City University, Ireland

Charlotte Donaldson
Booz Allen Hamilton, Inc., USA

Paul J. Edelson
State University of New York –
Stony Brook, USA

Palitha Edirisingha
University of Leicester, UK

Ashok Gaba
Indira Gandhi National Open
University, India

D. Randy Garrison
University of Calgary, Canada

Thomas Hülsmann
University of Oldenburg, Germany

Alistair Inglis
Victoria University (Sunbury
Campus), Australia

Insung Jung
International Christian University,
Japan

Heather Kanuka
Athabasca University, Canada

Diana G. Oblinger
EDUCAUSE, USA

Von V. Pittman
University of Missouri, USA

Ormond Simpson
Open University, UK

Mark J. Smith
University of New Mexico, USA

Jade Nguyen Strattner
IBM, USA

PREFACE

This text includes a collection of articles contributed by internationally known leaders, researchers, and practitioners of distance learning, online learning, and technology-enabled education and training. The book provides, for the first time, a comprehensive overview of the developments in the organizational models and the changing nature of distance and online learning, both from international perspectives and from the point of view of economic planning, costing, and management decision making. It discusses economic factors and costs of distance and online learning, covering the following areas: Funding policies, sources, and consequences; methodological frameworks and cost structures; models of distance and online learning; cost-effectiveness and quality of educational and training provisions in single-mode and dual-mode higher education institutions; the economics of virtual universities and the business models they propose; cost and quality of online/networked learning; cost-benefit of distance training; cost and economics of the emerging areas of open schooling, virtual schooling, and open basic and non-formal education; and the methodological issues in researching economics and costs of distance and online learning. The book points to directions for further research and development.

The organization and presentation through critical analysis and reflection of educational innovators, leaders, and researchers across the globe provides a convergence among existing economic models and theories, educational models and management imperatives, and organizational and institutional practices. These lead in turn to further reflection, debate, and sound decision-making in strengthening and reforming technology-enabled education in the emerging scenario of competition and globalization. The economic issues confronting management decision making and organization, and delivery of instruction, are examined in the contexts of reduced public funding, increasing student demands for education and training, and the diversified nature of organizational and educational provisions.

The book has considerable utility and significance. There have been increasing pressures on governments of nation states, educational and training organizations, and curricular departments within organizations to diversify, reform, and change their educational methods and learner support systems. The change is observed in a number of ways, including flexibility in meeting diverse client needs and needs of diverse groups of learners; innovativeness in the use of resources and technology; and responsiveness to changing socioeconomic needs and globalization. The technology of distance and online learning is being developed to ensure a smooth and productive technology-wrought change, and to meet diversified client needs and national development imperatives. Educational leaders, training managers, and teachers and trainers are under pressure to diversify their educational and training provisions, and to introduce technology to facilitate change, but at a low cost. This is often done not only to achieve economy of scale, but also to efficiently deploy and utilize resources; and to maintain a surplus, available to expand and implement diverse organizational planning and innovations.

The book brings together the economic, management, and pedagogic imperatives with critical analysis and reflection of the contributing authors, so that a comprehensive view is taken in effective planning and management of higher and further education in general, and distance and e-learning in particular. Authors are from many corners of the globe: Australia, Canada, Germany, Great Britain, India, Ireland, Japan, and the United States. We are deeply indebted to the contributing authors, who have achieved recognition in their field and offer consistently insightful contributions to the book — and without whom this collection of an emerging, complex area of study, and significant area of concern, would not have materialized. We thank them immensely for their patience, as well, with the lengthy schedule for completing the book.

The introductory chapter of the book include an overview of organizational structures for distance and online learning contributed by the book's editors, William Bramble and Santosh Panda. Chapters 2 through 5 include: Changing distance learning and changing organizational issues by Canadians D. Randy Garrison and Heather Kanuka; online learning and the university by Chris Curran of Ireland; virtual schooling and basic education by Thomas Clark of the United States; and distance and online learning in American society by Paul J. Edelson and Von Pittman, also of the United States. Chapters 6 and 7 address funding of distance and online learning in the United States by U.S.-based Mark J. Smith and William Bramble, and from the perspective of a developing country by Santosh Panda and Ashok Gaba from India. Cost structures and models are the focus of chapters 8 through 10 on cost and quality of online learning by Alistair Inglis of Australia, costing virtual university education by Insung

Jung currently in Japan, and cost-benefit of student retention policies and practices by Ormand Simpson of the United Kingdom. Chapters 11 and 12 address distance training, and the cost-benefit of distance training by Zane Berge and Charlotte Donaldson of the United States, and corporate e-learning and embedded training by Jade Nguyen Strattner and Diana Oblinger, also of the United States. The cost and economics of open and basic education is addressed in chapter 13 by Palitha Edirisingha of the UK. Research and development is the focus in chapter 14 on methodological issues in researching economics of distance and online learning by Thomas Hülsmann of Germany. The book closes with a review of the main issues discussed in the book and addresses implications for planning and management, coauthored by the book's editors.

The special contribution of this book is several-fold. First, it addresses both organizational issues and economics of a range of applications of distance and online learning in an international array of settings and from the points of view of authors representing many parts of the globe. Readers are thus able to envision organizational and cost issues from a variety of perspectives and settings. The book presents much of the current thinking about organizational and management issues in distance education. For example: How varied factors such as technology choice, throughput, drop-out rates, and system objectives, among many others, affect costs; how various countries view the imperatives for distance learning approaches; and the implications of presentation alternatives (entirely online, blended, and hybrid courses) relate to costs. The book presents up-to-date information about sophisticated economic models for calculating costs. It distinguishes between costing scenarios in education vs. training in business and government. And, because of the diversity of its authors, it provides critical information about the interpretation of organizational and economic issues in various international settings.

The book was designed during 2003, when Professor Santosh Panda visited the University of New Mexico as a Fullbright Scholar. He was a guest lecturer in Professor Bramble's course on the management of distance education, where we became acquainted and learned of our shared interests in distance education management and cost analysis. From that shared interest, the idea for the book was born. Once designed, we set out to interest some of the world's best thinkers on these topics to contribute to a quality volume of edited works. We were extremely blessed by the cooperation of the contributors and by the quality of their contributions. The completion of the book was a logistical challenge, given the dispersion of the authors around the globe, several unpredicted intervening events in the lives of the co-editors, and the editing and formatting of a large amount of submitted material. In this effort, we were ably and energetically assisted by the invaluable contributions of Mr. Mark Smith, a doctoral student of the Organizational Learning and Instructional Technology program at the University of New Mexico.

The resulting book has significance for the international community. It is intended for several audiences. Its academic character is appropriate for students and instructors of distance education and online learning. However, it also contributes to the knowledge base of distance education management and economics, promoting critical reflection on the part of administrators, practitioners, and researchers of distance education. We warmly recommend it to you and hope you enjoy the content as much as we have.

1

ORGANIZATIONAL AND COST STRUCTURES FOR DISTANCE AND ONLINE LEARNING

William J. Bramble

University of New Mexico

Santosh Panda

Indira Gandhi National Open University

INTRODUCTION

Distance education has today evolved from the earlier (and still continued) practice of *correspondence* education, which is supposed to have been initiated at the University of Wisconsin in the United States, or Pitman's correspondence school in the United Kingdom (Rumble & Latchem, 2004). Distance education has passed through and embraces many applications including open education/open learning, distributed learning, flexible learning, virtual education/online learning, and blended learning.

It has been argued that if universities do not want to face the fate of the dinosaurs, they need to go beyond conventional methods of teaching and learning, and their hierarchical and bureaucratic academic structure, and adapt to alternative educational provisions (Taylor, 2004). Post-secondary institutions—even if they are new to the field of distance education—tend to embrace online education and training, many of them skipping significant grounding in the theory and practice of distance learning. E-learning has made inroads into the traditional bastions of education and training, too; and the new providers aiming at the market niche include virtual universities, for-profit universities, and national and international consortia and alliances, among others (Bates, 2005).

It is important to appreciate how distance education, as understood and practiced today, has evolved and what organizational delivery mechanisms have been adopted to sustain and expand it. It is also important to understand their management and economic implications.

GENERATIONS OF DISTANCE EDUCATION

There have been many significant and worthwhile attempts by scholars to explain the developmental cycles of distance education. While all of them have viewed Distance Education (DE) developments from pedagogic, managerial, technological, and other perspectives, the most widely used classification from the technological point of view is that of Taylor (2001), who identified five global generations of distance education technology:

1. Correspondence model
2. Multimedia model
3. Telelearning model
4. Flexible learning model
5. Intelligent flexible learning model

Taylor has provided a comparative analysis of these models based on flexibility (with regard to time, place, and pace), learning materials, interactive delivery, and institutional variable costs (see Table 1.1).

First Generation: Correspondence Model

This is the earliest form of distance education, which used structured instructional materials based on sound principles of learning and instructional design, postal correspondence, and occasional face-to-face, radio, or telephone contact sessions.

Second Generation: Multimedia Model

The second generation of distance education benefited from developments in communication and information technologies. Though printed materials are still being used, distance teaching institutions the world over adopted media mixes and media integration using audio, video, computer-supported learning, and interactive video, among others. A variety of media, including print and the human teacher, are used based on supplementary, complementary, and integrated approaches.

These two generations of distance education embarked upon and reinforced industrialized processes in education (Peters, 1983). The industrial production principles of specialization, division of labor, line management,

Table 1.1 Flexible Delivery Technologies – A Conceptual Framework

Models of distance education and associated flexible delivery technologies	Characteristics of delivery technologies					
	Flexibility			Highly refined materials	Advanced interactive delivery	Institutional variable costs approaching zero
	Time	Place	Pace			
First Generation – The Correspondence Model						
• Print	Yes	Yes	Yes	Yes	No	No
Second Generation – The Multi-media Model						
• Print	Yes	Yes	Yes	Yes	No	No
• Audiotape	Yes	Yes	Yes	Yes	No	No
• Videotape	Yes	Yes	Yes	Yes	No	No
• Computer-based learning (e.g. CML/CAL)	Yes	Yes	Yes	Yes	Yes	No
• Interactive video (disk and tape)	Yes	Yes	Yes	Yes	Yes	No
Third Generation – The Telelearning Model						
• Audio teleconferencing	No	No	No	No	Yes	No
• Videoconferencing	No	No	No	No	Yes	No
• Audiographic communication	No	No	No	Yes	Yes	No
• Broadcast TV/radio and audio teleconferencing	No	No	No	Yes	Yes	No
Fourth Generation – The Flexible Learning Model						
• Interactive multimedia (IMM)	Yes	Yes	Yes	Yes	Yes	Yes
• Internet-based access to WWW resources	Yes	Yes	Yes	Yes	Yes	Yes
• Computer mediated communication (CMC)	Yes	Yes	Yes	No	Yes	No
Fifth Generation – The Intelligent Flexible Learning Model						
• Interactive multimedia	Yes	Yes	Yes	Yes	Yes	Yes
• Internet-based access to WWW resources	Yes	Yes	Yes	Yes	Yes	Yes

(continued)

Table 1.1 Continued

Models of distance education and associated flexible delivery technologies	Characteristics of delivery technologies					
	Flexibility			Highly refined materials	Advanced interactive delivery	Institutional variable costs approaching zero
	Time	Place	Pace			
• CMC, using automated response systems	Yes	Yes	Yes	Yes	Yes	Yes
• Campus portal access to institutional processes and resources	Yes	Yes	Yes	Yes	Yes	Yes

Source: Taylor (2005)

mechanization, packaging and delivery, and, to a considerable extent, "quality control," were applied to the contexts of distance education. A host of people including writers, editors, designers, graphic specialists, audio and video producers, tutor-counselors, evaluators, and coordinators/managers were involved in what is called "team distance teaching." The first two generations of distance education have been criticized as perpetuating Fordism (based on the mass production methods by which the Ford car is produced) and instructional industrialism, due to mass production and delivery and their largely linear approaches. Critics adhering to postmodernism and constructivism also argue that such DE restricts openness, emancipatory learning, and education for transformation.

Third Generation: Telelearning Model

The telelearning model introduced conferencing—audio, video, and computer—to facilitate human contact and human interaction, both synchronous and asynchronous. Group and collaborative learning at a distance was possible. All these methods enriched educational discourse, and dispelled the notion of distance education as extant (Annand, 2006).

Fourth Generation: Flexible Learning Model

With continuing technological developments—especially the World Wide Web, Computer Mediated Conferencing (CMC), online synchronous communication, and access to unlimited resources—interactive multimedia and other technology applications were possible within distance education. New pedagogic and delivery models were tested and applied; and the faculty was put at the forefront of the innovation, lest technology drive humans. Further, digitally-mediated asynchronous interaction was found pedagogically more enriching and effective. An important development has been the emergence of virtual universities across the globe.

Fifth Generation: Intelligent Flexible Learning Model

Besides the features of the fourth generation technology-enabled distance education, the fifth generation introduced automated and dynamic student access and response/advice systems through "multiple types of media outputs from a single source document" (Annand, 2006). This not only provided enhanced flexibility and freedom to the learners but also reduced cost considerably.

MODELS OF DELIVERY

In addition to defining the generations of distance education, there have been numerous interpretations of the ways distance education is delivered. This, of course, depends on the institutional vision and mission; the philosophical/ideological stance on the nature of client groups and the curricular provisions; the state of technological preparedness, geographical coverage, and the institutional strategic niche, among other factors. In a recent work, Otto Peters (2003) describes eight models which are briefly outlined as follows.

Examination Preparation Model

Citing examples of the University of London, U.K., and the Regents of the University of New York, Peters traces the initial development of educational delivery at a distance through the external examination model. It provided open access to education based on the liberal ideas of the contemporary times (i.e., equality of educational opportunity); the curriculum was very flexible; it allowed greater learner pacing; and it represented a traditional version of today's distributed learning.

Correspondence Education Model

As underlined above, the correspondence model supports learners through printed teaching texts, assignments, postal correspondence, and examination. Examples of this method include University of South Africa, Toussiant-Langenscheid in Germany, and Ecole Universelle in France, among others. Open access was provided, even if it raised significant economic considerations for the institution; interaction was ensured through built-in self assessment tests in the learning materials and tutor feedback on assignments. As noted earlier, this model initiated the process of an industrialized system of education.

Group Distance Education Model

This model includes group learning at a distance, where groups of students receive course content through radio and television, and undertake pre- and post-telecast group activities. The Central Radio and Television

University (CRTVU) of China, as well as China's provincial radio and television universities, the University of the Air of Japan, and others use this model. Since the telecasts are open, they are also available to individual citizens. However, the most significant limitation is that individualized instruction and special needs of individual learners take a back seat to the emphasis on *massification.*

Learner-Centered Model

This model, sometimes referred to as "contract learning," is quite flexible in order to meet individual learning needs. It makes learning self-directed and promotes continuing education. As an off-campus learning activity, the learner registers with the institution and negotiates with an assigned tutor for interaction and instruction. Learning packages include prescribed literature, online courses, and assistance at learning resource centers, among others. Empire State College (ESC; http://www.esc.edu) of the State University of New York (SUNY) is one of the best examples of this model. This program operates in a highly sophisticated network of institutions, campuses, and resource centers.

Multiple Mass Media Model

The advent of the open university system has combined traditional correspondence education with independent study through the use of a variety of mass media, such as radio, television, and other related audio and video forms. The United Kingdom Open University (UKOU; http://www.open.ac.uk/) has led the movement. It has been followed by more than 45 open universities around the globe. *Open learning* has been the basic premise of the learning organization. Flexibility is introduced through multiple media and multiple modular system credit accumulation. The open university model includes specialist teams working together to assist the individual learner.

Network-Based Distance Education Model

With advances in digital technology, there has been considerable digitization of learning environments. In this model, students basically study at a distance through self-learning multimedia CDs, digital resource repositories, online resources and databases, virtual seminars, online chats, and online collaboration. Learning is largely self-directed and individualized. There are multiple learning pathways since the students engage in a variety of means to retrieve, assimilate, reflect on and create information and knowledge. The Fern Universitat of Germany (http://www.fernuni-hagen.de/), ESC of SUNY and University of Maryland University College in the United States, UKOU in the U.K., and others have been developing this model of flexible pedagogical structure for quite some time now.

Technologically Extended Classroom Teaching Model

This is another form of distributed learning where studio classes are distributed across multiple campuses and multiple institutions without disturbing the quality of interaction, dialogue, and—therefore—of learning. Videoconferencing and teleconferencing are used to distribute instruction and to facilitate interaction. The University of Maryland University College (http://www.umuc.edu) has been extensively using this, though many other U. S. universities using this model point to its limited scalability as a challenge. Many multinational private companies are using this model of distance education, though this has recently been extended to include virtual training.

Virtual University Model

This is the latest form of digital technology-enabled distance learning where all aspects of the study—managerial, logistic, pedagogic, organizational, and others—take place virtually with the help of multimedia, Internet, conferencing, or by using the latest versions of the mobile phone technology. Activities undertaken for students include teaching, research, "top news," shop, cafeteria, office, library, and information. Peters notes that, "So far, there is not yet a real virtual distance teaching university. The term 'virtual university' is quite often used when a single course or part of a teaching program is presented via the Internet by campus-based universities for experimental reasons or as part of the regular teaching" (Peters, 2003, p. 25).

MANAGEMENT AND COST CONSIDERATIONS

As will be discussed in this volume, there is a variety of management and cost considerations when assessing the economics and economic viability of distance and online learning systems. Moore and Kearsley (1996), in discussing cost-effectiveness, remind us that "the research questions of primary interest to educational administrators are about how to organize resources of people and capital in ways that will produce good results at the lowest costs" (p. 71). This statement raises a set of corollary questions: What are the resources that are to be managed? Do these vary by system and context? How are the costs of the resources and their particular application determined? Is *cost-effectiveness* the only relevant cost measure? What are "good results," and how are these results measured? And finally, what level of costs can be managed by a given system?

In his now classic text, Rumble (1997) discusses a host of topics related to cost analysis. These include cost issues in the design of courses, the costs of media and materials, the costs of student support, comparison of the costs of distance and traditional education, and issues related to the financing of distance education. These themes are echoed by the contributors to this text. Cost levels for course design take on special significance in online courses, where the traditional emphasis on the costs of instructors is exceeded by the costs of course development. Demands for greater levels of interactivity can contribute to cost increases associated with both the supporting technology and further demands on an instructor's time. Student support and approaches to student retention carry their own demands for resources.

The following list describes several factors that can influence costs in distance and online learning systems.

International Aspects

Countries vary in the robustness of their economies, their ability to pay for new learning systems, the availability and costs of technical and human resources, the maturity of their educational systems, the educational models that are followed, the locus of control for education, the perceived relationship of education to economic development, and the geographic densities of their populations, etc. All of these factors contribute to the specifics of design for new learning systems and their resultant costs.

System Design

Various designs can be employed for distance and online educational systems. One program might serve tens of thousands of students, relying heavily on print, video transmissions, and staff at local support centers, as in the case of Indira Gandhi National Open University (IGNOU). A program at a U.S. university might serve several hundred students in one or more specialized areas and require high-bandwidth internet connectivity and sophisticated computers for each student. The distributions of capital and operating costs, and the opportunities for economies of scale will differ for the two systems. Systems also differ in the volume of students they serve, the instructional design employed, the process for developing and delivering the instruction, the degree of interactivity offered to students, support services offered to students, and the role of faculty in the instructional process. These factors influence the pattern of costs for a given system.

Organizational Type

Distance learning and online education systems have various homes. Some systems are located within traditional systems of education. This is common in the United States, wherein there is a large, well-established base of K–12 schools and two- and four-year institutions of higher learning. Distance and online learning systems are often overlaid on the existing educational institutions, creating dual-mode systems. In such cases, the newer system is usually seen as an overlay to the institution's budget as well, rather than as a unique and separate entity. The implications for funding and costing are many.

A second type of institution is the *single-mode* provider. In this case the learning institution is established specifically for the purpose of providing distance education programs. The institution serves as its own cost center and is not subsumed under the auspices of a larger system. With single-mode providers, management systems must be established from scratch. The same distinction, single- vs. dual-mode, applies in a general way to the case of business and government *workforce* training. Some training is offered through a training program under the umbrella of a corporation or government agency (in dual mode), whereas some business-related training is offered through separate corporations that serve the training needs of other corporations or government entities. These corporations operate more like single-mode institutions. An interesting wrinkle in corporate training is that training can be conducted, as needed, as a part of the work process, as *embedded training*, or at a separate off-site time and location. Collaborative efforts across organizations bring their own unique considerations to the table.

Curriculum Focus

Systems vary in terms of the curriculum areas they address and the clients they serve. A system may address the needs of K–12 education with its unique funding and accounting processes. A system might alternatively address the various programmatic areas of post secondary education: Liberal arts, engineering, sciences, education, health sciences, vocational training, etc. Each of these areas brings special concerns to the table when considering their costs. Client groups can vary from elementary and secondary school courses for home-schooled children to professional development for engineers and medical doctors—each group with its own special concerns and cost factors.

APPROACHES TO STUDYING COSTS

Researchers have used a variety of tools and approaches for studying the economics of distance and online learning systems (see Kearsley, 1982; Bramble & Rao, 1998; Rumble, 2003). Many of these are illustrated in the contributions to this book. Some examples follow.

Cost Categories

It is useful to separate costs into categories when studying instructional systems. In so doing, the researcher can get a more detailed and often more useful picture of costs. Some ways of categorizing costs are as follows.

Capital and Recurrent Costs Capital costs include such expenses as those associated with purchasing basic hardware and software needed to build a system. We often think of these costs as part of the cost of start-up, although capital items will have to be replaced according to a schedule of depreciation. Recurrent costs are those experienced with the ongoing nature of the operation. These include such items as salaries for personnel, communications costs, materials needed for course development, and so forth.

Production and Delivery Costs We can also separate system costs into the elements having to do with production and those having to do with delivery. This allows the researcher to differentiate costs according to the functions they serve.

Fixed vs. Variable Costs It is useful to separate the costs of learning systems into their fixed and variable cost components. Fixed costs are such things as capital costs and content development, while variable costs are materials and services that vary according to the number of students served.

Types of Cost Analysis

Cost Benefit Analysis This is a method to determine the *feasibility* of a system or the services it offers by weighing the expected costs against the expected benefits (see Whalen & Wright, 1999). If a researcher has some basic information about cost, he or she may be able to determine the likely cost of a system or new feature of a system. The researcher also has to have a systematic way to estimate expected benefits. In this way, a system developer can determine ahead of time the likely viability of a new system based on its likely cost.

Cost Efficiency This type of analysis relates cost inputs and outputs. Wagner (1972) notes that inputs are associated with the costs of providing learning, and outputs are the number of students taught or graduates. An efficient system is one that maximizes the number of students served at the lowest cost.

Cost Effectiveness Cost effectiveness takes this notion a bit further. In this type of study we are interested not only in the efficiency of a system but in its success or effectiveness. A cost effective system is one that minimizes cost and maximizes effectiveness of outcomes. Cost effectiveness fits well in the business environment, where one can measure the level of production of goods or revenues generated from their sales. It works less well in educational settings where the ultimate benefits of a learning system are way down the line—career success, lifetime earning capacity, a more lawful society, and so forth.

Cost Comparisons   Finding cost effectiveness studies difficult due to the difficulty of establishing good effectiveness measures. Many studies of costs for educational applications of distance and online learning address the topic of cost comparisons. The questions addressed here are: Given alternative possible approaches for delivery of instruction, which is advantageous in terms of cost? Or given two competing systems to provide a given set of training or education, which is least costly?

Return on Investment   Another approach to studying costs is Return on Investment (ROI; see Osiakwan & Wright, 2001). This approach originated in the business world where it can be applied very directly. ROI attempts to determine the value of a learning approach by considering the ratio of benefits to costs. As in cost effectiveness studies, the researcher needs to be able to quantify benefits and this is difficult in education. There are methods that researchers have used to try to quantify effectiveness for educational systems; gap analysis or having students set goals for themselves and then determining how well these goals are met.

CONCLUSION

As the reader can see, there are many factors influencing the costs of learning systems and alternative ways to study these costs. The contributors to this volume offer insights into these phenomena in the chapters that follow. The authors write from a variety of perspectives, contexts, and types of expertise. As a set, these chapters offer a level of insight into the economics of distance and online education that is new and unique in the field. It is well worth the time taken by the reader to study their contributions.

REFERENCES

Annand, D. (2006). Changing the academy. *Staff and Educational Development International, 10*(1), 1–18.

Bates, A. W. (2005). *Technology, e-learning and distance education*. London/New York: RoutledgeFalmer.

Bramble, W. J., & Rao, L. (1998). A model for cost analysis of a distance education programme. In D. Shomaker (Ed.), *Distance learning in professional education* (pp. 113–132). Salisbury, UK: Quay Books.

Kearsley, G. (1982). *Costs, benefits, and productivity in training systems*. Reading, MA: Addison-Wesley.

Moore, M. G., & Kearsley, G. (1996). *Distance education: A systems view*. Belmont CA: Wadsworth.

Osiakwan, C., & Wright, D. (2001). Distance training for operating equipment: A cost-benefit and return-on-investment analysis. *The American Journal of Distance Education, 15*(1), 69–79.

Peters, O. (1983). Distance teaching and industrial production: A comparative interpretation in outline. In D. Sewart, D. Keegan, & B. Holmberg (Eds.), *Distance education: International perspectives* (pp. 95–113). New York: Routledge.

Peters, O. (2003). Models of open and flexible learning in distance education. In S. Panda (Ed.), *Planning and management in distance education* (pp. 15–27). London/New York: RoutledgeFalmer.

Rumble, G. (1997). *The costs and economics of open and distance learning.* London/New York: RoutledgeFalmer.

Rumble, G. (2003). Modeling the costs and economics of distance education. In M. G. Moore, & W. G. Anderson (Eds.), *Handbook of distance education* (pp. 703–716). Mahwah, NJ: Erlbaum.

Rumble, G., & Latchem, C. (2004). Organisational models for open and distance learning. In H. Perraton & H. Lentell (Eds.), *Policy for open and distance learning* (pp. 117–140). London/New York: RoutledgeFalmer.

Taylor, J. C. (2001, April). Fifth generations distance education. Keynote address at the ICDE 20th World Conference, Dusseldorf, Germany.

Taylor, J.C. (2004, February). *Will universities become extinct in the networked world?* Plenary panel introduction at the ICDE 21st World Conference on Open Learning and Distance Education, Hong Kong.

Wagner, L. (1972). The Economics of the Open University. *Higher Education, 1,* 159–183.

Whalen, T., & Wright, D. (1999). Methodology for cost-benefit analysis of Web-based telelearning: Case study of the Bell Online Institute. *The American Journal of Distance Education, 13*(1), 23–44.

2

CHANGING DISTANCE EDUCATION AND CHANGING ORGANIZATIONAL ISSUES

D. Randy Garrison

University of Calgary, Canada

Heather Kanuka

Athabasca University, Canada

INTRODUCTION

Both on- and off-campus institutions of higher education around the world have been on the front end of being profoundly impacted by communication and Internet technologies during the 1990s and into the new millennium. Internet technologies, for example, have already greatly influenced administrative and research activities, with the greatest organizational change to occur with the design and delivery of teaching and learning. While the full impact is yet to be experienced, traditional open and distance education institutions are using online learning to provide opportunities for sustained interaction at the same time as traditional campus-based institutions are providing greater independence and access through online learning activities.

Currently, there are few exemplary models of both traditional on- and off-campus institutions that have successfully confronted and embraced creative and innovative models of online approaches. Rather, most institutions continue to experience barriers to planning and managing the integration of communication and Internet technologies. Yet, almost all higher education institutions are challenged with some, or all, of the following pressures: Increasing demands by mature students for more accessible learning opportunities; decreasing funding and resources; and the need to maintain or increase the quality of learning experiences to recruit and retain the best and brightest students.

The purpose of this chapter is to explore the influence of online learning approaches and the concomitant redesign of educational experiences. It will be shown that the integration of online learning marks the convergence of distance and campus-based educational organizations. These changes will inevitably have a profound influence on the organization of both traditional distance and campus-based institutions. Organizational changes and leadership challenges will also be discussed.

TWO DIVERGENT MODELS

It is important to identify the essential differences that have historically distinguished the practices and processes of distance and campus-based education. Early distance education models were driven by issues of access made possible by scalability and technology. Indeed, distance education had its genesis in correspondence study, which was based on mail and transportation technologies of the time. Distance education has always been reliant on technology. While correspondence education extends back over 150 years, correspondence institutions began to proliferate in the late 1800s. However, it was not until the early 1970s, with the introduction of the British Open University, that correspondence education evolved into what we know today as distance education. With the advent of the Open University model came legitimacy and recognition.

In the late 1960s and early 1970s, distance education became a focus of study—emerging first in the United Kingdom, followed shortly thereafter in North America and elsewhere. During this time, Otto Peters compared distance education to an industrialized production process (Keegan, 1994). This analogy was apparent with the highly systematized approach of the open universities to achieve economies of scale through the production of prepackaged, independent self-study course materials accessible to the masses. Teaching, in essence, was done by the institution through the mass produced course package. The design of the course package was to increase access to education by enhancing the independence of the learner and reducing the need for face-to-face communication. The result, however, was the "objectivization" of the teaching process (Peters in Keegan, 1994, p. 111).

On the other hand, the traditional campus-based educational approach has as its ideal a face-to-face collaborative community of learners. More specifically, the emphasis is on interaction and the socio-linguistic construction of knowledge through reflection, discourse, and collaboration. The underpinning assumption in the traditional campus-based model is that sustained face-to-face communication is necessary for higher levels of learning—the *sine qua non* of a university education. Here the educational process is seen as an opportunity to actively engage in verbal discourse to explore, confront, and integrate information for the purpose of achieving understanding and constructing new knowledge. A core element is the direct interaction with teachers and collaboration with fellow students. However, for some time now teaching in postsecondary settings has, unfortunately, become equated with lecturing and learning with note taking—as can be witnessed in the typical large undergraduate university course.

Nearing the end of the 20th century, traditional distance and campus-based educational models and approaches were on opposite ends of an independence-interaction spectrum. There seemed to be a clear divide as to their goals and what constitutes a quality learning experience. Distance educators argued that a well-designed course package could anticipate and address the educational needs of the learner. The condition, however, was narrowly-defined objectives and the acquisition of specific, well-defined concepts. This model did not address the unexpected and changing needs of the learner, particularly with ill-defined subject matter. In the conventional distance education model (e.g., self-paced and independent study), there is little opportunity to explore possible (mis)understandings or changing needs and interests. On the other hand, traditional campus-based approaches are also being challenged as to whether they are providing opportunities for interaction and discourse they so strongly profess to value. Fiscal constraints and an increasing focus on flexible access also raise serious questions as to the quality of the educational process. Lewis (2002) observes these growing issues from a UK perspective:

> Easier access to learning is also being demanded (somewhat ironically) by students who are supposedly learning full-time, on campus. Given increasing financial pressures resulting from the cessation of maintenance grants and the imposition of tuition fees, conventional full-time younger students are behaving increasingly like part-time distance learners, funding their way through university to pay fees and living expenses. Traditionally, part-time employment was a part of vacation life; now it is eating into term-time. Hence students sometimes cannot attend lectures because they are working in supermarkets, pubs, or other places of casual employment. Other ways than physical attendance at classes, and tutorials, thus have to be found to sustain the learning of such students. (pp. 5–6)

Case studies published by the Open Learning Foundation provide further evidence of these issues and the ensuing need for institutions of higher education to confront the changing landscape of higher education. Within the UK, the results have forced tertiary providers to develop innovative models that have resulted in erosion of the distinction between "distance" and "face-to-face"—though, as Lewis (2002, p. 1) notes, "barriers still remain to a more radical approach to provisions as a whole."

Alternatively, in China the use of web-based technologies in both dual-mode conventional and single-mode universities has been enthusiastically embraced (Zhang, Niu, & Jiang, 2002). Indeed, the use of Internet information and communication technologies has provided wider access to higher education, increased the sharing of quality resources between staff and students, and inspired new ways of teaching and learning. Yet, here too, China is experiencing barriers. These barriers include student access to computers and associated costs to the provision of Internet access; a shortage of online instructional resources, effective management and support centers, and teacher training; and reaching out to remote and economically disadvantaged areas.

Within Europe, many higher education institutions have effectively managed the use of new information and communication technologies, and ensuing organizational issues. In Germany, for example, and as in the UK, Internet technologies are forming a new type of university that is replacing both established on-campus and off-campus facilities:

> Complementary or supporting or supplementary environments refer to face-to-face instruction enriched by online technologies, a trend that is emerging both in open universities and in campus-based universities... In other words, both types of university are acquiring online components, digitalizing individual course offering, adding additional features and resources via the online mode, to existing course offering. Meanwhile, distance education programs at campus-based universities are following the same line of action. (Kappel, Lehmann, & Loeper, 2002, p. 16)

Though, even in this example, it is noted by the authors that while resistance to e-learning has not been expressed by German university faculty, concerns have been expressed that online instruction is monopolizing resources. The authors also note that a potential problem for existing distance education units in Germany is whether or not they will be able to legitimize their right to existence if traditional on-campus facilities can operate successful off-campus learning activities.

An overview of international perspectives on the changes occurring in current distance education practices, in both traditional distance and on-campus delivery, reveals there is considerable investment in convergent models of distance and campus-based institutions and—as might be expected—with varying degrees of success (Grepperud, Støkken, & Toska, 2002; Guri-Rosenblit, 2002; Kappel, Lehmann, & Loeper, 2002; Lewis, 2002; Shale, 2002; Zhang, Niu, & Jiang, 2002).

While all institutions experience problems and barriers, resistance to change, it appears, is particularly stalwart in North America—though resistance has also been witnessed in Germany, Spain, and Israel—where academic freedom is highly valued and different teaching practices and/or operating controls have been viewed as an infringement on academic freedom (Guri-Rosenblit, 2002).

CONVERGENCE AND THE RESISTENCE TO CHANGE

While developments in communication and Internet technologies have been a catalyst for exploration in both distance and campus-based institutions, invariably they have been on the margin and consisted largely of adding onto existing practices. Thus far technology use has, more often than not, resulted in yet another layer of costs with minimal gains in the quality of the learning experience. In Norway, for example, "one of the most prominent features of ICT development… is that it is accompanied by rhetoric that typically promises much more than it can deliver" (Grepperud, Støkken, & Toska, 2002, p. 5). Moreover, one of the most basic resistors to teaching online in Norway has been the competition over time between teaching and research. Research is what gains the faculty member promotion and the institution status—which is, of course, not unique to Norway.

While acknowledging the barriers and resistance to change, it is becoming increasingly evident to both distance and campus-based institutions that they must address quality of education concerns. While concerns about the quality of higher education are not new, the effects of globalization are forcing national universities to recognize that they are increasingly under threat of having their student market eroded (Mason, 2003). A report commissioned by the UK government (CVCP, 2000, p. 87) states:

> Innovative, non-traditional providers stress their commitment to the adult learner, point to pedagogically sound and professional relevant curricula and exemplary student services. The charge is made that much traditional higher education largely falls on these counts.

Likewise, an Australian study concluded the following (Cunningham et al., 1998, p. xv):

> There is a widespread perception that traditional institutions are not meeting the needs of the lifelong learning cohort and that the field is open for new providers to meet market demands. One obvious, and problematic, outcome of this segmentation is that traditional institutions may be left serving the less profitable traditional undergraduate market (18–24), which is largely government-funded or family-funded, in a time when governments are increasingly endeavouring to cut public outlays.

These reports reveal the need for national universities to be flexible, adapt-able, and portable in their course and program offerings (Mason, 2003). In Brazil, for example, while the public sector has been unable to meet these increasing demands, the private sector has begun to invest heavily using distance education to address the problem (Litto, 2002).

Distance education institutions are also under threat. While providers of distance education have traditionally offered flexible, adaptable, and portable courses and programs, they have done so at the expense of inter-active/collaborative/cooperative learning environments. As such, distance educators are finding themselves in competition with "a new wave of com-petitors using forms of quasi distance education" (Evans & Nation, 2003, p. 777)—who also have the capacity to provide their students with interac-tion and communication.

At the heart of a quality learning experience is interaction and com-munication; it has been shown that interaction is a predictor of perceived learning and satisfaction (Swan, 2001; Rovai, 2002). Moreover, the widely adopted and accepted communication and Internet technologies gener-ally are raising questions as to why there is not greater interaction and discourse. That is, it is unclear as to why students either study in isolation in their homes or lecture halls when other options, such as the thoughtful blend of online activities and face-to-face encounters are available. There is no longer an issue of having to choose between access (independence) and quality (interaction). It is now possible for students to learn collaboratively any time, any where. The online communication and conferencing capa-bilities of computer mediated technologies are providing opportunities to revolutionize higher education.

This blending of on- and off-campus modes of learning is transforming both traditional distance and campus-based education. We are beginning to see distance education approaches shift from organizational to transac-tional approaches (Garrison, 2000). Traditional campus-based institutions are also recognizing the need and opportunity to shift to more transac-tional approaches (Garrison & Kanuka, 2004). In distance education there is talk of the "post-industrial era," while in conventional campus-based institutions it is more "back to the future" in trying to recapture the sense of community and engagement in exploring and creating ideas that have been lost with the increased dominance of the lecture. Both are rethinking and rediscovering what the possibilities are in terms of a flexible, multi-dimensional/mediated, and fully engaged teaching and learning transac-tion. There is a convergence toward more differentiated communities of learners who are not constrained by ideological and rigid designs.

Shale (2002) argues that the interactive potential of communications and Internet technologies reveal a "growing convergence between conven-tional and distance learning modes, leading to the hybridization of higher education…" (Introduction). This hybridization has perhaps been led by the dual mode institutions, such as Deakin in Australia, where half of their students study at a distance with mixtures of on-campus and off-campus learners (Calvert, 2001). Another organizational example capitalizing on a hybrid approach and filling this middle ground are private institutions, such as the University of Phoenix (US) and Royal Roads University (Canada). Traditional dedicated distance and open learning institutions, such as Athabasca University (AU) in Canada, are also recognizing that education is more than information transfer and are moving to integrate online learning. In this regard, Davis (2001) identifies issues of quality and the adoption of new communication technologies for a recent change in culture at AU and a movement to collaborative online learning. If this convergence continues, it is going to become much more difficult to distinguish distance and campus-based institutions based upon pedagogical approaches and designs. In the near future, distinctions may well only exist in terms of programs and target audiences.

NEW MODELS—BLENDED LEARNING

The convergence of traditional distance and campus-based institutions is based upon the blending of online and face-to-face learning experiences. The potential of blending online and face-to-face designs is causing traditional higher education institutions to confront their established and time-honored paradigms—and to re-examine what a quality learning experience could be—indeed, *needs* to be, in a knowledge society. The undemanding task of information assimilation, whether it be through independent study packages or passively listening to a lecture, falls short of providing students with the skills to effectively function in a knowledge society, where the ability to think critically and creatively are essential.

The essence and appeal of blended learning is its simplicity of taking the best from both online and face-to-face instructional designs. It recognizes that Internet and communication technologies have removed the traditional barriers of time and space. There is no longer a need to choose between independence and interaction. Blended learning offers an open system that provides opportunities for educators to reflect on meaningful learning experiences—without artificially limiting one's options in the design of a constructive, engaged educational experience.

The practical reality, however, of the elegant simplicity of blended learning is the complexity of selecting and thoughtfully integrating appropriate methods and techniques. Most importantly, it is not simply layering technology on existing and often deficient practices. It is a fundamental rethinking of the educational possibilities, purpose, and goals. Notwithstanding the challenges of understanding the possibilities, the potential is there for an instructor to design a course that can uniquely meet the needs of specific learners as well as the demands of the content and goals of a particular course. In the end, it represents an opportunity to examine our educational values and come closer to realizing our educational ideals.

In higher education, the educational ideal is that of a community of learners fully engaged in critical inquiry for the purposes of constructing and confirming knowledge. For both distance and campus-based institutions, blended learning offers the possibility to create communities of inquiry, whether the dominant mode is face-to-face or online. Communication and Internet technology can support asynchronous and synchronous written and verbal communication, wherein spontaneous and reflective properties are differently matched to specific educational activities. Communities of inquiry are of growing importance as information proliferates and technology creates the conditions to socially isolate.

The arguments for blended learning and its potential to transform go beyond the strong theoretical analysis. There is growing evidence that under certain circumstances, blended learning can provide effectiveness and efficiency gains (Dziuban et al., 2004; Heterick & Twigg, 2003; Owston, Garrison, & Cook, in press). Compared to the traditional large lecture-based classroom model, the results of blended learning have revealed an increase in achievement on objective tests, higher completion and retention rates, and improved student satisfaction—in addition to offering learners a more flexible, efficient, and varied learning experience. This is largely due to an ability to appropriately match interactive learning experiences with specific learning outcomes (Garrison & Cleveland-Innes, 2004). There is good reason to believe that these findings can be transferred to distance delivered courses.

Blended learning goes well beyond its impact on a course or program. Blended learning is a disruptive technology in that it has the potential to overcome the resistance to change of any large educational institution. It will overcome this resistance by virtue of its proven methodology and congruence with the values and ideals of higher education. While blended learning is inevitable if survival is the choice, this will not happen without visionary and courageous leadership.

MANAGEMENT ISSUES

Most senior academic officers of distance and campus-based education institutions are aware of the forces for change due to reduced funding, increasing quality expectations, and technological development in society generally. Notwithstanding current developments, it is uncertain whether senior academic leaders are prepared to re-examine and position their institutions for new and emerging models and methodologies such as blended learning. There is a serious question as to whether there is the willingness and sufficient commitment to strategically confront the organizational challenges, policies, and practices.

If educational institutions are going to thrive, it is imperative that there is strong and creative leadership that recognizes the possibilities of fusing independent and interactive learning, as well as the blending of online learning and face-to-face experiences. This demands a new kind of leadership that supports systemic change—which most educational institutions have not yet experienced. It is a form of creative leadership prepared to critically examine current practices, envision new possibilities, and havethe courage and commitment to engage in fundamental and sustained change. Unfortunately, to date, many senior leaders have chosen to spread existing resources thinner and thinner, rather than invest in fundamental change that will bring both efficiency and effectiveness. Many current leaders are not able to see beyond what already exists.

Successful leadership of complex organizations in times of change requires more than a charismatic leader and fundraiser. At the core of this leadership is a visionary and a team leader who has a deep knowledge and appreciation of the educational process, is fully engaged in the process of transformation from beginning to end, and prepared to be held accountable. It is essential that leaders provide clear direction and lead from the front. Higher education is an international enterprise, and once it is recognized that the nature and characteristics of successful leadership in a communication and Internet age has changed, educational institutions will find themselves in a very competitive market for leadership at all levels of the organization.

It is generally recognized that online learning is crucial to a long-term strategy. What is less certain is what it might look like and how to plan for this future. Most institutions are far from drafting a comprehensive policy and plan that will position them for the future. From an institutional perspective, it is important to have a policy framework that will lay out the vision, goals, and rationale that describe in general terms what needs to be done, and why. The creation and adoption of such a document provides an opportunity to raise awareness and gain support. It is important to take the next step of drafting an action plan if this is to be more than an inert document. An action plan must have the clear support of the senior leadership. It is not sufficient for senior leadership to simply proclaim that it shall be done and walk away from it. There must be a strategic selection of projects with accompanying resources, support, and recognition. The plan must also reflect a long-term commitment, such that activities can ramp-up in a reasonable manner, and where lessons can be learned and adjustments made.

The greatest challenge for senior administrators will be coping with inherent resistance to change. As described earlier, resistance can manifest in a variety of ways, but the most common will be to demand unrealistic resources. The University of Central Florida (US) has shown that it is possible to transform an institution with modest investment when "initiated and supported at the highest administrative levels" (Dziuban et al., 2004, p. 143). Online learning at the University of Central Florida accounts for over 46,000 enrolments. This represents a 32% increase since 2001–02, and growth projections are strong. A similar example of a top-down strategy, which has been very successful at facilitating and sustaining effective use of information and communication technologies in the learning process, is in Israel. In an effort to avoid random and sporadic technology integration by a handful of enthusiastic individuals, Israel created a macro-level systemic change that resulted in a serious shift of existing learning infrastructures and overhauling the institutional commitment to new technology uses. To achieve this, Israel:

> ...took into consideration the long-standing reluctance of academics to external intervention, and their sensitivity in relation to their individual academic freedom. In such a way, bottom-up elements were triggered by a top-down initiative, enabling individual enterprise under a central sponsorship. (Guri-Rosenblit, 2002, p. 13)

In the case of Israel, senior administrators who understand and value the academic culture and are sensitive to academic freedom can, in turn, also trigger a bottom-up response that results in a top-down and bottom-up action to technology use. Failure to appreciate and integrate the academic culture (such as academic ethos, organizational infrastructures, and unique needs and characteristics of relevant constituencies) will likely result in a top-down model to a "passive teaching community, initiating changes only in response from orders from above"—as is the case in Brazil (Litto, 2002, p. 4). Thus, while a top-down approach is essential to effecting successful technology use, it must be conducted in such a way that will also generate a bottom-up movement.

We can see from these examples that online and blended approaches represent a major challenge for faculty and students, as well as for administrators. If these new approaches and models are to be more effective and efficient, then faculty and students must be afforded sustained support. This clearly is an important resource implication for the institution and can become a major challenge, even when systematic change has been effected. As in the case of Israel, for example, cost issues associated with online learning continue to be a major hindrance to large scale implementation (Guri-Rosenblit, 2002). Yet, while cost issues are complicated and unique for each institution, an essential first step begins by collaboratively exploring redesign possibilities and providing technical support. It is naïve to think that faculty members have the time to master the technological tools at the same time they are coping with significant shifts in approaches to teaching and learning. Until there is a critical mass of prototypes and experienced faculty who can mentor their colleagues, there will need to be considerable investment in faculty support and development for facilitating online learning—for both traditional distance and on-campus institutions.

The inevitable resistance to change for both distance and campus-based educational institutions will most assuredly open opportunities for private institutions that have the agility and management style to address emerging students' needs—as is currently happening in Brazil (Litto, 2002) and elsewhere—with perhaps the most cited example being the University of Phoenix. Even with convergence, private, for profit, institutions will fill the void between these two models and occupy the middle ground on the continuum between traditional distance and campus-based approaches.

For both distance and campus-based educational institutions, leaders must realize that they are not immune to competition for students and faculty. For campus-based institutions, there is considerable competition for the best students, and the reputed quality and convenience of course work will increasingly become an issue. Distance education students, of course, are not restricted by place and, therefore, will likely select the institution based on the quality and reputation of the institution. Competition for qualified faculty will be no less a challenge with predicted shortage of faculty in the near future. As distance education institutions converge with campus-based institutions in terms of offering blended learning experiences, they will find themselves increasingly competing for the same qualified faculty.

CONCLUSION

Communication and Internet technologies have precipitated the adoption of online learning in both distance and campus-based educational institutions. While this adoption has been pervasive, in general it has not yet resulted in widespread course redesign reflected by significant re-conceptualization of the teaching-learning process. As exogenous factors such as changing outcome expectations and budget constraints come into play, we shall see new instructional models and a true convergence of distance and campus-based institutions.

This convergence will generate a full spectrum of instructional approaches and models. The distinction amongst educational institutions will dissolve. The future will be more eclectic, not unlike the blending of fashion today. Diversity will be more acceptable and the distinction between distance and campus-based institutions will become blurred. The concept of blended learning best describes the new model of learning on the core of this convergence. This transformation must not be underestimated and represents an enormous challenge for educational institutions and their leadership.

Educational institutions must not be immune to issues of diminishing quality, advances in communication technologies, and emerging redesign methodologies. Institutions that are reluctant to step out of their restrictive paradigm will likely experience increasing sustainability pressures resulting from other educational providers, such as: "corporate universities, private for-profit universities, virtual universities and a wide range of education brokers" (Mason, 2003, p. 745). The threat for campus-based institutions is from world-class and well recognized campus-based institutions that have enhanced the quality of the learning experience—and their reputation—through appropriate integration of online learning. Of course, there will always be those institutions that distinguish themselves by remaining at the extremes of the continuum, but it will become increasingly difficult to resist the adoption of communication and Internet technologies as they become integral to the design of a quality educational experience.

REFERENCES

Calvert, J. (2001). Deakin University: Going online at a dual mode university. *International Review of Research in Open and Distance Learning, 1*(2). Retrieved June 12, 2007, from http://www.irrodl.org/index.php/irrodl/article/view/20/360.

Cunningham, S., Tapsall, S., Ryan, Y., Stedman, L., Bagdon, K., & Flew, T. (1998). *New media and borderless education: A review of the convergence between global media networks and higher education provisions, 97/22.* Canberra, AU: Department of Education, Training and Youth Affairs.

CVCP. (2000). *The business of borderless education: UK perspectives.* Retrieved June 12, 2007, from http://bookshop.universitiesuk.ac.uk/downloads/Borderless-Summary.pdf.

Davis, A. (2001). Athabasca University: Conversion from traditional distance education to online courses, programs and services. *International Review of Research in Open and Distance Learning, 1*(2). Retrieved June 12, 2007, from http://www.irrodl.org/index.php/irrodl/article/view/19/358.

Dzuiban, C., Hartman, J., Moskal, P., Sorg, S., & Truman, B. (2004). Three ALN modalities: An institutional perspective. In J. Bourne & J. C. Moore (Eds.), *Elements of quality online education: Into the mainstream,* (Vol. 5 in the Sloan C Series). Needham, MA: The Sloan Consortium.

Evans, T., & Nation, D. (2003). Globalization and the reinvention of distance education. In M. G. Moore & W. G. Anderson (Eds.), *Handbook of distance education* (pp. 777–792). London: Erlbaum.

Garrison, D. R. (2000). Theoretical challenges for distance education in the 21st century: A shift from structural to transactional issues. *International Review of Research in Open and Distance Learning, 1*(1), 1–17.

Garrison, D. R., & Cleveland-Innes, M. (2004). Critical factors in student satisfaction and success: Facilitating student role adjustment in online communities of inquiry. In J. Bourne & J. C. Moore (Eds.), *Elements of quality online education: Into the mainstream* (Vol. 5 in the Sloan C Series, pp. 47–58). Needham, MA: The Sloan Consortium.

Garrison, D. R., & Kanuka, H. (2004). Blended learning: Uncovering its transformative potential in higher education. *The Internet and Higher Education, 7*(2), 95–105.

Grepperud, G., Støkken, A., & Toska, J. (2002). Out of the shadow and into the spotlight—The development of distance teaching in Norwegian higher education. *International Review of Research in Open and Distance Learning, 2*(2), 1–13.

Guri-Rosenblit, S. (2002). A top down strategy to enhance information technologies into Israeli higher education. *International Review of Research in Open and Distance Learning, 2*(2), 1–16.

Heterick, B., & Twigg, C. (2003, February 1). *The learning MarketSpace.* Retrieved June 12, 2007, from http://www.center.rpi.edu/Newsletters/Feb03.html.

Kappell, H-H., Lehmann, B., & Loeper, J. (2002). Distance education at conventional universities in Germany. *International Review of Research in Open and Distance Learning, 2*(2), 1–21. Retrieved June 12, 2007, from http://www.irrodl.org/index.php/irrodl/article/view/62/127.

Keegan, D. (1994). *Otto Peters on distance education: The industrialization of teaching and learning.* London: Routledge.

Lewis, R. (2002). The hybridization of conventional higher education: UK perspective. *International Review of Research in Open and Distance Learning, 2*(2), 1–13. Retrieved June 12, 2007, from http://www.irrodl.org/index.php/irrodl/article/view/58/120.

Litto, F. (2002). The hybridization of distance learning in Brazil—An approach imposed by culture. *International Review of Research in Open and Distance Learning, 2*(2), 1–14.

Mason, R. (2003). Global education: Out of the Ivory Tower. In M. G. Moore & W. G. Anderson (Eds.), *Handbook of distance education* (pp. 743–752). London: Erlbaum.

Owston, R., Garrison, D. R., & Cook, K. (in press). Blended learning at Canadian universities: Issues and practices. In C. Bonk & C. Graham (Eds.), *The handbook of blended learning.* Hoboken, NJ: Wiley.

Rovai, A. P. (2002). Sense of community, perceived cognitive learning, and persistence in asynchronous learning networks. *The Internet and Higher Education, 5*(4), 319–332.

Shale, D. (2002). The hybridization of higher education in Canada. *International Review of Research in Open and Distance Learning, 2*(2). Retrieved June 12, 2007, from http://www.irrodl.org/index.php/irrodl/article/view/64/131.

Swan, K. (2001). Virtual interaction: Design factors affecting student satisfaction and perceived learning in asynchronous online courses. *Distance Education, 22*(2), 306–331.

Zhang, W., Niu, J., & Jiang, G. (2002). Web-based education at conventional universities in China: A case study. *International Review of Research in Open and Distance Learning, 2*(2), 1–14. Retrieved June 12, 2007, from http://www.irrodl.org/index.php/irrodl/article/view/63/129.

3

ONLINE LEARNING AND THE UNIVERSITY

Chris Curran

Dublin City University, Ireland

INTRODUCTION

This chapter examines the potential impact of online education on universities. Observation of operational strategies in some 30 universities in Europe and the United States suggests that rapid growth, pervasive spread among tertiary institutions, and an inherent adaptability in application, are among the more prominent features of the contemporary development of online education. This adaptability on the one hand, and the unique institutional context of application on the other, are reflected in a diversity of institutional strategies. The chapter reviews some current evidence with respect to the impact of online education on the university, with particular reference to the impact on pedagogy, on resource allocation, on staff, and on various aspects of institutional strategies. It is concluded that the diverse strategies adopted by universities reflect, rather than influence, institutional ethos, and that by virtue of its capacity to adapt to different contexts, online education may be more malleable—and so less threatening—to traditional values and academic mores, than some observers fear.

ONLINE LEARNING

Online education has been variously defined, but it can be simply described as a learning process in which learners can communicate with their instructors and their peers, and access learning materials over the Internet or other computer networks (Oakley, 2000). It therefore provides a means through which the ubiquitous computing and communications technologies—so powerful and pervasive in other areas of economic and social life—can be applied to tertiary education and, perhaps, to addressing some of the contemporary challenges facing universities.

Online learning is the latest in a succession of technology-based innovations in higher education that go back almost a century, to the use of radio in Wisconsin in 1917 (Wood & Wylie, 1977)—some might say back earlier still to the innovative exploitation, for correspondence teaching, of contemporary developments in printing: Low-cost paper-production and the introduction of the "penny post" in 19th century Britain. As in the case of earlier applications of technology (e.g., television, radio, computer-based learning, satellite-based communications, and computer conferencing), the potential impact of online learning on higher education is the focus of much speculative interest. Many of the expectations recently advanced in respect to online education—the potential to widen access, reduce cost, transform pedagogy, and the like—were similarly advanced with respect to earlier applications of technology (as can be seen from the substantive literature on their use and efficacy in education).

While most of these technologies undoubtedly enriched the process of tertiary teaching and learning, and some continue to do so, few if any have had the radical impact on higher education envisaged by early enthusiasts. Notwithstanding the undoubted contribution of these technologies to teaching and learning, initial expectations of their transformative influence now seem unduly sanguine; and the anticipated change in tertiary teaching (however desirable or otherwise one might view it) remains, at best, only partially realized. In spite of the ubiquity—and undoubted benefits—of some practical aids to teaching and learning (e.g., the overhead projector, xerographic reproduction, the personal calculator and, more recently, easy access to digitized bibliographic databases, e-mail, and personal computers), the essential process of teaching in universities and colleges has continued largely unchanged for a century or more (and in some fundamental respects for very much longer).

Moreover, while rare radical innovations in tertiary education—such as the establishment and successful operation, for more than three decades, of the European Open Universities—have influenced higher education in significant, if often subtle, ways; the prevailing pedagogy of traditional teaching in universities and colleges has remained largely unchanged and unchallenged, at least until now.

And yet, the promise of online learning seemed somehow different, if only because of its intimate association with two of the most influential and pervasive technologies of the day: Computers and telecommunications.

Already by the mid 1990s, awareness of the pedagogic opportunity presented by these technologies was growing among educators. This awareness is increasingly stimulated by the declining cost, increasing speed, and expanding storage capacity of computers; by the greater bandwidth of computer networks; and by the extraordinarily rapid growth of the Internet, when compared with earlier technologies. In this last case, for example, Naughton (2000) notes that while it took radio 37 years and television about 15 years to reach an audience of 50 million, the World Wide Web had a similar number of users in *just over 3 years.*

The pervasive dispersion of computer access—however uneven, most notably in the United States (U.S. Department of Commerce, 2000; Gladieux, 2000)—was, no doubt, a further stimulant to awareness of the opportunity presented by these new technologies. As were the official and powerful voices raised in support of using technology in education—in Europe (European Commission, 2000), in the United States (Web-Based Education Commission, 2000), and in many nation states (MacKeogh, 2001). This support found practical expression in a diversity of strategies, education policies, and funding programs to promote the application of these new technologies in teaching and learning.

GROWTH OF ONLINE EDUCATION

By the late 1990s, there were few institutions of higher education in developed countries without recourse to these technologies to support institutional operations as diverse as marketing programs, registering students, posting course related information online, sourcing data, accessing library services, communicating with staff and students, and a host of other activities beside. Awareness in tertiary institutions of the power of these technologies, coupled with the opportunity to access essential hardware and software infrastructures, were (no doubt) an initial stimulus to faculty interest and experimentation in teaching and learning online. It is hardly surprising, then, that so many early pedagogic programs were developed by staff in departments of computer science, informatics, or education, where the synergy between research and teaching was strongest and facilities for course development most readily available.

The pervasive spread of the new technologies in the wider economy, the availability of external funding to support pilot projects, and the speculative boom in technology stocks of the 1990s—with a related fear of "missing the boat" through failure to invest in online education—were, no doubt, among the more proximate incentives to institutional engagement in online education. As awareness of online learning became ever more pervasive, the potential (perceived or presumed) to improve on existing pedagogies, to communicate interactively with distance students, to respond more speedily to student inquiries, and to facilitate a collaborative mediated learning environment, was a further stimulus to course development.

United States

An initial pilot phase quickly led to wider provision. An early initiative in the United States by the Sloan Foundation involved the development of online versions of a few courses in 1993. This quickly grew to embrace 571 courses—one-third leading to awards—by 2001, and to 300 full degree and certification programs by 2002 (http://www.sloan-c.org). A later survey on the quality and extent of online education indicated that some 81% of all U.S. institutions of higher education "...offer at least one fully online or blended course" and that complete online degree programs "...are offered by 34 percent of the institutions" (Allen & Seaman, 2003, p. 2).

Enrolment Growth

Broadly similar trends were evident in enrolment growth. Enrolment in "for-credit" distance-education courses in the United States., a high proportion of which used online technology as a primary or supporting medium of instruction, more than doubled over a 3-year period—from 1.3 million in 1997–98 to 2.9 million in 2000–01, with some 2.4 million enrolments in undergraduate distance education courses (Waits, Lewis, & Greene, 2003). Allen and Seaman's (2003) survey on online education indicated that about 11% of U.S. higher education students took at least one course online in fall of 2002, and that over one-third of these students took all of their courses online. Data on enrolment at an institutional level is even more striking; at least three U.S. universities have reported *annual* rates of enrolment-growth of 50–100% in their online programs.[1] This is an exceptional growth rate, even when regard is had to the established track record of the particular institutions in developing and marketing programs (e.g., Hudgins, 2000).

A more recent survey of more than 400 institutions compiled a list of graduate level programs in Business, Education, Engineering, Library Services, Nursing, and Public Health. Analysis of the data shows that the 58 institutions listed had a total enrolment, across these six postgraduate subject-areas, of 128,961 students. The 10 institutions with the highest enrolment accounted for 95,767 students. The authors additionally suggest that more than 3 million people are "pursuing degrees online from institutions of higher learning across America today" ("Education online," 2006, p. 62).

Online Learning in Europe

Directly comparable data on online learning in Europe are unavailable; however, a recent strategic study carried out on behalf of the EU Commission showed that the integration of information and communication technologies (ICT) in teaching had increased greatly over the preceding two years. And while strategies vary between institutions (PLS RAMBOLL, 2004) and scale of diffusion varies between countries (Martin & Jennings, 2002), e-learning activity in Europe continues to grow. A survey of the use of e-learning in training and professional development showed that some 14% of total spending by users of training went to e-learning-related content in 2001—"appreciably more than two years earlier when the figure was under 10%" (CEDEFOP, 2001). Similarly, e-learning was estimated to be responsible for about one-third of the total income of training suppliers, from the supply of training content and material, in 2001—markedly higher than just under 18% two years earlier (CEDEFOP, 2001).

A recent survey of about 1,000 adults in each of 10 European Union member states, conducted in early 2005 using computer assisted telephone interviews, shows that, on average, about 12% of the adult population makes use of the Internet as part of purposeful organized learning activities—for example, doing research as part of a course, exchanging messages with co-learners, and downloading dedicated learning content. The take-up of online courses, in which a significant part of the learning content is transmitted via the Internet, is more modest, at about 2% of the adult population, excluding students in fulltime education. As might be expected, learning-related use of the Internet is much more developed among formal and full-time students. The survey showed that some 78% of students use the Internet in the course of organized learning activities and, on average, 8% take an online e-learning course in any year (http://www.euser-eu.org).

ONLINE EDUCATION: CURRENT STATUS

It will be clear, even from this brief review, that online learning has grown from modest early initiatives to establish a substantive presence in higher education, with programs of one kind or another provided by a high proportion of tertiary institutions. True, the long-term significance of this presence in the context of core *credit-based teaching activity* in the university sector as a whole is still difficult to assess. The scale of online education in the totality of *university for-credit, degree level* teaching and learning is difficult to estimate; given the scarcity of data, still early stage of development, and significant sectoral variation in activity. Nonetheless, rapid growth and a pervasive presence in tertiary institutions, especially in U. S. public universities, are among the more striking features of the early development of online education.

THE MODERN UNIVERSITY

But what long-term effect, if any, is online learning likely to have on traditional pedagogy in universities? And how might it impact on still more fundamental issues of mission, ethos, and the professional autonomy of faculty? Before addressing these questions directly, it may be helpful to consider briefly the rather special character of that ubiquitous but conceptually unique institution, the modern university. The literature on the history, nature, and idea of the university is extensive, and even the briefest review would take us beyond the aims of this paper. But a few salient points relevant to the application of online education should be noted.

Influence of Tradition

First, even a cursory consideration of the modern university should have regard to the continuing influence of a long-standing and exceptional heritage. This unique tradition—embracing institutional autonomy, independent of Church and State; an intellectual focus on teaching and the generation of knowledge; an ethos grounded in creative, ethical, and cultural values; and with the exceptional rights and privileges conferred on the university "by King and Pope" (Barnett, 1992)—has served to set the university apart from other institutions and continues to do so.

This continuity is important. Ashby (1958), writing just a few decades ago, notes that:

> The features, which today distinguish the University from other social institutions in Ghana, in Germany, and in Australia, are similar to those, which distinguished it from other social institutions in the fourteenth century... Through wars, revolutions, and reformations... [the university] has continued to fulfill its function in society and it has done so without losing that pattern which identified it as a university. (p. 3)

In spite of many contemporary challenges, notwithstanding the influence of change and manifest contemporary institutional diversity, the university in essence remains a special kind of social institution, with a continuity of purpose and identity extending back over some six centuries to its origins in medieval Europe.

Intensification of Social Role

Second, the unique tradition of the university has not diminished its social role and significance, nor curtailed engagement with the wider community. Institutional autonomy has continued to be seen as intrinsic to the roles and rights of the university, even as for a century and more, the realisation of social goals became increasingly dependent on state-university collaboration, and universities increasingly dependent on state-funding. Most universities are institutions created or substantially maintained by the state. For many, their primary purpose is "to service social, economic and cultural needs defined essentially in national contexts" (Scott, 1998).

Moreover, the social role of the university has intensified in the decades since World War II, as tertiary education came to be universally recognized as critical to economic growth (Bowman, 1966; Sobel, 1978), "inextricably linked to social and economic development" (van der Molen, 1996), and as a means of conferring important public goods "that must be accessible to all strata... [and] all peoples" (Ramphele, 2002, p. xi). Today, in an increasingly "knowledge-intensive" age, few states feel free to ignore an institution as socially relevant as the modern university.

Influence of Change

Further, even the briefest review should have regard to the impact of change, in particular expansion and diversification, on the modern university. Gellert, writing in the early 1990s, noted that most European countries experienced an unprecedented expansion of their institutions of higher education over the preceding 30 years, with a quadrupling of the number of post-secondary students in many of them. Staff in universities and other institutions of higher education, as well as government funds for teaching and research, increased at a similar rate (Gellert, 1993). Many universities experienced significant expansion in the scale and scope of their activities, some becoming the most significant economic units in their cities or regions (Scott, 1998).

Experience in the United States was broadly similar. Bender describes the half-century following World War II as the "golden age" of the American university and notes that "between 1940 and 1990, federal funds for higher education increased by a factor of twenty-five, enrollment by ten, [while] average teaching loads were reduced by half" (Bender, 1997, p. 21). In the three decades after 1945, American undergraduates increased by almost 500% and the number of graduate students increased by nearly 900% (Menand, 2001).

Diversification

For most universities, expansion was accompanied by diversification. In the post-WWII period, new curricula and disciplines emerged; student populations changed, in many countries from an initial small, mainly elite, student body, to provision for mass education; and enrolment of mature and part-time students became increasingly significant. New pedagogies were adopted, notably distance learning, and universities took on new and novel roles such as the development of technology parks and entrepreneurial incubation units. Kerr (2001), in his seminal text on the multiuniversity, notes that the University of California had operating expenditures of nearly $500,000,000, a total employment of over 40,000 people, operations in over 100 locations, nearly 10,000 courses in its catalogues, approaching 100,000 students—30,000 of them at graduate level, 200,000 students in extension courses, and "some form of contact with nearly every industry, nearly every level of government, [and] nearly every person in its region" (p. 6).

Expansion in enrolment growth was accompanied by a restructuring and diversification of the higher education sector as a whole, with new types of universities and institutional forms of advanced learning being set up in most countries (Gellert, 1993): Community colleges in the United States, Polytechnics in Britain, and *Fachhochschulen* in Germany (Teichler, 1996). This change no doubt introduced to protect universities, perhaps inevitably led to increased competition for scarce resources, and obliged individual universities to review their particular role and strategic positioning. A necessity made all the more urgent by the failure of state funding to keep pace with growth in activities over the last decade or so, and by a growing demand, in a number of countries, for more intense scrutiny of university outputs and internal processes, for greater accountability in the use of scarce resources, and for more formal assessment of quality. One significant effect of these changes was to increase the diversity of institutions calling themselves universities.

An Exceptional Institution

The modern university, therefore, can be seen as an exceptional institution—heir to a long and continuing tradition of unique social relevance, and subject to continuing, even intensifying, change. As a result of these manifold, often conflicting influences, the university might aptly be described as a diverse, multifaceted, complex, ill-defined—even (in Scott's telling phrase) "schizophrenic"—institution (Scott, 1998). But it is an institution nonetheless well adapted to inducing and coping with change, and well practiced in responding to the contemporary needs of the communities it serves. And doing so, moreover, while continuing to respect the ethical, cultural, and intellectual values that are its *raison d'être.*

ONLINE EDUCATION AND THE UNIVERSITY

What then are the effects of the substantive growth and pervasive spread of online education on that exceptional institution, the modern university? How significant is this development? And will its impact on traditional pedagogy be more far-reaching and lasting than earlier forms of technology-based teaching? Will it, as some observers suggest, not only induce change in traditional pedagogy (Newman & Scurry, 2001; Young, 2002), but additionally have an impact on cost, academic productivity and still more fundamental issues of university mission and ethos, and the professional autonomy of faculty?

Effect on Traditional Pedagogy

The scale of online provision, noted above, may not yet be overly substantial relative to the totality of teaching and learning in the university sector as a whole, but it is clearly growing in scale and significance. The impressive data on the growth of online education points to a rapidly increasing level of activity, especially in the United States—but how indicative is it of seminal change in the pedagogy of tertiary teaching?

Diversity

Online education covers a diverse spectrum of activity. Allen and Sea-man (2003) classify online courses in three categories, ranging from "web-facilitated," where the proportion of content delivered online ranges from 1-29%; to "online courses," where the vast bulk of content (80+%) is delivered online—indicating a wide range, not just in activity, but also in the potential impact on traditional pedagogy. Zemsky and Massy (2004) adopt a somewhat different classification and, more to the point, identify a number of overlapping adoption cycles, ranging from "enhancements to traditional course/program configurations" (p. 11) which do not change the basic mode of instruction; to new course/program configurations, "... which result when faculty and the institutions re-engineer teaching and learning activities to take full and optimal advantage of the new technology" (p. 11).

Observation of operational programs in universities in the United States and Europe reaffirms the perception of diversity. Pedagogic strategies can range from a minimalist use of technology to support contiguous teaching, to programs where virtually all course materials are disseminated, all communication exchanged, and all collaboration conducted online. More significantly still, perhaps, tutor student interaction can range from tightly scheduled and directive interaction, to an open-ended, exploratory pedagogic strategy in which the student progressively learns to acquire knowledge independently, and to develop and apply it.

Nonetheless, much online education, as currently practiced, might be appropriately described as traditional pedagogy, suitably enhanced in one way or another, but not essentially different to long-standing instructional practice. Zemsky and Massy (2004) note that neither illustrated lectures, nor the use of Blackboard or WebCT to distribute learning materials, need constitute electronically mediated learning—and for the most part, faculty who make e-learning a part of their teaching do so "...by having the electronics simplify tasks, not by fundamentally changing how the subject is taught" (p. 52). It would be helpful to know how much online education is of a more potent kind. Unfortunately, I know of no data that would support an unambiguous estimate of the extent to which online education is inducing fundamental change in university pedagogy; even if such data were available it would constitute, at best, an uncertain guide to future development.

Quality of Teaching

That online education is capable of re-engineering teaching and learning is hardly in doubt. There is increasing (if still somewhat sparse) evidence to show that universities—including the oldest and most prestigious institutions—can use technology to facilitate the adoption of an innovative pedagogy (Curran, 2004) or to support a richer pedagogy, firmly grounded in the principles of effective instructional design and developed around the concept that "students learn best when they act as independent critical researchers within their discipline" (p. 12). Many online educators aspire to using technology to support student-centred learning; some, adopting an essentially constructivist view, contrast the potential of online education with traditional teaching practice, much of which they perceive to essentially involve the transmission and rather passive absorption of institutionalized knowledge.

Quality of Output

This perception has not gone unchallenged, nor has the aspiration to a richer student-centred pedagogy absolved online educators from critical comment—much of it focused on (a presumed) absence of teacher-student, and student-peer, interaction (of the kind common in traditional pedagogy). A particular concern with respect to the quality of online teaching, relates to the "unbundling" of the teaching process that allows a "content expert" to prepare materials to be subsequently delivered by a "facilitator," effectively disrupting or precluding the critical interaction between students and faculty members over time (Perley & Tanquay, 1999).

Unbundling the teaching process is not new; it has, for many decades, been an established part of distance education strategies, especially in large-scale distance teaching systems. Interestingly, this pedagogic dichotomy has not, of itself, impaired the quality of instruction in distance teaching. The European Open Universities, for example, have an excellent reputation for the quality of their teaching—the UKOU is consistently placed in the top 20% of national quality rankings, acclaimed for the excellence of its teaching in subjects like Music, Earth Sciences, and Chemistry (Daniel, 1998). True, the open universities (and most other distance education systems) effectively operate *in parallel* with traditional education, providing for the needs of predominantly mature students—who, other things being equal, are more likely to possess the characteristics of maturity and motivation required for success in this alternative mode of instruction.

Nonetheless, notwithstanding this unbundling, there is a good deal of support for the view that the pedagogic output of distance education is equivalent—or at least not significantly different—to traditional teaching, at least when assessed on the basis of student grades and test scores; or of course-participants' attitude to, or experience of, learning at a distance. Russell's (1999) text is perhaps the most cited source on evidence on "no significant difference," but by no means the only such review to come to a positive (if qualified) view of the evidence on the effectiveness of distance education (cf. Moore et al., 1990). Moreover, there is a long standing and not insubstantial literature on the (at worst) neutral impact of media on learning, culminating—explicitly, if not chronologically—in Richard

Clark's (1983) often cited observation that media do not influence student achievement "any more than the truck that delivers our groceries causes changes in our nutrition" (p. 445). True, Clark's view has not gone unchallenged, and (more to the point) many of the studies reporting positive conclusions with respect to the pedagogical effectiveness of distance education have been, if not dismissed, at least seriously questioned, because so many were subject to inherent methodological flaws (Phipps & Merisotis, 1999).

Wider Dimension

Moreover, most critics of online pedagogy are less concerned with equivalence in terms of outputs (e.g., student grades or test scores) than with a wider dimension; measured (if at all) by significant, if subtle, metrics, such as the degree to which students have opportunities for peer-discourse, interaction with tenured faculty, and—more generally—meaningful participation in a community of learners. Whether such measures represent a realistic view of traditional pedagogy as experienced by most students today—or, indeed, whether they accurately reflect the objectives of more mature and part-time student populations—is a source of continuing contention by online educators.

Overall, we might conclude that online education has the *potential* to improve traditional pedagogy—at least, as currently practiced in many tertiary institutions. Whether, for the most part, it will do so in practice may depend on a range of factors, not least the availability of adequate resources to support effective student-centred learning (a provision notably absent in some earlier manifestations of technology-based teaching); a commitment, of sufficient degree and extent, by tenured staff to the development and practice of online teaching; and, perhaps, on the extent to which the practice (as distinct from the concept) of online education proves compatible with the enduring, fundamental aims and ethos of the university.

Effect on Staff

A good deal has been written on possible negative consequences of online learning for staff, in particular academic staff, in universities. Much of the initial concern seemed to reflect a general unease in response to change of unknown scale and consequence, reflecting faculty fears of loss of tenure, replacement, or simply that the use of technology will mean more work for faculty members, or "more time on teaching and less on research" (Bates, 2000, pp. 104–105). Noble (2001) argues that the use of technology extends working time and intensifies work "...as faculty struggle at all hours of the day and night to stay on top of the technology and respond, via chat rooms, virtual office hours, and e-mail, to both students and administrators to whom they have now become instantly and continuously accessible" (p. 32).

There is a good deal of anecdotal evidence to show that involvement in online learning can, indeed, increase faculty workload, even substantially so in some cases; but just how much of this extra workload is due to an initial positioning on a learning curve is still unclear. Some part of the additional work load is probably a consequence of the unstructured (and so less controlled) character of much staff–student interaction in online learning. But whether, and to what extent, any difference in work-load will persist in the longer-term, as faculty gain more experience of online education, remains to be seen. Other barriers to faculty participation, identified in one study, were: Release time to develop courses; lack of promotion and tenure to reward additional teaching; money to pay for time and equipment in up-front development of courses; and lack of incentives or rewards for participation in online education (Ellis, 2000).

Professional Autonomy

The wider implications of online learning for the professional autonomy of faculty is a specific, and critically important, concern—given the close links between professional autonomy and academic freedom—"the key legitimating concept" of the university (Menand, 1996, p. 4). This concern finds expression in various ways: The ownership of copyright to course materials developed by faculty, for example, with an attendant fear of teachers' control of pedagogical duties being diminished to the point where they are "...reconceptualized, without their consent, as workers for hire" (Katz, 2001, paragraph 10), or concern that teaching activities may be restructured through technology to reduce faculty "...autonomy, independence and control over their work" (Noble, 2001, p. 32). Or, more generally, that the "commodification" of instruction will inevitably lead to deprofessionalization of the professoriate (Noble, 2002) and to the "casualization" of academic staff.

What lessons can we draw from earlier innovations? No doubt the dichotomous approach to course development and teaching adopted in a number of open universities—with multi-skilled course teams responsible for developing courses and related courseware, and a predominantly separate team of mostly part-time tutors and counselors responsible for student-support—had some, even significant, impact on the traditional role of faculty. But there were important factors constraining any negative consequences. The open universities, by and large, were scrupulous in observing the established norms of university practice in related areas: The academic content of programs, the qualifications of staff, the duration of courses, and the commitment to research as an integral element of faculty work, were all consistent with the established norms of traditional university practice.

Social Benefits

Was the difference in approach to course development necessary? Almost certainly so; it is highly questionable whether an alternative approach, based solely or primarily on traditional teaching practice, could then have been as successful in widening access. In the three decades prior to 2001, the UKOU alone "...served more than two million students" (Daniel, 2001, p. B24); in achieving similar student success rates in attaining course credits or graduation (Perry, 1996); or, in many cases, operating at a unit cost (per fulltime-equivalent student) lower—in some cases significantly lower—than that for similar courses in traditional universities (Curran, 1996). The critical question, then, would seem to be whether the erosion of faculty autonomy (if indeed such erosion occurred) was more than compensated by the significant extension of access to educational opportunity and the adoption of a successful pedagogy? No doubt the majority of Open University graduates would think so (and an objective observer might argue that this is yet another illustration of the university acting as an adaptable social institution).

Similar questions would seem to arise in the case of online education: Is the risk to faculty autonomy sufficient to outweigh the wider social (and to the students concerned highly personal) benefits of wider access and—perhaps—of more effective pedagogy? Moreover, online education seems to involve a less radical departure from traditional teaching practice (than was the case for the open universities); for the most part, the approach adopted by universities to teaching their students online involves a less radical break with traditional teaching practice. Much current online teaching seems to have emerged, more or less naturally, from traditional teaching, or operates happily in tandem with it, in the form of "blended" or "hybrid" programs (Young, 2002; Carnevale & Olsen, 2003).

This being so, one might expect that fears, of the kind outlined above, would abate with experience of online learning, but clearly some faculty still have reservations. In response to a recent survey in the United States, more than one in four academic leaders at private non-profit schools stated that their faculty questions the value and legitimacy of online learning. The percentage, however, was markedly lower at public institutions, a difference, the report-authors suggest, that may be due to "...the longer experience that these schools have in delivering online courses and programs" (Allen & Seaman, 2003, p. 14). Overall the fact that 59.6% of respondents expressed the view that their faculty accepts the value and legitimacy of online education suggests that such fears may be in decline.

Faculty Influence

The institutional benefits of faculty commitment to online education are considerable, and in at least some universities, probably indispensable. In practice, the extent of faculty influence can vary greatly from one institution to another, sometimes in subtle but significant, ways. Universities are rather special institutions, strongly influenced by their particular traditions and ethos. In most traditional universities, and in particular in research intensive universities, the influence of faculty is an important determinant of pedagogic strategy. This is exercised through enduring internal structures, which for many universities means the department as the basic organizational unit (Bender, 1997), and through a process of collective, consensual decision-making. Influence of this kind might be expected, other things being equal, to act as a natural brake on the erosion of faculty interests or autonomy. On balance, one might reasonably conclude that much depends on the particular ethos and internal decision-making structures of individual universities. Other things being equal, research-intensive universities, with strong academic departments and established traditions of consensual decision-making, are less likely to develop strategies that threaten faculty autonomy.

Effect on Resource Allocation

Much of the early development of online education was initiated by enthusiastic faculty, working as individuals in small groups. It is not too surprising, given the interest of faculty and often the availability of grants or other external funding to support the activity, that little regard was given to the substantive commitment of time and other resources involved in these early initiatives. Where such concerns were raised at all, the difficulty of identifying and allocating costs (e.g., of faculty-time and technology-use) was a significant disincentive to the assessment of cost effectiveness.

Even later, as departments and institutions as a whole became involved in the process, the pressures of getting courses up and running meant that little attention was directed to the cost—still less to the cost-effectiveness—of online learning. For many institutions, this seems still to be the case; in a recent U.S. survey, only 18% of public four-year institutions indicated that reducing per-student costs was an important goal of their distance education programs—a high proportion of which use online learning (Waits, Lewis, & Greene, 2003).

University Aims

A degree of disinterest in the cost of online learning is not altogether surprising. Although, viewed from an economic perspective, universities generate revenue-producing outputs, the process of production is markedly different to that of competitive industry. And their primary outputs (graduates and research) have external effects that generate benefits beyond those captured, however indirectly, by market prices. As a consequence of these characteristics, universities in general are different from the profit-maximising form of traditional microeconomic theory and, in practice, most lack many of the forces that serve in other industries to promote the efficient utilisation of resources (Attiyeh & Lumsden, 1974). Universities, in common with Marc Blaug's observation on education, pursue "...multiple objectives, none of which include maximisation of profits, or any proxy for profits ... [and operate] ... with a fairly rigid handicraft technology, in large part self-imposed by custom and tradition" (Blaug, 1970).

Nor can it be assumed that universities will naturally seek to lower costs—not to suggest that responsible faculty will not seek to ensure that resources are allocated as efficiently as possible—only that the preferred aim may be to *improve the quality* of teaching or other aspects of the program, rather than to *reduce costs*. Much experience to date suggests that technologically induced gains in "productivity" have almost always been realized, as Bowen (2001) notes, "...in the form of better research, improved access to information, and so on... rather than in the form of savings in inputs."

Cost Effectiveness

Still, interest in the cost analysis of online education has grown, much of it initially focused on methodology (Ehrmann & Milam, 1999; Bacsich et al., 1999; Milam, 2000; Fisher & Nygren, 2000; Ash, Heginbotham, & Bacsich, 2001), with (still rather sparse) empirical studies focused on a comparison of unit costs relative to more traditional modalities of instruction (Bacsich et al., 1993). One might expect, *a priori*, a higher per-student cost for online education (relative to traditional contiguous teaching) as a consequence of additional infrastructural costs (e.g., technology use, learning platforms, technician support, and 24 hours, 7 days-a-week student support) and a possibly higher—or at best uncertain—staff-student ratio. Rumble (1989), in an early study of computer mediated learning at the UKOU, concluded that "...nobody knows at present how much time tutors spend off-line preparing and reading messages, whether value for money was achieved, or whether tutors were grossly underpaid for the hours they actually spent on the course" (p. 158). And there is a good deal of anecdotal—and some empirical (Schelin & Smarte, 2002)—evidence to support the view that staff-student ratios can be higher in online education, relative to similar courses taught in contiguous classroom mode. Many faculty members are of the view that online teaching is both time and labour intensive. And, as one faculty report concluded, that teaching the same number of students "...at the same level of quality as in the classroom requires more time and money" (University of Illinois, 1999, p. 2).

Economies of Scale

How cost-effective is online education? A number of earlier studies of technology-based teaching (notably those on the European and other Open Universities) showed substantive economies of scale, with significantly lower unit costs per-student, relative to more traditional modes of contiguous teaching. In general, however, these institutions achieved economies of scale by enrolling substantial student numbers (sometimes with hundreds, even thousands, of students in a single course). Additionally, they operated with a distinctly different course production process than that adopted by most universities involved in online learning. It would be unwise, therefore, to assume that the cost experience of earlier modes of technology-based education is relevant to online education—not least, having regard to the diverse strategies universities adopt in online teaching, and to sometimes marked differences in their respective scale of course enrolments.

In keeping with these earlier studies, particular interest has centred on identifying the "break-even point," at which unit costs are equivalent, in the two systems being compared (i.e., traditional and online teaching). The results of this research, overall, might best be described as mixed. Bates (2000), citing experience at the University of British Columbia, suggests that a standard Web-based course, with a mix of pre-prepared Web materials, online discussion forums, and required texts, becomes increasingly more cost-effective (than contiguous teaching) at relatively modest enrolment levels—as per-class numbers increase beyond 40 per year over a 4-year period (Bates, 2000). Other studies of have come up with somewhat different estimates (cf. Rumble, 2001); much depends on context.

Faculty Productivity

Increasing, faculty productivity is a closely related topic of interest. Massy and Zemsky (writing now more than a decade ago) expressed the view that, while information technology has the potential to enhance teaching and learning, "...there is no agreement on how that technology should be used to boost academic productivity—or even whether such an increase is in itself a valid goal if its enhancement means substituting technology for the more traditional, labour-intensive rhythms of higher education." Raising the question, "What can IT contribute to increasing learning productivity?" they suggest that it offers economies of scale, and mass customization. Posing two scenarios—adaptive and non-adaptive—they conclude that the impact on productivity will depend less on the technology, than on the response of institutions, and not least on their capacity to restructure and re-engineer activities and to optimize the use of information technology (Massy & Zemsky, 1995). Massy and Wilger (1998) pick up that theme; they suggest that technology's long-term economic advantage lies in its capacity to open up more options, more ways of adapting teaching and learning processes to "...whatever financial conditions may ensue." They go on to note that "providing the institution always optimizes its technology, having these additional options can never make it worse off" (p. 52).

Empirical research in this area is still somewhat sparse, but some recent studies on the teaching of large enrolment classes offer some tentative indications of success (Arvan et al., 1997; Twigg, 1999; Harley et al., 2003). As in earlier studies of technology-based teaching, much depends on perspective. Where account is taken of the cost of students' time, of qualitative differences (e.g., higher grade average), or of reaching out to particular (otherwise inaccessible) students, online learning, other things being equal, is more likely to provide a cost-effective alternative to more traditional learning modalities.

Economies of Scope

Interestingly enough, some of the early programs, especially those with a strong research orientation, may well have enjoyed economies of scope arising from the joint production of research and courseware, rather than the more costly separate production of each (Panzar & Willig, 1981)—of the kind found in related areas of university education (e.g., in the joint production of undergraduate and graduate instruction in American research universities (de Groot, McMahon, & Volkwein, 1991). Similarly, where online education is used with external students (or in hybrid format with internal students), there is good reason to expect potential savings on physical infrastructure, relative to traditional, contiguous teaching (i.e., even if the effect on teacher-productivity is negative, the effect on *total-factor-productivity* could still be positive) by virtue of more efficient use of buildings and equipment.

Effect on Institutional Strategies

A distinguishing characteristic of online education is the diversity of institutional strategies universities adopt, and the extent to which these vary from one institution to another (Curran, 2004). The resulting differences are perhaps most evident with respect to program aims; arrangements for the management and governance of e-learning activities; the extent to which online programs are, or are not, an integrated part of regular internal academic structures; and the pedagogic approaches adopted to instruction and student-support. These differences in approach—some easily seen, others less obvious—are influenced in part by institutional goals (e.g., widening access, reaching new students, enhancing the quality of teaching, reducing costs, and increasing academic productivity); and in part by institutional constraints (e.g., the need to reconcile divergent goals and interests, to involve faculty in e-learning initiatives, and to have due regard to ethos, mission, and the economy of established methodologies).

Effect on Governance

This diversity can be observed in relation to arrangements for the governance and management of online education programs. Success in online education, in common with other forms of distributed learning, can require rather different organizational structures from those already existing in traditional institutions (cf. Oblinger, Barone, & Hawkins, 2001). Observations (by the author) of operational strategies in universities in Europe and the United States show a diversity of organizational structures which, in the interests of brevity, can be illustrated by three archetypal examples of online distance teaching; these are designated, for ease of reference, as "integrated," "quasi-independent," and "separate."

Integrated

In some universities, online education is an integrated part of regular university activities, routinely subject to the normal governance, management structures and processes of the institution. Practice varies somewhat from one institution to another, but a not atypical arrangement is one where academic departments are encouraged to submit proposals for the initiation of online programs (with related budgetary estimates), to a central committee for approval. Successful bidders are advanced the funds required to develop the program, in the form of a loan against anticipated income. Part of the additional income, accruing to the online version, is retained by the department responsible for developing and teaching the program.

With integrated programs of this kind, courses are often developed and, for the most part taught, by tenured faculty, and are usually based on existing courses taught on campus. Once developed, they typically form part of the standard university curriculum—often available to both on-campus and off-campus students. Often a dedicated unit is responsible for providing essential training and support to faculty in the development and delivery of programs.

Quasi-independent

Other universities adopt a broadly similar—but less tightly integrated—quasi independent strategy. Here again, particulars of the approach vary from one university to another, but an archetypal example is one where programs are primarily aimed at external part-time students, and are often career-related and targeted at familiar market sectors. Courses are generally based on those taught on-campus, with similar course-entry requirements, academic content, and assessment procedures—but, in the main, adjunct faculty are contracted to develop and teach courses, or full-time faculty may be paid a stipend to develop the course.

Teaching strategies can vary somewhat, but the approach to teaching generally includes designated texts, provision of additional course materials online, the completion of personal assignments—sometimes related to the student's work experience—and online peer discussion. Instruction tends to be predominantly text-based, with communication by email and an instructional focus on group and individual project-work. Courses generally are provided using a proprietary online platform with assistance, as required, from a special support unit, which often incorporates instructional designers and Web developers. A separate department or administrative unit is often responsible for the operational management of the online program as a whole, with technical support services sometimes outsourced to external providers. Online technologies tend to be used in a relatively simple mode, with the primary emphasis on easy access for students.

Separated

A few universities have set up *separate*, sometimes subsidiary institutions to provide online education programs. Here again, strategies vary quite widely, but the following example incorporates features found in a number of such institutions. The separate entity may be wholly owned by the parent university, but with a separate executive head and board. Courses are often developed by regular university faculty, and are based on those taught on-campus. Faculty may work with instructional and Web-designers, usually employed directly by the subsidiary-organisation, in adapting courses for provision over the Internet. The visual design and quality of courses is often of a very high order.

The pedagogic strategy is typically based on online interaction and collaboration, with asynchronous discussion, and sometimes synchronous conferences. Course content may be predominantly delivered online, sometimes with the additional use of standard texts and communication by email. Sometimes tutorial support is available to students, but in other cases there may be no tutorial support, no direct monitoring of students, and no examinations or accredited awards.

Consortia

Many universities adopt other, still more malleable, strategies that can more easily be made to fit in with their preferred (or existing) arrangements for governance and management. Participation in some form of consortium is one such strategy, often involving the exchange or joint production and delivery of online education programs. Strategies of this kind offer potential advantages in meeting the particular requirements of individual universities.

Participation in an online consortium, for example, allows universities to pool resources, share costs, and realize potential economies of scale in course development and delivery, while facilitating specialization of function between institutions (e.g., in staff training or the provision of technical support). Where appropriately structured a consortium agreement can additionally minimize investment risk and allow universities to make better use of resources while retaining direct control of the academic aspects of their programs. However, there are inevitably some disadvantages in consortia arrangements—not the least being potentially higher transaction costs and the difficulty of sustaining such partnerships, as evidenced by a number of costly and highly visible failures over the last few years. Nonetheless, a recent survey in the United States showed that some 68% of public four-year institutions participated in a distance education consortia in 2000–2001 (Waits, Lewis, & Greene, 2003).

Effect on Management

The impact of online learning on the management of some universities, especially those with a substantive institutional commitment to program development, can be demanding. Significant involvement in online education can require more active leadership and a willingness, on the part of responsible leaders, "...to use their influence and power with many different constituencies to move the agenda forward" (Hitt & Hartman, 2002).

Effect on Planning

Most forms of technology-based teaching typically involve three activities: Course development (e.g., the design of the curriculum; the writing and editing of course texts and other materials; and the design and preparation of any required master-copies); course production (e.g., the production of course materials and other courseware); and course delivery (e.g., the dissemination of course-content to students, and provision of tutorial or other support to students, with related monitoring and assessment). While some form of course planning and design is an essential preliminary to all forms of tertiary teaching, the planning and development of technology-based courses generally assumes a more central role and absorbs a higher proportion of staff time than contiguous modes of instruction. Other things being equal, the more complex the approach adopted, and the more limited the opportunity for in-course communication between course developers and students, the greater the need for prior planning and development.

Substitutability

Some forms of technology-based teaching, however, are malleable; that is to say they allow a high degree of substitutability between pre-course planning and the development of courseware on the one hand, and in-course teaching and student support on the other. This malleability, in effect, presents the course provider with the option of choosing, from the available operational strategies, the one that best suits the particular purpose and resources to hand. Observation of operational online programs in a range of universities suggests that online education is of this malleable kind, and so the extent of planning can vary from one program to another. In practice, of course, there are inevitable constraints that limit choice; much depends, in any particular case, on the aims of the program, on the academic content of the course, and on the nature and skills of the particular student population.

Effect on Mission and Ethos

Mission and ethos are intrinsically difficult to observe. However, the variety of aims that online education programs are designed to meet serves to illustrate one of the ways in which differences in mission and ethos, between institutions, finds expression. Some institutions provide courses primarily for on-campus students, often through some form of blended or hybrid program; some provide courses mainly for external distance learning students; and some do both. Some institutions provide only non-credit courses; others provide full undergraduate and/or postgraduate degrees online. Some institutions use online education essentially as a means of "topping up" their existing curriculum (e.g., by allowing students to access courses in other universities); others allow students to take all their courses online. The diversity of program aims is a striking illustration of the flexibility of online learning, and of the potential it offers universities to use it in ways compatible with the institution's particular mission and ethos.

CONCLUSIONS

Overall, this diversity in online education points to an inherent adaptability in use and flexibility in the application that, other things being equal, should facilitate its further growth and dispersion among tertiary institutions. More important still, this inherent adaptability of online education on the one hand, and the capacity on part of the modern university to respond to change on the other, suggests that radical or revolutionary change in universities as a consequence of the growth and pervasive spread of online education, is an unlikely prospect.

Moreover, viewed from the perspective of the university sector as a whole, one may surmise that the longer-term impact of online education will be hardly more profound than the change and diversification already experienced in the decades since World War II. For most traditional universities involved in online education, the related activities are, at most, a small part of their total operations, whether measured in terms of income, expenditure, or staff deployment—even in terms of enrolment (particularly where enrolment is measured in terms of full-time equivalent students). And it is not yet evident that this position will change substantially, in the short to medium term at least.

Experience to date suggests rather that the characteristics of adaptability, flexibility in application, and strategic diversity should (other things being equal) serve to facilitate individual universities in pursuing their particular mission and ethos. The inherent institutional constraints—of context, cost, and culture—should act as a brake on radical change.

Whether, and to what extent, these trends will coalesce with each other and with the wider forces of change and tradition acting on the university is an empirical question of great, and almost certainly continuing, interest—and an appropriate focus for longitudinal study.

NOTE

1. [a] www.apollogrp.edu [b] www.umuc.edu [c] *Chronicle of Higher Education*. (2003, Feb. 21). Letter to the Editor. (From Dr Jack Wilson, CEO UmassOnline).

REFERENCES

Allen, I. E., & Seaman, J. (2003). *Sizing the opportunity: The quality and extent of online education in the United States, 2002 and 2003*. Needham, MA: The Sloan Consortium.

Arvan, L., Ory, J. C., Bullock, C. D., Burnaska, K. K., & Hanson. M. (1997, September). The SCALE efficiency projects. *Journal of Asynchronous Learning Environments, 2*(2), 33–60.

Ash, C., Heginbotham, S., & Bacsich, P. (2001). *CNL handbook: Guidelines and resources for costing courses using activity based costing*. Sheffield, UK: Telematics in Education Research Group, Sheffield Hallam University.

Ashby, E. (1958). *Technology and the academics: An essay on universities and the scientific revolution*. London: Macmillan.

Attiyeh, R., & Lumsden, K. G. (1974). Educational production and human capital formation. In K. G. Lumsden (Ed.), *Efficiency in universities: The La Paz papers* (pp. 131–145). Amsterdam: Elsevier.

Bacsich, P., Ash, C., Boniwell, K., & Kaplan, L. (1999). *The costs of networked learning*. Sheffield, UK: Telematics in Education Research Group, Sheffield Hallam University.

Bacsich, P., Curran, C., Fox, S., Hogg, V., Mason, R., & Rawlings, A. (1993). *Telematic networks for open and distance learning in the tertiary sector* (Final Report:1–mimeo). Heerlen, Netherlands: European Association of Distance Teaching Universities.

Barnett, R. (1992). *Improving higher education: Total quality care*. Buckingham, UK: SRHE and Open University Press.

Bates, A. W. (2000). *Managing technological change: Strategies for college and university leaders*. San Francisco: Jossey Bass.

Bender, T. (1997). Politics, intellect, and the American university, 1945 to 1995. In T. Bender & C. E. Schorske (Eds.), *American academic culture in transformation: Fifty years, four disciplines* (pp. 17–56). Princeton, NJ: Princeton University Press.

Blaug, M. (1970). *An introduction to the economics of education*. Middlesex, UK: Penguin Books.

Bowen, W. G. (2001). *At a slight angle to the universe: The university in a digitized, commercialized age*. Princeton, NJ: Princeton University Press.

Bowman, M. G. (1966, Spring). The human investment revolution in economic thought. *Sociology of Education, 39*(2), 111–137.

Carnevale, D., & Olsen, F. (2003, June 13). How to succeed in distance education: By going after the right audience, online programs build a viable industry. *Chronicle of Higher Education, 49*(40), A31–A33.

CEDEFOP (2001). *E-learning and training in Europe* (CEDEFOP Ref series 26). Luxembourg: Office for Official Publications of the European Communities.

Clark, R. E. (1983). Reconsidering research on learning from media. *Review of Educational Research, 53*(4), 445–459.

Curran, C. (1996). Distance teaching at university level: Historical perspective and potential. In G. Fandel, R. Bartz & F. Nicholmann (Eds.), *University level distance education in Europe: Assessment and perspectives* (pp. 19–31). Weinheim, Germany: Deutscher Studien Verlag.

Curran, C. (2004, September). *Strategies for e-learning in universities.* (Research and Occasional Papers Series, CSHE 7.04). Berkeley, CA: UC Berkeley, Centre For Studies in Higher Education. Retrieved March 23, 2007, from http://repositories.cdlib.org/cshe/CSHE-7-04.

Daniel, J. (1998). Can you get my hard nose in focus? Universities, mass education and appropriate technology. In M. Eisenstadt & T. Vincent (Eds.), *The knowledge web: Learning and collaborating on the Net* (pp. 21–30). London: Kogan Page.

Daniel, J. (2001, September 7). Lessons from the Open University: Low-tech learning often works best. *Chronicle of Higher Education, 48*(2), B24.

de Groot, H., McMahon, W. W., & Volkwein, J. F. (1991, August). The cost structure of American research universities. *Review of Economics and Statistics, 73*(3), 424–431.

Education online [Cover story]. (2006, October 16). *U. S. News & World Report, 141*(14), 62.

Ehrmann, S. C., & Milam. J. H. (1999). *Modeling resource use in teaching and learning with technology.* Washington, DC: Teaching, Learning and Technology Group, AAHE.

Ellis, E. M. (2000). Faculty participation in the Pennsylvania State University World Campus: Identifying barriers to success. *Open Learning, 15*(3), 233–242.

European Commission (2000). *Designing tomorrow's education: Promoting innovation with new technology.* Brussels: Author.

Fisher, S., & Nygren, T. I. (2000). *Experiments in the cost effective uses of technology in teaching: Lessons from the Mellon program so far.* New York: Andrew W. Mellon Foundation, Cost Effective Uses of Technology in Teaching (CEUTT) Initiative.

Gellert, C. (1993). Changing patterns in European higher education. In C. Gellert (Ed.), *Higher education in Europe* (pp. 9–20). London: Jessica Kingsley.

Gladieux, L. E. (2000). *The virtual university and educational opportunity: Issues of equity and access of the next generation.* Washington, DC: The College Board.

Harley, D., Maher, M., Henke, J., & Shannon, L. (2003). An analysis of technology enhancements in a large lecture course. *Educause Quarterly, 26*(3), 26–33.

Hitt, J. C., & Hartman, J. L. (2002). *Distributed learning: New challenges and opportunities for institutional leadership.* Washington, DC: American Council on Education and EDUCAUSE.

Hudgins, S. (2000). *Never an ivory tower: University of Maryland University College, the first 50 years.* Adelphi MD: University of Maryland University College.

Katz, S. N. (2001, June 15). In information technology, don't mistake a tool for a goal. *Chronicle of Higher Education, 47*(40), B7–B9.

Kerr, C. (2001). *The uses of the university* (5th ed.). Cambridge, MA: Harvard University Press.

MacKeogh, K. (2001, June). National strategies for the promotion of online learning in higher education. *European Journal of Education, 36*(2), 223–236.

Martin, G., & Jennings, A. (2002). *The adoption, diffusion and exploitation of e-learning in Europe: An overview and analysis of the UK, Germany and France.* Dundee, Scotland: University of Abertay, Dundee Business School.

Massy, W. F., & Zemsky, R. (1995). *Using Information Technology to Enhance Academic Productivity.* National Learning Infrastructure Initiative (NLII) and Educom. Retrieved June 12, 2007, from http://www.educause.edu/ir/library/html/nli0004.html.

Massy, W. F., & Wilger, A.K. (1998). Technology's contribution to higher education productivity. In J. E. Groccia & J. E. Miller (Eds.), *New directions for higher education: No. 103. Enhancing productivity: Administrative, instructional, and technological strategies* (pp. 49–59). San Francisco: Jossey-Bass.

Menand, L. (1996). The limits of academic freedom. In L. Menand (Ed.), *The future of academic freedom* (pp. 3-20). Chicago: University Press.

Menand, L. (2001, October 18). College: The end of the Golden Age. *New York Review of Books, 48*(16), 44–47.

Milam, J. (2000). *Cost analysis of online courses* [2000 AIR Forum Paper]. Charlottesville, VA: University of Virginia, Curry School of Education.

Moore, M. G., Thompson, M. M., Quigley, B. A., Clark, G. C., & Goff, G. G. (1990). *The effects of distance learning: A summary of literature* (Research Monograph No. 2). University Park, PA: The Pennsylvania State University, American Center for the Study of Distance Education. (ERIC Document Reproduction Service No. ED330321).

Naughton, J. (2000). *A brief history of the future: The origins of the Internet.* London: Phoenix.

Newman, F., & Scurry, J. (2001, July 13). Online technology pushes pedagogy to the forefront. *Chronicle of Higher Education, 47*(44), B7–B9.

Noble, D. F. (2001). *Digital diploma mills: The automation of higher education.* New York: Monthly Review Press.

Noble, D. F. (2002, March). Technology and the commodification of higher education. *Monthly Review, 53*(10), 26–40.

Oakley, B. (2000). Learning effectiveness: An introduction. In J. Bourne (Ed.), *On-line education: Learning effectiveness and faculty satisfaction. Proceedings of the 1999 Sloan Summer Workshop.* Nashville, TN: ALN Center, Vanderbilt University.

Oblinger, D. G., Barone, C. A., & Hawkins, B. L. (2001). *Distributed education and its challenges: An overview.* Washington, DC: American Council on Education and EDUCAUSE.

Panzar, J. C., & Willig, R. D. (1981, May). Economies of scope. *American Economic Review, 71*(2), 268–272.

Perley, J., & Tanguay, D. M. (1999, October 29). Accrediting on-line institutions diminishes higher education. *Chronicle of Higher Education, 46*(10), B4–B5.

Perry, W. (1996). Distance systems in Europe. In A. Burgen (Ed.), *Goals and purposes of higher education in the 21st century* (pp. 62–68). London: Jessica Kingsley.

Phipps, R., & Merisotis, J. (1999). *What's the difference? A review of contemporary research on the effectiveness of distance learning in higher education.* Washington, DC: The Institute for Higher Education Policy. Retrieved June 12, 2007, from http://eric.ed.gov/ERICDocs/data/ericdocs2/content_storage_01/0000000b/80/11/6f/e4.pdf.

PLS RAMBOLL (2004, February). *Studies in the context of the e-learning initiative: Virtual models of European universities.* (Lot 1). [Draft Final Report to the EU Commission]. Copenhagen: DG Education and Culture.

Ramphele, M. (2002). Foreword. In R. Hopper (Ed.), *Constructing knowledge societies: New challenges for tertiary edu*cation (pp. ix–xi). Washington, DC: The World Bank.

Rumble, G. (1989). Online costs: Interactivity at a price. In R. Mason & A. Kaye (Eds.), *Mindweave: Communications, computers, and distance education* (pp. 146–165). Oxford: Pergamon.

Rumble, G. (2001, April 1–5). *The costs of providing online student support services.* UKOU Student Services at the UK Open University. Papers presented to the 20th World Conference of the International Council for Open and Distance Education. Dusseldorf, Germany.

Russell, T. L. (1999). *The no significant difference phenomenon.* Raleigh: North Carolina State University, Office of Instructional Telecommunications.

Schelin, E., & Smarte, G. (2002, March). A conversation with Tony Digiovanni of the University of Phoenix Online. *e-Learning, 3*(3), 42–44.

Scott P. (1998). Decline or transformation? The future of the university in a knowledge economy and a post-modern age. In P. Baggen, A. Tellings & W. van Haaften (Eds.), *The university and the knowledge society* (pp. 13–30). Bemmel, Netherlands: Concorde Publishing House.

Sobel, I. (1978). The human capital revolution in economic development: Its current history and status. *Computer Education Review, 19,* 187–201.

Teichler, U. (1996). Higher education and new socio-economic challenges in Europe. In A. Burgen (Ed.), *Goals and purposes of higher education in the 21st century.* London: Jessica Kingsley.

Twigg, C. A. (1999). *Improving learning & reducing costs: Redesigning large-enrollment courses.* Troy, NY: Centre for Academic Transformation, Rensselaer Polytechnic Institute.

University of Illinois. (1999, December 7). *Teaching at an Internet distance: The pedagogy of online teaching and learning: The report of a 1998–1999 University of Illinois faculty seminar.* Retrieved March 6, 2007, from the University of Illinois Web site: http://www.vpaa.uillinois.edu/reports_retreats/tid.asp.

U. S. Department of Commerce (2000). *Falling through the net: Toward digital inclusion.* Washington, DC: Author.

van der Molen, H. (1996). Creation, transfer and application of knowledge through the higher education system. In A. Burgen (Ed.), *Goals and purposes of higher education in the 21st Century* (pp. 13–23). London: Jessica Kingsley.

Waits, T., Lewis, L., & Greene, B. (2003). *Distance education at degree-granting post-secondary institutions: 2000–2001.* Washington DC: U.S. Department of Education, National Center for Education Statistics. (NCES 2003-017).

Web-Based Education Commission (2000). *The power of the Internet for learning: Moving from promise to practice: Report of the Web-Based Education Commission to the President and Congress of the United States.* Washington, DC: Web-Based Education Commission. [http://www.webcommission.org].

Wood, D. N., & Wylie, D. G. (1977). *Educational telecommunications.* Belmont: Wadsworth.

Young, J. (2002, March 22). 'Hybrid' teaching seeks to end the divide between traditional and online instruction. *Chronicle of Higher Education, 48*(28), A33–A34.

Zemsky, R., & Massy, W. F. (2004). *Thwarted innovation: What happened to e-learning and why.* Philadelphia: The Learning Alliance at the University of Pennsylvania. Retrieved March 23, 2007, from http://www.thelearningalliance.info/Docs/Jun2004/ThwartedInnovation.pdf.

4

VIRTUAL SCHOOLING AND BASIC EDUCATION

Thomas Clark

TA Consulting, Illinois, USA

INTRODUCTION

The primary focus of this chapter is the current status and trends of virtual schools and e-learning in elementary and secondary schools, and in basic education, with a particular focus on the United States. The context of online learning in schools and basic education is reviewed. Developments in the United States are highlighted, within the international context, and basic information on economic aspects of virtual schooling is presented.

CURRENT STATUS OF VIRTUAL
SCHOOLS AND E-LEARNING

Elementary and Secondary Education in the United States

In the United States, education of students between the ages of 5–18 usually occurs in early elementary or primary schools (Kindergarten–5th grade), in middle (late elementary) schools (5th–8th grade), and at the secondary level in high schools (9th–12th grade). Together these schools are referred to as K–12 schools. About 53.9 million students were enrolled in public or private K–12 schools in the United States in 2001, a number projected to increase about 4% annually to 56.4 million by 2013 (Gerald & Hussar,

2003). Public and private education is primarily regulated at the state level, with each of the 50 states having its own system. The organization of elementary and secondary education is very similar in the adjoining nation of Canada, where each of the 13 provinces and territories has its own educational system. However, Canada does not have a federal department of education.

Passage of the No Child Left Behind (NCLB) Act in 2001 had a major impact on U. S. public education. NCLB imposes federal standards for academic outcomes, assistance to disadvantaged students, school improvement, and teacher quality. Under NCLB, public schools must show academic progress annually, including for minority, disabled, and limited English proficient students. If they cannot, their district must fund alternative schooling options for students, called Educational Choice, after two years, and provide Supplemental Educational Services after three years. NCLB is not legally considered an unfunded mandate because state and local entities can opt out and decline federal funds. None has done so to date, although only about 8.3% of the $536 billion spent on public schools by U.S. taxpayers in 2004–05 was at the federal level (U. S. Department of Education, 2005a).

Virtual Schools and E-Learning

Clark (2001) defines a virtual school as "an educational organization that offers K–12 courses through Internet- or Web-based methods" (p. 1). Virtual schooling is a form of distance education, or formal study in which teacher and learners are separate in time or space. It is conducted primarily online, and intended for elementary or secondary learners. As noted by Watson, Winograd, and Kalmon (2004), a virtual school or online learning program offers formal instruction, not merely instructional resources or content. Many organizations, such as home schooling Web sites, provide e-learning resources but are not themselves virtual schools. Distance education may utilize both non-electronic media such as print and electronic media. Electronic media include telecommunications systems, such as audio and video conferencing networks, and "online" information technologies such as computers and the Internet. Distance education conducted via correspondence study, or via audio or video conferencing systems, is not considered here to be virtual schooling.

Virtual schooling is a type of e-learning. *E-learning* may be broadly defined as all the ways in which technology supports teaching, learning, and school improvement (Clark & Berge, 2005a). Internationally, the term *information and communication technologies* (ICTs) is commonly used to describe electronic media, which may be used in education, business, government, or daily life. In the United States, the term *technology* is often used in a similar sense. The general use of technology or ICTs in education is here referred to as e-learning. Some prefer to define e-learning as online learning only, but this usage is too narrow. E-learning may occur both in distance and conventional education and may involve electronic media that do not use online delivery. For example, integration of technology or ICTs in face-to-face classroom activities is e-learning, as are courses delivered via videoconferencing.

The actual extent of virtual schooling in the United States is hard to measure. It appears that most students take an online course or two while enrolled full-time in a regular school. About one-third of U. S. public school districts reported at least one student enrolled in a distance education course delivered by online, video, or other methods in 2002–03 (Setzer & Lewis, 2005). Clark (2001) estimated 40–50,000 K–12 enrollments in online courses in 2000–01 based on a survey of course providers. Peak Group (2002) surveyed virtual schools a year later and found 180,000 enrollments. In 2002–03, Eduventures estimated 300,000 enrollments (Newman, Stein, & Trask, 2003). Enrollments currently may be two or three times that number.

TYPES OF VIRTUAL SCHOOLS

Clark (2001) classifies virtual schools by controlling entity: State government, university, consortium, local school district, charter school, or private school. This organizational scheme is followed here. Virtual schools may also be organized by full-time or supplemental nature, accreditation status, curricular or instructional model, course offerings, or other characteristics.

State-Level Virtual Schools

These are virtual schools developed, administered, or funded in part by state government and intended to provide statewide online learning opportunities (Watson, Winograd, & Kalmon, 2004). By 2001, about 13 state-level virtual schools were in existence. By 2005, about 20 of the 50 U.S. states operated a virtual school (Table 4.1). Twelve were administered by the state education agency, and six by consortia; two were freestanding entities. State virtual schools are usually intended to provide supplemental courses to regular schools, although they may also serve homeschoolers. In most states, the local school acts as school of record and awards the final grade, allowing it to count enrollments toward state aid funding.

When Utah founded its Electronic School in 1994, it offered both online and video-based distance education opportunities for students. The next wave of state virtual schools focused on online education. Many virtual schools started in the last few years, such as the Iowa Learning Online (www.virtualacademy.k12.ia.us), combine online and video opportunities. Given extensive state investments in existing videoconferencing networks

Table 4.1 State-Sanctioned State-Level Virtual Schools: Operating Agency and Year Founded

Free-standing school	Operated by a consortium, state education agency a partner	Primarily operated by a state education agency	
Florida (1997)	Arkansas (2000)	Utah (1994)	New Mexico (2001)
Michigan (2000)	Alabama (2000)	Hawaii (1996)	Virginia (2003)
	Colorado (2001)*	Louisiana (2000)	Mississippi (2003)
	Illinois (2001)	West Virginia (2000)	Idaho (2003)
	Washington (2003)	Kentucky (2000)	Iowa (2004)
	Maryland (2004)**	North Dakota (2000)	Georgia (2005)

* *Consortium administered by state department of education, expanded to state-wide availability in 2001.*

** *First offered online courses in 2004; state department of education resource site prior to 2004.*

and programming, this recent trend of merging state e-learning systems via virtual schools is not surprising.

The largest state virtual school is Florida Virtual School (FLVS), which began as a cooperative program of the Orange and Alachua County school districts in 1996 through a $200,000 state grant. Funded through a line item budget by the Florida legislature from 1996 until 2003, the program became an independent educational entity in 2000. In 2003, FLVS obtained state approval to receive its state funding through a performance-based model, in which it receives state aid for each successful student completion. Tuition is free to local schools. As a result of this unique funding model, FLVS is one of the few virtual schools to directly control its own financial future. FLVS is a school district in its own right and recognized as a Parental Choice option under NCLB. Districts may not prevent students from participating if FLVS accepts their enrollment, and FLVS assigns final grades. The state of Florida authorizes FLVS to market its programs nationally and internationally, as a source of revenue to subsidize in-state operations. FLVS had 21,270 course enrollments in 2003–04 and 33,000 in 2004–05, with a completion rate over 90% (www.flvs.net). FLVS received about $8.5 million in state aid in 2003–04 and $14.9 million the following year, a 74% increase (Florida Department of Education, 2005).

Consortia

A consortium or collaborative can spread the costs of course development across participating agencies, facilitating development of a shared curriculum that follows common design standards (Cavalluzzo, 2004). Some state virtual schools, such as Colorado Online Learning, operate as consortia managed by the state education agency. Regional educational agencies have developed some virtual school consortia, such as Virtual Greenbush in Kansas. School districts also lead virtual school consortia. For example, Alaska Online is a 14-district consortium that operates directly via a line item in the Federal budget.

Perhaps the best known and longest-lived consortium is the Virtual High School (VHS). In 1996, a five-year Technology Innovation Challenge Grant was awarded to Hudson Public Schools to develop VHS in partnership with the nonprofit Concord Consortium. Unlike many federally funded projects, VHS succeeded in transforming itself into a self-sustaining non-profit (VHS, Inc.), established in 2001 to continue operations of the collaborative. It instituted fees for participation and instructor training, but continued to maintain a critical mass of participating schools—about 207 schools in 22 states and 14 countries participate (www.govhs. org). This online learning program uses a collaborative model, in which each participating school provides an instructor who is trained to teach an online class. In return, the school receives a classroom's worth of seats in virtual courses offered by VHS Collaborative schools. VHS used a 2003 grant to develop an Advanced Placement academy that targets low-income schools. In 2004, VHS partnered with the International Baccalaureate Organization and the Graded School of Sao Paulo to develop and deliver the first cross-national IB Diploma course, delivered entirely online. In 2003–04, VHS enrolled 5,069 students, and like Florida Virtual School, had a completion rate over 90%. Why do these two large virtual schools have such high completion rates? Both have strong standards for course development, delivery, and instruction; and both train teachers extensively and screen and pace students effectively. FLVS is only paid for completers, while the seat limit may help in VHS.

College or University-based Programs

A significant portion of virtual schooling is conducted by U. S. postsecondary or tertiary institutions. About one-half of school districts reporting distance education enrollments in 2002–03 had students enrolled in a course via a college or university. While not a form of virtual schooling or e-learning, correspondence or independent study is still an important K–12 distance learning method in the United States. Enrollments in independent study high schools increased through the 1980s and 1990s, reaching 164,000 in 1997–98 (Pittman, 2000). At least seven independent study high schools have developed an online curriculum, making them virtual schools as well.

The University of Nebraska-Lincoln, which established the first independent study high school in 1929, led the transition to online learning. From 1996–2001, the Federal Star Schools Program funded its CLASS (Communications, Learning, and Assessment in a Student-centered System) Project. The goal of CLASS was to produce a full high school diploma curriculum on the Web, incorporating interactive multimedia.

As grant funding ended, Class.com, a commercial entity, emerged as an Research and Development spin-off from the university that continues to be a national provider of online courses today (Clark, 2001). Other university-based online learning programs began outside of independent study units. Examples include Stanford's Education Program for Gifted Youth, which enrolls over 3,000 students from 23 countries (www-epgy.stanford. edu), and the University of California College Prep program (www.uccp. org) which offers Advanced Placement (AP) and other college preparatory courses online with the goal of increasing minority student eligibility for enrollment in the University of California system.

Virtual Charter Schools

Charter schools are underwritten with public funds and are operated under a charter by an eligible organization as defined under state law. They are exempt from many school laws applied to regular public schools, and under NCLB, are one of the options for Educational Choice. As public education entities, they are tuition-free. In 2005, 40 states and the District of Columbia had charter school laws in place. Approximately 3,400 charter schools were in operation across the United States, serving about a million students (Center for Education Reform, 2005). Sixteen of these states have permitted virtual schools to operate as charter schools, and in 2003–04, 86 cyber charter schools served about 31,000 students nationwide. Ten of these cyber charters operated in Pennsylvania in 2003–04, enrolling 6,885 students or 45% of all charter school students in the state (Chute, 2005).

Some for-profit companies partner with charter school organizations in multiple states to provide a virtual education where the student attends from home. Connections Academy, begun in 2001, operated 11 charter schools in eight states in 2005, serving approximately 3,000 students in grades K–8. Founded in 1999, K12, Inc. (www.k12.com) served charter schools in nine states by 2003 (Baker, Bouras, Hartwig, & McNair, 2005). Each started with a focus on early elementary grades, and both expanded to offer K–9 curricula in 2005–06. Both providers lend computers to participating families, which can pay for curriculum materials directly for use in home schooling or enroll their child in a tuition-free public school option. Parents conduct instruction using the provider's curricular materials and an individualized learning plan generated through periodic online assessment results. Certified instructors can track student progress through the curriculum via a learning management system. Some states without charter school laws have sanctioned cyber charter school-like activities. Florida's K–8 Virtual Pilot provides $4,800 per student, per year to virtual schools operated by K12, Inc. and Connections Academy to serve home-based students who have previously attended a public school. Students must show a year's progress on proctored state academic tests for their virtual schools to receive payment (Watson, Winograd, & Kalmon, 2004).

Home school families are generally of two minds about virtual charter schools. On one hand, some experienced home school parents are concerned about cyber charters as a form of public education imposing state standards on home instruction. On the other hand, some parents are more likely to undertake home schooling in a virtual school environment.

Local Education Agencies

A majority of online learning activity occurs in public schools. In establishing their local virtual school program, these schools may follow a variety of paths. Many elect to participate in a consortium; others offer access to the state's virtual schoo, or to courses from vendors. Some districts sponsor cyber charter schools. One example of a virtual school developed "from scratch" by a local school district is the Cumberland County School (CCS) Web Academy, located in Fayetteville, North Carolina. This school served about 1,600 North Carolina students in 2002–03. About 75% of students were in-district, while other students were enrolled in 76 of the 116 other school districts in North Carolina. Students may study in individual or supervised formats, as determined by their school district (Jordan, 2005). Other examples of virtual schools operated by local districts include Houston ISD Virtual School in Texas, which provides middle school and college preparatory courses, and the Wichita eSchool in Kansas, which provides an online high school curriculum.

Local virtual schools operate within varying state and local funding policies. CCS Web Academy receives no state aid, except for the small minority of students who study full-time. Most in-district students attend regular CCS schools and take Web Academy courses supplementally; out-of-district students pay tuition. Wichita eSchool charges only textbook fees to in-district students who attend from home full-time, but charges tuition and fees for out-of-district students. It does not serve in-district students who are enrolled in schools.

Private Schools

A number of nonprofit and proprietary private school entities offer virtual schooling. Because they are not associated with public education entities, obtaining accreditation recognized by colleges and employers is more of a challenge for private virtual schools. A growing number offer regionally or trans-regionally accredited high school diplomas, such as Christa McAuliffe Academy (CMA), Keystone National High School, and Laurel Springs School. CMA, based in the state of Washington, began offering Internet-based K–12 education in 1995. It began a decade earlier as a small local academy that offered its mastery learning-based curriculum via independent study, using computer and CD-ROM based materials. CMA is a non-profit corporation, funded from private sources and from contractual funding for services provided to school districts and charter schools. Students complete self-paced online tutorial-style lessons with the assistance of CMA mentors and participate in weekly meetings with their mentor in an online virtual classroom. Pennsylvania-based Keystone National High School, one of the oldest proprietary high schools in the nation, offers high school study online through its iSchool or through traditional correspondence study. Laurel Springs School, located in California, promotes a personalized distance education model through its Web- and text-based curricula. Students and parents are encouraged to complete a learning style profile.

Some for-profit companies that focus on providing online courses for school districts have decided to become private schools themselves. For example, Apex Learning became regionally accredited in 1999 as a distance education school. It continues to follow a non-diploma model of providing supplemental courses to local schools, taught by a certified Apex instructor or local teacher. Many companies have become e-learning solutions providers, offering online content, infrastructure, instruction, and other components of a virtual school.

VIRTUAL SCHOOLS AND E-LEARNING IN OTHER NATIONS

School networking infrastructure, or "schoolnet," is a common frame of reference in many nations for the process of communicating and collaborating via ICTs across schools and nations, to share activities, content, and curricula (Naidoo & Isaacs, 2004). For example, Canada's SchoolNet (www.schoolnet.ca) was the first to connect public schools and libraries to the Internet across an entire nation, in 1999, while the European Schoolnet (www.eun.org) is operated by 26 ministries of education and their partners. Similar multinational efforts are underway in other regions of the world. Schoolnet consortia often lead initiatives to build ICT infrastructure and provide standards and training. Attempts to create a national schoolnet-type structure in the United States have not succeeded. Instead, school networking efforts occur mainly at the state level. About 34 states have joined the Internet2 K–20 initiative (http://k20.internet2.edu), established to share high-bandwidth educational projects on their K–12 or K–20 networks.

Given its relatively open border with the United States and shared language and educational traditions, it is probably not surprising that Canada has considerable virtual schooling underway. Examples of well-established virtual schools operated by public school districts include Durham Virtual School in Ontario and Fraser Valley Distance Education School in British Columbia. Virtual schools may act as home school providers under supervision of a public or private school board in Alberta. Examples include School of Hope, a Catholic online school, and Rocky View Virtual School, operated by a public school district. These home-based schools appear to play a role similar to cyber charter schools in the United States. So far,

Alberta is the only province that permits charter schools, all of which appear to operate conventionally.

Other nations with a history of K–12 distance education, such as Australia and England, have a limited number of online learning programs at the elementary and secondary levels. For example, A School Without Walls, or ASW2 (www.asw2.net), a program of the Southbank International School in London, officially opened its doors in 2003. ASW2 offers six Level A subjects and six International Baccalaureate subjects online on a supplemental basis for students enrolled in other schools. Virtual School for the Gifted, founded in Melbourne in 1997 (now closed), offered online enrichment courses.

The high levels of technology access and use in the United States and Canada are often given as an explanation for the growth in virtual schooling there. Despite similar levels of technology access and use, online learning programs at the elementary and secondary level do not appear to be a major focus in Europe. However, ICT is part of the compulsory minimum curriculum of pupils virtually everywhere in Europe, and almost two-thirds of 15-year-olds reported using computer regularly in school in 2000 (Eurydice, 2004). Why is virtual schooling largely a North American phenomenon? There appears to be a number of interrelated factors involved, none of which is sufficient on its own to explain its emergence and growth there.

FACTORS IN THE GROWTH OF VIRTUAL SCHOOLS AND E-LEARNING IN THE UNITED STATES

Technology Access and Use in Schools

Most schools in the United States have fairly high levels of technology access and use, due in part to federal and state efforts. By 2003, nearly all U. S. public schools had access to the Internet, and over 9 in 10 instructional rooms were connected. Four-fifths of public schools provided professional development in technology integration that school year, and 43% indicated one-half or more of their teachers participated (Parsad & Jones, 2005). In 2001, about 68% of American children 5–17 reported accessing the Internet at school (Debell & Chapman, 2003). Without this level of technology access, it is unlikely virtual schooling would have grown as quickly as it has. Federal support has helped build this access.

National Policies and Planning

The Web-Based Education Commission (2000) showed the evolving federal interest in online learning. It began with a mission to assess educational software, but received additional direction to assess policy issues in the use of Web-based learning at the K–12 and postsecondary education levels. One thing that distinguishes current U. S. e-learning efforts from other nations is a focus on using technology to document student achievement under NCLB. Prior to passage of NCLB by the U. S. Congress in 2001, the primary focus was on expanding educational opportunities via technology (*Education Week*, 2005). The federal vision sees e-learning and virtual schools as a strategy for implementing NCLB. In 2005, the National Educational Technology Plan (NETP) was released. One of seven NETP action goals for improving the use of educational technology is "support e-learning and virtual schools." Five recommendations support this strategy:

- Provide every student access to e-learning
- Enable every teacher to participate in e-learning training
- Encourage the use of e-learning options to meet NCLB requirements for highly qualified teachers, supplemental services, and parental choice
- Explore creative ways to fund e-learning opportunities
- Develop quality measures and accreditation standards for e-learning that mirror those required for course credit. (U. S. Department of Education, 2005b, pp. 41–42)

After the NETP was released, the President's Budget for 2005–06 proposed elimination of a key federal funding source, the Enhancing Education through Technology program. This has raised questions about federal commitments to help states, districts, and schools implement the NETP, and lent renewed urgency to efforts by technology leaders at all levels to advocate effectively for their goals.

One such effort is the North American Council for Online Learning (www.nacol.org), founded to provides support and advocacy for online learning. NACOL grew out of a series of meetings of online learning organizations. Its first board was announced in 2003 and included administrators of leading virtual schools and experts in the field from the United States and Canada. NACOL's Web site includes an Online Learning Clearinghouse of U. S. K–12 online learning programs.

Federal Support

Federal funds for technology connectivity have mainly been provided via the E-Rate program. E-Rate provides discounts of 20–90% on the costs of Internet and telecommunications connectivity for eligible entities, with high-poverty urban and rural locations receiving the largest discounts. Schools, school districts, and libraries may apply individually or as a consortium. E-Rate is funded through a federal tax on end user telephone bills. From 1998 to present, about $2.2 billion has been authorized each year for payments by E-Rate to connectivity service providers (www.e-ratecentral. com). Recent connectivity gains in high-poverty schools can be attributed in part to E-Rate funding. In 2000, schools where at least three in four students were in poverty reported that only 60% of their classrooms had Internet access. By 2003, they reported Internet access in 90% of classrooms, close to the national average of 93%. However, charges of fraud and mismanagement in the E-Rate program continue to be an issue, and its future is uncertain.

Another major federal funding source is the Enhancing Education through Technology (EETT) program, which provides grants to states. In 2002, EETT replaced the Technology Literacy Challenge Fund program, which since 1995 had been annually funded at around $400 million. Appropriations under EETT began at $700 million annually, but declined to $496 million in 2004–05; they have continued to decline since, with program elimination a possibility each year. Under EETT, states distribute one-half of their funding to school districts based on poverty and one-half based on competitive priorities. Funds can be used for online courses, hardware and software, testing, and data reporting. At least 25% of EETT funds must be devoted to staff development in technology use.

A number of smaller federal technology programs were proposed for elimination by the Administration when EETT was introduced in 2002. The Technology Innovation Challenge Grant program, which funded the Virtual High School, peaked at $149 million annually in 2000; its funding ended in 2005. The Star Schools program began in 1988 with an emphasis on video-based distance learning for rural schools, and shifted its emphasis over time to online learning programs, such as the CLASS Project. Expenditures peaked at $59 million in 2001. Star Schools has enjoyed bipartisan popularity, and Congress has continued funding through Fiscal Year 2006. It is also facing possible program elimination. Both VHS, Inc. and Class. com achieved a "critical mass" of participating schools and funding commitments prior to the end of their federal seed funding. They are probably the most successful federally funded virtual school experiments.

State Policies and Support

Most states continue to apply policies developed to regulate physical schools to online learning. For example, state aid to school districts has traditionally been based on seat time, with the average daily attendance of students being used to calculate payments. States do not set quality or special education standards for online learning used by local schools. This *ad hoc* policy approach is leading to a variety of online education practices that may later be proscribed or seen as undermining public education (Watson, Winograd, & Kalmon, 2004).

States are primarily responsible for integrating technology use into their educational systems. A number of states have focused on providing free or reduced-cost access to online learning courses and resources via a state virtual school, as a way of making online learning affordable (Cavalluzzo,

2004). Some states complement the federal E-Rate with programs to assist with connectivity needs that it does not address. For example, the California Teleconnect Fund uses a state tax on telephone bills to subsidize high-bandwidth data lines in schools, libraries, hospitals, and community agencies.

Most departments of education in the United States offer portals to curriculum resources and conduct statewide initiatives to disseminate technology and training. A good example is the state of South Dakota, which since the mid-1990s has linked schools via the Digital Dakota Network, seeded school technology funding, and used workshops and academies to build technology integration skills of educators (Simonson, 2005). In 2005, this rural state had the highest per-student school Internet connectivity in the U.S. (*Education Week*, 2005).

Another is Ohio Schoolnet (www.osn.state.oh.us), the only state e-learning agency in the nation that bears the SchoolNet name familiar internationally. Reflecting an emphasis on NCLB, its mission is "to provide leadership, coordination and accountability in the use of technology to improve schools and raise student achievement." Three of its seven priorities are accountability related, including developing a decision support system, increasing school administrator skills in data-driven decision making, and assessing the impact of technology on achievement. OSN also builds and supports state technology infrastructure, provides professional development resources, fosters collaboration, and seeks to maximize technology funding and cost savings. Like many state e-learning agencies, Ohio SchoolNet also administers video-based distance learning efforts.

Equity Concerns

When the state of California was sued over inequitable access to Advanced Placement (AP) courses in rich and poor public schools, states looked to virtual schooling as one way to address this national equity issue. AP allows students to take college-level courses in high school and sit for exams that give them early college credit. In many school systems, an "A" in AP counts as a "5", not a "4" on a student's grade point average. With the elimination of race-based preferences in university admissions, increasing AP opportunities for disadvantaged students was seen as a way to improve their college chances. Many entities sought funding through the federal Advanced Placement Incentive Program (www.ed.gov/programs/apincent) to start their virtual school efforts. In 2005, APIP provided about $29 million for online and on-site AP activities.

POLICY INFLUENCERS

Education Market Vendors

Online education vendors may be driving policy and practice in some states and in some cases compete with public schools for funding (Watson,

Winograd, & Kalmon, 2004). For example, national providers of charter school content partner with in-state charter operators to obtain state aid for their cyber charter schools. These for-profit organizations work closely with states and districts and play a role in policymaking and planning. Educational need, not vendors, should drive the planning process for educational agencies considering online learning (Clark & Berge, 2005b). At the same time, a significant portion of the technology investments in schools has come through in-kind donations from technology vendors.

Consumer Interest

The role of parental or student interest in creating a demand for K–12 online learning should not be overlooked. AP and other online college-level courses can give college-bound students an early start, both in college credits and online learning experience. By fall 2004, an estimated 2.6 million U.S. college and university students enrolled in at least one online course (Sloan Consortium, 2005).

Stakeholder Perceptions

Most "cyber charter school" students are homeschoolers. Only about 850,000 students, less than 2% of all school age children, were home schooled in 1999 (Bielick, Chandler, & Broughman, 2001). Opinion polls have shown that only about 30% of U. S. adults support allowing students to earn high school credits over the Internet without attending a regular school, compared with 41% who approved of home schooling (Rose & Gallup, 2002). However, this poll did not ask about supplemental use of online courses by students attending regular schools, the most common mode of virtual schooling. Many supplemental virtual schools seek, through public relations efforts, to counter the public image that all virtual schools are charter schools taking dollars away from public education.

Quality and Accreditation

With the emergence of virtual schools, policy makers at all levels are revisiting the perennial issue of whether distance education is as effective as conventional education, this time at the K–12 level. Studies have shown no significant difference in the academic outcomes of distance and conventional K–12 education, including a recent rigorous meta-analysis by Cavanaugh, Gillan, Kromrey, Hess, and Blomeyer (2004). A number of organizations have developed quality measures for online K–12 courses, including National Schools Board Association and its partners, the Southern Regional Educational Board, and the Texas IQ Project. Five of six regional accrediting associations and the National Council for Private Schools Accreditation have developed a Council for Trans-Regional Accreditation (www.citaschools.org), one of whose services is providing standards and accreditation for distance education schools. While not perfect, accreditation assures a basic level of quality.

Demographic Issues

Geographic location is associated with different kinds of virtual school use. Virtual schooling, like other forms of K–12 distance education, continues to appeal to small and rural schools seeking to expand their curriculum (Clark, 2003). Large urban schools have become more active users of online learning as a strategy for meeting No Child Left Behind goals. Suburban schools often use virtual courses for college preparatory purposes. Projected increases in student populations have been used as a justification for funding state virtual schools in Florida and elsewhere, but to date the utility of online learning as a strategy for relieving overcrowding in schools or lowering class size has not been conclusively demonstrated.

Costs and Funding Models

Declining state revenues have impacted state-level funding for technology, while federal funding for technology is shifting to a focus on measuring student achievement. While many virtual school programs and e-learning initiatives have received start-up funding from external sources, their long-term sustainability is unlikely without a viable funding model. Most state virtual schools start with a legislative appropriation but transition to a tuition or subscription model for sustainability (Cavalluzzo, 2004). As noted previously, state policies often determine the viability of funding models. There have been few studies of the costs of online K–12 learning in the United States and none on cost/benefit or return on investment. The cost of a virtual school operation is essentially its fixed costs, plus variable or recurrent costs, times the number of students served. Cavalluzzo provides a good overview of the costs of online learning programs that follow different organizational models. Cost categories cited by this author include: (1) courseware, platform, and delivery system, (2) instruction, and (3) management and administrative functions. Adsit (2003) analyzed the costs of virtual schools and found them to average $6,000–6,400 per pupil annually, the same as (on a per-pupil basis) or more than conventional schools. Like Cavalluzzo, Adsit found that the costs of courseware varied widely and often accounted for variances in per-pupil cost.

Approaches to Virtual School Planning

Clark (2001) identified nine issues or components important in virtual school success: Access/equity, funding, curriculum, technology, instruction/teacher development, academic services, administration and policy, marketing and public relations, and program assessment. Several recent works have focused on virtual school development. Morris (2002) provides a good overview from the program administrator's viewpoint of the process of creating the Wichita eSchool. Eduventures (Newman, Stein, & Trask, 2003) provides a virtual school planning framework focused around assessing needs and making "build or partner" decisions on components. While valuable, this report was funded by vendors and has a focus on partnering with them. Cavanaugh and colleagues (2004) and Berge and Clark (2005) compiled case studies from virtual schools on their planning and management strategies and lessons learned.

VIRTUAL SCHOOL PROGRAM PLANNING CHECKLIST

Is there a "roadmap" for virtual learning? There are no hard and fast rules for those planning a virtual school, especially given the wide range of organizational models and purposes served. The following checklist for the local school thinking about starting a program was adapted from Clark and Berge (2005b). It reflects a belief that a decision to develop a virtual school program should be based on school needs rather than vendor-driven.

1. Determine if needs warrant consideration of a virtual school
   - Create a planning group, identify school improvement and equity needs
   - Identify academic content to meet needs
   - Identify student audiences and desired academic outcomes
2. Determine if a virtual school program is the best option to meet identified needs
   - Consider alternatives for meeting needs
   - Develop a basic cost/benefit analysis
   - Determine stakeholder readiness
   - If a viable option, develop case for a virtual school

If program is approved by the appropriate authorities:

3. Establish internal processes
   - Set program goals and objectives
   - Develop internal/external communication plan
   - Establish development teams
   - Consider appropriate curriculum and instruction models
4. Consider external partnerships
   - Consider whether to "build or buy" key components
   - Consider and select virtual learning providers and external partners
   - Select initial technology solutions
   - Build curriculum and instructional capacity
5. Plan to measure success
   - Institute performance assessment measures at the beginning

- Continually evaluate the program for improvement and justification purposes
- Demonstrate and communicate your success

E-LEARNING IN ADULT BASIC EDUCATION

Informal basic education for children has been available in the U. S. for many years through educational television programs such as *Sesame Street*. More recently, mobile interactive learning games such as Leapfrog (www.leapfrog.com) have become widely available for use with children as young as infants and toddlers. In developing nations, a primary education may be considered the end point of basic education, while in developed nations, it is secondary education. Basic literacy and learning the country's primary language are intermediate steps toward a basic education. In the United States, due to the near-universal participation of youth in compulsory education, the focus of basic education efforts has primarily been on adults.

Basic Education for Adults in the United States

Adult basic education programs serve individuals 16 or older who are not enrolled in secondary school, lack sufficient mastery of basic educational skills, do not have a high school diploma or its recognized equivalent, or are unable to speak, read, or write English (20 USC 92 9202(1)). These programs are commonly provided by community (two-year) colleges and school districts. Offerings include General Educational Development (GED) preparation, high school diploma, English as a second language, adult literacy and community education.

Educational agencies in the United States and Canada participate in the American Council for Education's GED Testing Service (www.gedtest.org), which allows school leavers to earn a certificate demonstrating high school graduate level knowledge and skills. GED preparation providers are unaffiliated with the Testing Service, which administers the GED exams via local testing centers. Some states and provinces award a high school diploma based on the GED. Out-of-school youth are also served by programs such as Job Corps, which combines GED and diploma study with vocational training.

Many states have developed mechanisms to support the use of distance learning methods in adult basic education. For example, under a law passed by the California legislature in 1993, adult education programs may expend up to 5% of their block entitlement grant from the state on distance learning, independent study, and other innovative programs. In 2003, 78 adult basic education programs offered a distance learning program, reporting about 44,000 unduplicated enrollments. Online learning was still an emerging method. Based on courses made available in participating adult schools, videos were the most popular instructional delivery mode, followed by workbooks and study packets. Computer based training was fourth, while online courses ranked ninth out of 12 media listed (Porter, 2004).

Many states use LiteracyLink (http://litlink.ket.org), an online resource for adult basic education students and their teachers that combines video, Internet, and print materials. The state of Kentucky developed LiteracyLink with the Public Broadcasting System and the National Center for Adult Literacy. LiteracyLink resources include GED Connection and Workplace Essential Skills, which combine programs offered via broadcast and videotape with print workbooks and an online management system. The portfolio-based online system contains pre-tests, lessons, and activities for learners aligned with the workbooks. Teachers can manage their student's progress online. LiteracyLink also offers online professional development resources for instructors, such as ESL/CivicsLink.

Preparation programs for GED testing increasingly offer fully online learning options. State level two-year (community) college boards usually sponsor GED training in their states. Mississippi GED Online (www.colin.edu/gedonline) offers an online GED course free to state residents. Documentation of prior completion of the Test of Adult Basic Education is required, with students scoring at 8th grade reading level or below required to start their study in on-site classes. Online GED instructors conduct the virtual course. The Illinois GED Online program (www.gedillinois.com) offers participating GED programs the opportunity to use an online GED curriculum with their local instructors, an increasingly common method of using e-learning to support local on-site instruction.

There is a long history of using courseware such as Plato and NovaNet with alternative, remedial, and school leaver populations in supervised computer lab settings. The structured nature of online learning can be used to encourage self-directed learning skills and personal responsibility. These individualized learning programs are increasingly available online. For example, The Kentucky Virtual Education Initiative (www.kyvae.org) offers the Plato Web Learning Network (PWLN) to adult education programs across the state for use in GED preparation and workforce skills training. In 2003, 10,793 students, or 10% of adult education students statewide, enrolled in PWLN (Plato Learning, 2004). Will online learning come to play a larger role in North American adult basic education? These examples suggest that it can.

REFLECTIONS ON THE FUTURE OF VIRTUAL SCHOOLING

The use of e-learning or ICTs in elementary and secondary education is growing around the world, but whether online distance education via virtual schools will catch on outside North America is an open question. With an established technology infrastructure in place, better state policies may be the most pressing need for virtual schools to reach their full potential in the United States. However, the American public is not sure about the quality or desirability of virtual schools, due in large part to the rise of cyber charter schools and fears that virtual schools will drain funds from traditional public schools. Today's students are less worried. They live in a virtual learning environment, in and out of class, and use the Internet as a "virtual backpack, locker and notebook" (Levin & Arafeh, 2002, p. 13). They are more at ease with technology and online learning than their "digital immigrant" parents and teachers (Prensky, 2001). When today's virtual students are themselves parents, a new type of e-learning may arise, in which schools, students, and parents share responsibility for learning.

LESSONS LEARNED FROM POLICY AND PRACTICE

Virtual schooling, or K–12 online distance education, started in the United States as a way of expanding educational opportunity, and has since been enlisted to support education reform. E-learning, or use of ICTs in education, is a more global phenomenon spurred by growth in ICT access and SchoolNets. Virtual schools operate within state systems of education in the U. S. federal system. How they are funded and operated varies widely. School improvement needs, not external forces, should drive the planning of virtual school programs. Basic education programs have a long history of use of distance learning and independent study, which is moving online and serving new audiences. Future growth in U. S. virtual schooling and e-learning will require updated state policies and may depend on societal attitudes about the role online learning should play in elementary, secondary, and basic education.

REFERENCES

Adsit, J. (2003). *Funding online education: A report to the Colorado Online Education Programs Study Committee*. Retrieved June 12, 2007, from http://www.cde.state. co.us/edtech/download/osc-fundingonline.pdf.

Baker, J., Bouras, C., Hartwig, S. M., & McNair, E. R. (2005). K12, Inc. and the Colorado Virtual Academy. In Z. L. Berge & T. Clark (Eds.), *Virtual schools: Planning for success* (pp. 133–142). New York: Teachers College Press.

Berge, Z. L., & Clark, T. (Eds.) (2005). *Virtual schools: Planning for success*. New York: Teachers College Press.

Bielick, S., Chandler, K., & Broughman, S. (2001). *Homeschooling in the United States: 1999-2001*. Washington, DC: U.S. Department of Education, National Center for Education Statistics. (NCES 2001-033).

Cavalluzzo, L. (2004). *Organizational models for online education*. Alexandria, VA: CNA Corporation. Retrieved June 1, 2005, from http://www.cna.org/documents/P&P109.pdf.

Cavanaugh, C., Gillan, K. J., Kromrey, J., Hess, M., & Blomeyer, R. (2004). *The effects of distance education on K–12 student outcomes: A meta-analysis.* Naperville, IL: Learning Point Associates. Retrieved June 1, 2005, from http://www.ncrel. org/tech/distance/k12distance.pdf.

Center for Education Reform (2005). *National charter school directory.* Washington, DC: Author.

Chute, E. (2005, May 8). Cyber schools spring up in state. *Pittsburgh Post-Gazette.* Retrieved June 1, 2005, from http://www.post-gazette.com/pg/05128/500990. stm.

Clark, T. (2001). *Virtual schools: status and trends.* Phoenix, AZ: WestEd. Retrieved June 1, 2005, from http://www.wested.org/online_pubs/virtualschools.pdf.

Clark, T. (2003). Virtual and distance education in American schools. In M. G. Moore & W. G. Anderson (Eds.), *Handbook of distance education* (pp. 673–699). Mahwah, NJ: Erlbaum.

Clark, T., & Berge, Z. L. (2005a). Perspectives on virtual schools. In Z. L. Berge & T. Clark (Eds.), *Virtual schools: Planning for success* (pp. 9–19). New York: Teachers College Press.

Clark, T., & Berge, Z. L. (2005b). Planning for success: A road map to the future. In Z. L. Berge & T. Clark (Eds.), *Virtual schools: Planning for success* (pp. 201–216). New York: Teachers College Press.

DeBell, M., & Chapman, C. (2003). *Computer and Internet use by children and adolescents in 2001.* Washington, DC: U.S. Department of Education, National Center for Education Statistics. (NCES 2004–014).

Education Week. (2005, May 5). *Technology counts 2005.* Special edition. Retrieved June 1, 2005, from http://www.edweek.org/ew/toc/2005/05/05/index.html.

Eurydice, European Commission (2004). Key data on information and communication technology in schools in Europe. Brussels: Author. Retrieved June 12, 2007, from http://www.eurydice.org/resources/eurydice/pdf/0_integral/048EN.pdf.

Florida Department of Education (2005). *2004–2005 FEFP.* Tallahassee, FL: Author. Retrieved June 12, 2007, from http://www.fldoe.org/strategy/pdf/ 0405final. pdf.

Gerald, D. E., & Hussar, W. J. (2003). *Projections of education statistics to 2013.* Washington, DC: U. S. Department of Education, National Center for Education Statistics. (NCES 2004–013).

Jordan, A. (2005). Cumberland County Schools Web Academy. In Z. L. Berge & T. Clark (Eds.), *Virtual schools: Planning for success* (pp. 143–158). New York: Teachers College Press.

Levin, D., & Arafeh, S. (2002). The digital disconnect. Washington, DC: Pew Internet in American Life Project/American Institutes for Research. Retrieved June 1, 2005, from http://www.pewtrusts.com/pdf/vf_pew_internet_schools.pdf.

Morris, S. (2002). *Teaching and learning online: A step-by-step guide for designing an online K–12 school program.* Lanham, MD: Scarecrow Press.

Naidoo, V., & Issacs, S. (2004, February). Focus on schoolnets. *Connections & Ed Tech News.* Commonwealth of Learning. Retrieved June 12, 2007, from http://www. col.org/colweb/site/pid/124.

Newman, A., Stein, M., & Trask, E. (2003, September). *What can virtual learning do for your school?* Boston, MA: Eduventures.

Parsad, B., & Jones, J. (2005). *Internet access in U.S. public schools and classrooms: 1994–2003.* Washington, DC: U.S. Department of Education, National Center for Education Statistics. (NCES 2005-015).

Peak Group (2002). *Virtual schools across America.* Los Altos, CA: Author.

Pittman, V. (2000). Waiter, there's a school in my university! *Journal of Continuing Higher Education,* 48(1), 46–48.

Plato Learning (2004). *Kentucky Virtual University uses PLATO Learning.* Retrieved June 1, 2005, from http://www.plato.com/downloads/implementations/kyvu.pdf.

Porter, D. (2004). *California adult education 2002–2004 innovation and alternative instructional delivery program.* Dominguez Hills, CA: California State University.

Prensky, M. (2001, October). Digital Natives, Digital Immigrants. *On the Horizon,* 9(5), 1–6.

Rose, L. C., & Gallup, A. M. (2002). 34th annual Kappan/Gallup poll on the public's attitudes toward the public schools. *Phi Delta Kappan,* 84(1), 41–56.

Setzer, J. C., & Lewis, L. (2005). *Distance education courses for public elementary and secondary school students: 2002–03.* Washington, DC: U. S. Department of Education, National Center for Education Statistics. (NCES 2005-010).

Simonson, M. (2005). South Dakota's statewide distance education project: Diffusion of an innovation. In Z. Berge & T. Clark (Eds.), *Virtual schools: Planning for success* (pp. 183–199). New York: Teachers College Press.

Sloan Consortium (2005). *Entering the mainstream: The quality and extent of online education in the United States, 2003 and 2004.* Needham, MA: Author. Retrieved June 1, 2005, from http://www.sloan-c.org/resources/ entering_mainstream.pdf.

U.S. Department of Education. (2005a). *10 facts about K-12 education funding.* Retrieved June 1, 2005, from http://www.ed.gov/about/overview/fed/10facts.

U.S. Department of Education. (2005b). *The national educational technology plan.* Retrieved June 1, 2005, from http://www.ed.gov/technology/plan.

Watson, J. F., Winograd, K., & Kalmon, S. (2004). *Keeping pace with online learning.* Naperville, IL: Learning Point Associates.

Web-Based Education Commission (2000). *The power of the Internet for learning.* Retrieved June 1, 2005, from http://interact.hpcnet.org/webcommission.

5

HISTORICAL PERSPECTIVES ON DISTANCE LEARNING IN THE UNITED STATES[1]

Paul J. Edelson

State University of New York – Stony Brook, USA

Von V. Pittman

University of Missouri, USA

INTRODUCTION

Distance learning represents the most dynamic sector of higher education, particularly in the United States where World Wide Web (WWW)-based electronic delivery is fast becoming a dominant mode of instruction. This trend will almost certainly apply around the world. Other forms of distance learning persist, of course. Turkey's Anadolu University (according to the World Bank, the largest university in the world) enrolls more than 500,000 students, mostly through correspondence. The same is true for the United Kingdom Open University (UKOU) and Indira Gandhi National Open University (IGNOU), both of which are still heavily dependent on correspondence study. However, at the moment, there can be no question that computer-mediated asynchronous distance learning is the medium of choice in the development of new academic courses and programs delivered at a distance.

U.S. NATIONAL CONTEXT

The dramatic growth of electronic distance education initially caught faculty and administrators in the United States by surprise. According to the Federal Government's National Center for Educational Statistics (NCES, 2003), in academic year 2001–2002, 91% of public four-year and two-year colleges reported that they planned to offer at least some courses at a distance. By far the greatest number of colleges said they will offer web-based courses.

Students and faculty in the United States who experience online teaching and learning report enthusiasm for—and satisfaction with—the medium. Between 1994–97, online courses tallied an overall growth of 116% among all institutions, and 204% in public four-year schools. According to this NCES trend line, by 2009–10, online courses are projected to account for 31% of *all* course enrollments at the postsecondary level. Student demographics indicate equal popularity among both full- and part-time students. E-learning is proving itself to be, to use Christensen's term, a "disruptive technology" in U.S. higher education; it is following the classic trend lines of growth for new technologies, thereby reshaping all of higher learning (Christensen, 2000).

CORRESPONDENCE STUDY MODELS AND E-LEARNING

Today's educators, particularly in the United States, frequently fall into the error of "presentism," or living in the moment. They imagine this period, and their own experiences, as *sui generis*, unique unto themselves. This is not the case. In many respects, the development of electronic distance education is reminiscent of the history of correspondence education in the United States. This first distance teaching format appeared in university-level instruction in the late nineteenth century and quickly became a major phenomenon, particularly in adult education. It enabled students to study and learn at a distance and to accrue academic credit. They could, if they wished, bring the credits with them if they decided to relocate to a campus. Correspondence study proved incredibly popular, particularly in the first three decades of the twentieth century.

Two distinct sectors of correspondence study—university programs and profit-oriented commercial schools—appeared at virtually the same time and grew up as rivals. Universities intended their correspondence courses to extend access to college education to people living far from any campuses. Commercial, or "proprietary," schools operated for the sole purpose of making money for their owners. In terms of quality, the latter schools ranged from very good to fraudulent. Commercial schools began offering secondary level diploma programs in the early part of the century.

Some universities, located mainly in rural states, also adopted this practice beginning in the 1920s. The two sectors grew up together, the first emphasizing the accumulation of academic credits, the second geared to the accumulation of knowledge and skills necessary in trades and vocation.

Because of correspondence study's accessibility to people of all classes and income levels, and the aggressive advertising campaigns of some of its practitioners, it enrolled people in huge numbers. In 1924, four times as many people were enrolled in proprietary correspondence schools than in all resident colleges, universities, and professional schools combined (Noffsinger, 1926).

The rise of correspondence education coincided with the proliferation of advancing job opportunities in a variety of occupations, especially in technical and professional areas, and in response to state licensing requirements, which relied on test performance. These developments favored the acquisition of specific, occupationally related knowledge and certificates of completion. Both the proprietary correspondence schools and university "home study" departments, most notably at the University of Wisconsin, addressed this need for specialized skills and knowledge. Even today, universities continue to teach applied vocational skills via correspondence. Pennsylvania State University's lawn sprinkler courses enroll large numbers of golf course greens keepers and cemetery maintenance supervisors. Like the correspondence study medium, many e-learning programs also are credential and certificate driven. They are intertwined with opportunities in e-commerce and in virtually all fields of employment.

Correspondence study, a system that allowed—even encouraged—common people to take charge of their own learning and guaranteed access to all who desired it, complemented a persistent theme in American political philosophy: the exaltation of the common citizen. In U.S. political history, this theme is often called "Jacksonian Democracy," after Andrew Jackson, the country's seventh president, a noted champion of the "common man" who urged his followers to resist intimidation by the social and political elite that had previously governed the country. Thus, correspondence study was a tool of a movement one scholar called "the democratization of knowledge" (Kett, 1994, p. 36).

Some prestigious institutions entered correspondence study early on. The University of Chicago, a world-class, research-orientated university from the day it opened in 1892, integrated correspondence study into its original design. Its founding president, William Rainey Harper, had been academic principal of the Chautauqua Institute's College of Liberal Arts, which made extensive use of correspondence study. Even before that, he had built up a huge correspondence program for teaching the Hebrew language at the Baptist Union Theological Seminary, in Chicago. This program became the basis of the American Institute for Sacred Literature, which he had taken to Yale as a professor, then returned to Chicago when he assumed its presidency. Chicago's early program, consisting primarily of languages and the liberal arts, also flourished. Indeed, between 1893 and 1923, the University of Chicago enrolled 32,000 students in home study sociology courses alone (MacLean, 1923).

The University of Chicago was not alone among prestigious American universities in offering correspondence study. A number of the most respected public universities featured extensive offerings. For many, most notably the University of Wisconsin, this mode of study represented a manifestation of democratic ideology, a feature of their "land-grant" origins. As agencies of their states, the land-grant universities had the mission of serving all the citizenry, not just those people who could relocate to a campus for full-time study. In the last decade of the nineteenth century and the first two decades of the twentieth, such major institutions as the Universities of Wisconsin, Illinois, Minnesota, and Iowa established or revitalized their correspondence programs. At Pennsylvania State University and other schools with colleges of agriculture, the faculty developed detailed courses of study for people engaged in farming and agribusiness (United States Department of Agriculture, 1900). A number of smaller public colleges that mainly served to train teachers also began to offer correspondence study (Jenkins, 1953). Thus, the collegiate correspondence programs served two publics: those interested in a traditional liberal arts curriculum and those who needed more applied professional or vocational training.

In Wisconsin, a legislative agency investigated the numerous commercial correspondence schools that were enrolling thousands of the state's residents. The investigators found many of those schools suspect, ineffective, or even fraudulent, but nonetheless highly profitable. They proposed that the University of Wisconsin establish a vocationally oriented program to provide a high quality alternative for the state's citizens. The University's Board of Regents duly enacted such a program, which it promoted as a consumer protection measure. However, the legislature also demanded that the correspondence courses generate revenues in excess of their cost. This return could then be used to further subsidize the education of workers in Wisconsin's businesses and industries (Rosentreter, 1957; Fitzpatrick, 1944).

While correspondence study has a long history within a number of large universities, most of them have treated it as a marginal enterprise. They have required that their correspondence study programs operate in a self-sustaining financial mode. Within this funding scheme, tuition receipts have had to cover all faculty stipends for developing and grading courses, delivery costs, and staff payroll. Some universities, including Wisconsin and Chicago, sometimes demanded that their correspondence programs generate a profit that could be used to support less lucrative outreach or extension activities. And, because students had to pay in excess of 100%

of the cost of these courses, correspondence departments were essentially small, profit-oriented businesses within large public, taxpayer-supported institutions. They became "cash cows" for their universities.

While this circumstance has been demeaning in some ways, it has not been totally irredeemable. At the University of Chicago, President Harper professed great respect for—and commitment to—the Extension Division, including the correspondence department. But he insisted that all Extension departments pay their own way; he refused to contribute funds from the University's general budget to them. In the end, however, home study was the only part of Harper's extension division that survived his presidency. All of the other outreach departments failed, not because of public indifference or instructional quality, but because they could not cover their expenses with their revenues (Dunkel & Fay, 1978). And it is almost certain that many correspondence departments would not have survived the Great Depression of the 1930s had they not generated their own funding. The low pay to the professors who taught the courses also helped university correspondence departments to survive. And while they did survive, it would be an exaggeration to say they prospered.

Modern American postsecondary institutions vary greatly in their enthusiasm for distance education. Some elite schools, notably private institutions, have limited their involvement in e-learning to the marketing of their brand names for income-producing, non-credit offerings, while limiting their high-status degree programs to conventional delivery formats. This strategy is both described and recommended in Lloyd Armstrong's article in *Change* (2000). On the other hand, equally illustrious schools are offering their "big ticket" programs at a distance. Duke University and Purdue University's renowned Krannert School, for example, are offering their highly regarded Master's of Business Administration (MBA) degree programs via the Internet.

In spite of the lessons of history, the advocates for today's e-learning often try to promote it as a source of immense potential profits. While this prospect cannot yet be ruled out, neither has it yet become a reality. So far, university e-learning operations are more notable for their purported earning potential than for their profit margins.

One operational principle of many early correspondence programs was to rationalize the course design and production processes in order to deliver curricula at the lowest possible cost. This mechanical approach to multiplying productivity—and thus profitability—became known as the "industrial model." Indeed, some scholars concluded that distance education could succeed only through this approach (Peters, 1983). This strategy has dominated commercial correspondence school course development. The heavy reliance on standardization has made it especially attractive to the military. Some colleges also adopted it. The University of Missouri's Computer-Assisted Lesson Service (CALS), developed in the 1970s, is especially notable. In this case, the industrial model enabled Missouri to develop the first large-scale use of the computer in collegiate correspondence study (Young & Phillips, 1982). It should be noted, however, that neither the University of Missouri nor any other major university ever converted *all* of their courses to an industrial or computer-evaluated model.

While some universities adopted the industrial model, at least in part, others took an entirely different approach. They developed courses that mandated intense and frequent one-to-one interaction between student and instructor, using this feature as a justification of the medium and as a marketing feature. These programs based their instructional strategies upon principles not unlike those William Rainey Harper set down in 1885 (Vincent, 1886/1971). Harper's orientation and philosophy evolved into a system sometimes called the "author-editor model," whereby a professional editor or instructional developer works with a professor on a one-to-one basis. As a team, they converted the professor's conventional class to a correspondence format. Under this model, they create a study guide, either in print or online. The function of this document has been described as

> ...Not a substitute for the professor, but only for his or her physical presence. A good study guide extends an instructor's style, point of view, and to some extent, personality to students never met in person. At the same time, it should also reflect the instructor's standards, degree of rigor, and determination to make the course worthwhile. (Pittman, 1987, pp.198–199)

Today, the same controversies over course development are being played out in the creation, communication, and promotion of online courses, with a great deal of confusion ensuing in the process. For example, the term "asynchronous" has become ambiguous. Online course administrators and designers use it in two vastly different ways. The first defines "asynchronous" in a manner reminiscent of traditional correspondence study. Students may enroll at any time and usually set their own pace, all within a time frame that extends a set number of months—usually nine or twelve—from enrollment. This format differs from the usual term of study, with fixed start and stop dates. Within this definition of asynchronous learning, some universities rely on the industrial model of course construction, while others feature the intense student-teacher interaction described above. Neither model provides for student-to-student interaction.

Other administrators, professors, and distance education professionals use "asynchronous" in a more restricted manner. Their courses take place within a conventional school term, with fixed beginning and completion dates, and thus operate as classes with frequent, mandated student-to-student interaction. In this manner, asynchronous means that instructors and students neither gather in one place, nor gather in real time. They interact with each other, even to the point of participating in joint projects, via online bulletin boards and other forms of delayed communications, at their convenience but within definite periods. Most often, the week is used as a pacing mechanism. For such courses, the term "semi-asynchronous" might be more appropriate. However, this term is unlikely to catch on.

As noted above, while some of the more aggressive promoters of online teaching have promised abundant financial returns from their classes, to date such results have been rare. Indeed some institutions, usually under faculty pressure, have imposed restrictions, such as small class sizes, that limit profitability. The emphasis on revenue generation from the perspective of many institutions stems from the fact that both correspondence and e-learning are viewed as areas of "soft pedagogy" by many administrators and professors. Too often, they view students taking courses at a distance as occupying the educational fringe, not as participants in fulfilling the university's academic mission. It should be noted that this perspective is definitely not that of the continuing education units charged with operating these programs. Generally, they are advocates of both distance education courses and the students who choose to enroll in them. Nor do institutions for which e-learning is the primary instructional format, view it as a marginal activity. This is especially true within two-year community colleges.

In spite of its consignment to the margins of the university, correspondence study—more often called "independent study" since the 1960s—has enhanced the structural edifice of continuing education in the United States. In fact, the large number of independent study students flowing into American higher education initially provided a major *raison d'etre* for collegiate continuing education units, which were charged specifically with administering, bringing cohesion to, and improving the quality of distance learning. E-learning follows the same pattern, and is usually housed within schools and divisions of continuing education. It attracts the greatest interest there, since its primary appeal is to the same audience of working adults found in other part-time programs, including independent study.

Further, it should be remembered that this progression has some paradoxical elements. The strongest independent study and online education programs were—and still are—located at research-oriented flagship and land-grant universities, which are also the most likely to view distance education as peripheral to their mission. At any rate, correspondence study generated the greatest share of employment in early university outreach. Online teaching is having the same effect on today's continuing education divisions and departments.

While some universities offered large correspondence programs, they did not satisfy the popular demand for courses. And given that the greatest interest was in vocational and applied skills courses, realistically they could not. With a few notable exceptions, such as the University of Wisconsin and Penn State, they offered only academic subjects. The commercial schools filled the vacuum. Indeed, because these schools emerged at roughly the same time as mass media advertising, they played a large part in *creating* the demand, which turned out to be extensive. For example, the International Correspondence Schools of Scranton, Pennsylvania, founded in 1891, could claim more than 4,000,000 alumni by 1930. Today, due to the emergence of dedicated large-scale distance education institutions such as UKOU and IGNOU, annual enrollments—numbering up to 500,000—are beginning to rival those of the American proprietary schools of the early twentieth century. Even though the bulk of this work is by correspondence, it is definitely shifting towards e-learning. In the United States, the University of Phoenix, now the nation's largest private university in terms of enrollments, is aggressively expanding its online program (Klor de Alva, 1999–2000).

BREAKS WITH THE PAST—PREDICTIONS

To this point we have argued that online education has numerous antecedents in the instructional format of correspondence study, particularly as practiced in university departments of continuing education. Those similarities will continue to apply. However, we also expect to see some definite changes.

Educators and students will increasingly view distance education as beneficial to all students, full-time as well as part-time, resident as well as nonresident. The distinction between such arbitrary categories of students will become ambiguous. More young students will work; more older working people will enroll in colleges and universities. This is not an entirely new phenomenon, of course. Physical distance is not the only factor that draws students to independent study courses. Some university independent study directors have long noted that resident, full-time students have accounted for upwards of 40% of their enrollments. Students who encounter scheduling problems when they register for resident courses often opt for an independent study course to fill out their semesters. This strategy has provided many students with a means of staying on track when closed out of a required or badly needed course on campus. Still, to this point, such classification of students has been possible, if imprecise. Soon, such categories as "resident," "off-campus," and "distance" will have become so thoroughly mixed that any rigorous delineation will no longer be possible. Nor, would it serve any useful purpose.

Today's online education is institutionally ubiquitous. Through the 1990s, approximately 70 University Continuing Education Association (UCEA) schools dominated independent study enrollments, numbering about 250,000 annually. The U.S. National Center for Education Statistics (NCES, 1997) accurately predicted that by the end of 2001, 91% of public institutions and 65% of all institutions would participate in electronic distance education. Two reasons for this are the almost universal allure of e-learning and the notion that little capitalization is required. In other words, it looks easy and cheap, but seems to promise a large return. Advocates of e-learning frequently overstate this position. Actually, the increased server and network capacity needed for large-scale operations are not inexpensive. And the payroll costs of instructional developers, graphic artists, and technical support personnel can be considerable. By any measure, developing online courses is more costly than creating the conventional print-based independent study counterparts of these courses—or additional classroom sections on campus, for that matter. However, some for-profit companies, including publishing houses, will enter into partnerships in which colleges produce the content for courses, and publishers do all the design, production, and marketing work. McGraw-Hill, one of the United States' largest publishing houses, provides a good example of this type of vertical integration.

Online courses are far more popular among faculty than were (and are) independent study courses and other distance education formats, such as television. The allure factor again applies. Also, most young faculty have grown up with computers and have little difficulty in integrating them into their academic disciplines. Indeed, elements of distance education, such as class web pages and bulletin boards, are now commonplace in conventional classrooms.

This is not to say that faculty acceptance is a given. No sector of the work force is without Luddites. Indeed, we have begun to see signs of a backlash that could become considerably larger than the anti-correspondence course feelings on many campuses. It is not unusual to see anti-distance educational polemics and diatribes with titles such as "Digital Diploma Mills" (Noble, 2001). Independent study has provoked little resentment, probably because the large universities that have operated the largest programs have so effectively marginalized them that, while they have continued to operate, they have drawn little notice.

Online programs, by contrast, are attracting considerable attention, in both the academic press and in the general news. Some faculty, as a result, have begun to express concern. The most obvious feature of online education is that individual professors cannot maintain the degree of control they have enjoyed for centuries in the conventional classroom. They frequently need instructional designers to help them adapt their expertise to a more dynamic medium. The asynchronous pacing, or lack of it, results in a drastic loss of control. Courses become student—rather than faculty—centered. Further, some professors know that many—if not most—of the students they will encounter will be their superiors in terms of computer literacy and Web literacy.

Far more threatening for some professors are fears that their employers will steal or misappropriate their intellectual property. With this wrongfully gained courseware, universities will then attempt to increase productivity by foisting more students upon them, these faculty members fear.

Some professors have taken the exploitation theme even further. Professor David Noble, of Toronto's York University, has developed a Marxist critique of distance education. He has said that universities have formed partnerships with corporate enterprises in order to further exploit labor—in this case, professors. By using private capital to set up and offer courses online, universities can reduce the value of professors' work and deprive them of their autonomy in curriculum and governance. Indeed, Noble and his fellows at York succeeded in winning a provision in their union contract that forbids the university to force professors to teach via distance education (Noble, 2001). The problem of faculty backlash will probably abate with time. But in the short run it will generate considerable tension and general unpleasantness on some campuses.

E-learning and e-commerce will converge on a wide scale. As the population in general becomes more familiar with e-mail and the Internet, their comfort level with Web-based learning will increase, massively and quickly. Colleges, universities, and other education providers will combine e-learning with other educational innovations—such as compressed scheduling and outcomes assessment—aggressively to provide greater flexibility, thus removing or diminishing some barriers to participation. Indeed, it is this very flexibility that already draws many resident college students to independent study, telecourses, and other conventional distance education media. E-learning will not only take advantage of these measures of flexibility, it will far surpass them.

MYTHS AND MISPERCEPTIONS

E-learning has inspired or provoked a number of arguments from both advocates and skeptics, creating glee among the former and dread among the latter. Some are clearly myths, others merely exaggerations.

E-learning will replace traditional education. Class cohorts, campuses, and face-to-face teaching will not disappear. Innovators, pioneers, and enthusiasts for the various educational media have long proclaimed that total revolution was just around the corner. Harper, in 1885, proclaimed, "The day is coming when the work done by correspondence will be greater in amount than that done in the classrooms of our academies and colleges..." (Vincent, 1886/1971, p. 193). He would come to regret this widely publicized utterance in his own lifetime. In 1894, Thomas Edison introduced motion pictures, which he proclaimed would replace textbooks (Ohles, 1985). More recently, management expert Peter Drucker joined enthusiasts of distance education when he warned of the impending obsolescence of campus physical facilities (Lenzner & Johnson, 1997). Just recently James J. Duderstadt, president of the University of Michigan, told an academic audience that digital instruction might well doom conventional postsecondary education. "Will this university as we know it now exist a generation from now? That's a disturbing question, but a question we have to ask" (Carlson & Carnevale, 2004).

This will not happen. There will always be an essential place for real-time, cohort-based learning, especially in fields that rely upon apprentice-based training, where people are the expert systems, where the problems of practice are too unpredictable, and where the human cost of error is unacceptable. Additionally, campus-based learning will always be a preferred option for students whose parents seek for them a traditional collegiate experience. The conventional college will continue to provide socialization for 18- to 22-year-old students. Indeed, as they always have, parents will continue to insist that society provide a place for their children that is well removed from them. But even within conventional institutions, many students will take some e-learning courses as the supply expands.

E-learning will democratize higher education by enhancing access. In their book *The Social Life of Information*, Brown and Duguid (2000) argue that distance learning advocates often neglect "social distance" when they think about e-learning in purely geographical terms. "Minorities, women, and the poor [all have] to struggle across this distance for access," they write. "It is not overcome by a few strokes of the keyboard" (p. 224).

E-learning will improve quality. The jury is still out on this matter. In 1999, Thomas Russell published a bibliography of 355 research studies produced between 1928–1997 that compared the effectiveness of teaching formats. He included studies that compared the traditional classroom to correspondence, correspondence to television, television to "teaching machines," and so on. These research studies have compared virtually every possible juxtaposition of teaching formats. The overwhelming conclusion of these studies provided the title for Russell's book; in terms of learning outcomes, he found that the choice of medium made *No Significant Difference* (Russell, 1999). At least to this point, there is no indication that e-learning is either inferior or superior to other types of instruction.

More recently, Russell has begun to gather a few studies that have found significant differences, usually to the advantage of electronic formats. To this point, however, the generalization of "no significant difference" continues to apply. And, of course, it should be noted that not only have researchers not found a significant difference in favor of e-learning or any other distance education format, neither have they discovered any advantage in favor of the conventional classroom, lecture hall, or seminar room. In the long run, there may be grounds to substantiate the case for e-learning, but they have not yet been established.

Critics of e-learning, like those of other distance education formats, base much of their argument on the absence of visceral clues in teaching within the virtual classroom. This is reminiscent of the argument that acting on stage is superior to acting on film or television, in that the former is "more real," and happens before a live audience. The implied comparison provides a model of teacher as performer. Yet this is essentially a "straw man" argument unless proven by analysis of outcomes. The state of research at present is such that we cannot assert that online teaching is superior to that of any other format. But the reverse is also true; there is no evidence that conventional teaching is in any way superior to online teaching. Scholars should continue to test the effectiveness of all teaching formats, but to this point, traditionalists have produced no empirical evidence of the superiority of their preferred methodologies.

E-learning will speed tendencies toward globalization. E-learning may make it easier to see what other institutions are doing, and thus intensify competition. It should not erode national markets except where there is no comparable national product. Even so, there are barriers to trade within certain countries, with respect to the value of foreign degrees. UKOU students outside the United Kingdom and IGNOU students outside India tend to be nationals of those countries living abroad. In many countries, foreign degrees have a limited appeal and negotiability except for students who intend to emigrate.

FORECASTS

Within the United States, registration in online courses could rise to 50% of all enrollments. This would include graduate as well as undergraduate students. To some extent, this will depend upon the development of a uniform nomenclature. Currently there is no universally accepted definition of "online course." Even many more-or-less conventional courses include online components. At some colleges and universities they are labeled online; at others they do not qualify for this category. Either way, the Web will be ubiquitous in all instructional formats. According to Gleick (1999), "faster is better." The preference of many students for greater speed, in order to finish their degrees in a shorter time span, enhances the appeal and marketability of e-learning.

The U.S. government will provide increased support for students learning at a distance. Federal aid will be made independent of the number of class hours taken per week. Until 2002, the "12-hour rule" required that students must be in class 12 hours per week to qualify for government aid. In the future, financial aid will be based upon the number of credits, or course load. Current financial aid policy, parts of which have been relaxed, is one of the reasons that correspondence study never became a major factor in American higher education. The success of online instruction will be dependent upon the further liberalization of financial aid regulations.

E-learning students will be highly mobile, at least in terms of the institutions from which they choose to take courses, programs, and degrees. This will lead to greater competition between established institutions and new virtual colleges. Supply may catch up with demand due to lower capitalization costs for electronic distance education. For faculty who enjoy and relish teaching, online instruction provides another area for mastery. For those who shun teaching, e-learning has no intrinsic appeal. Newer schools will specialize; many schools will offer only a few courses. Currently, many small liberal arts colleges in the United States are already struggling with declining budgets and enrollments. Some are closing; more will. While e-learning has not been a factor in this phenomenon to this point, it will accelerate the pace. Many of these smaller institutions will attempt to go online; few will succeed. This sector of the educational marketplace will definitely shrink. While e-learning courses are not responsible for this trend, neither will they reverse it.

E-learning will alter the higher education landscape for the better. It will do so by promoting outcomes-based assessment that will measure *what* is learned, rather than concerning itself with where or how the learning takes place. For example, the University of Phoenix (UOP), a proprietary institution, offers online academic programs that have been highly successful in enrolling students. However, faculty and administrators in many conventional universities have either dismissed it out-of-hand or ridiculed it. The founder of UOP, John Sperling, in essence has challenged its detractors to "put up or shut up," that is, to prove their points. UOP launched a peer-reviewed journal, *Assessment and Accountability Forum* (AAF), now operated by Inter Ed, in which it publishes studies of innovative programs and teaching formats based primarily on the assessment of learning outcomes. According to its explicit statement of purpose, "AAF was founded to enhance the science and practice of accountability and quality management in higher education only." Conventional institutions have traditionally shied away from evaluation based on learner outcomes. However, they will find it increasingly difficult, and perhaps even embarrassing, to continue avoiding comparisons based on actual results.

E-learning will expedite the development of more robust multimedia learning environments based upon the widespread integration of technology and learning. In turn, a rich e-learning environment will facilitate the emergence of a continuous learning environment, one in which the teaching-learning process never ends. The e-learning environment provides a platform for the combinations of text, voice, and video that is compatible with divergent learning styles and inclinations. This feature will promote repeated use and heavy demand.

E-learning will make "scientific learning," which stresses maximum efficiency, an important goal. Indeed, it will be as important as "scientific management" in the workplace. All concerned will devote more attention to the "science" of teaching and learning. They will also give greater attention to measurement of learning outcomes.

Electronic distance education will reshape the professoriate. The impact will be as profound and as wrenching as current changes in the practice of medicine have been for physicians and related health professionals. The new faculty model will no longer provide for the high degree of autonomy that tenured professors now enjoy. It will give more power to institutions. This change will be neither easy nor pretty. The counterrevolution is underway; indeed, it has already become nasty.

CONCLUSIONS

Distance learning can provide an educational environment every bit as demanding as the traditional face-to-face class. Quality resides in the worth of the effort put forth by faculty and students. There are—and always have been—poor face-to-face classes, just as there are—and long have been—inferior distance learning classes. This is not a question of format. Instead, discussions of quality and its pursuit must be waged on an individual basis, course-by-course.

Change will continue to build rapidly. James Gleick's book *Faster* analyzes the incredible acceleration we are experiencing within technology-based cultures. But earlier generations have also faced this situation. Alvin Toffler's (1970) *Future Shock* gave a comparable warning to the 1960s generation. Today's—and tomorrow's—online education provides some major opportunities, problems, and challenges. But while they may be profound in degree, they are not entirely new in kind. The founders of distance education—the administrators and faculty who made correspondence study/independent study programs work—faced many of the same issues, including asynchronous communication, rolling (non-term-based) enrollment, and constant skepticism about quality and standards.

NOTES

1.. An earlier version of this chapter appeared as Edelson, P. J., & Pittman, V. V. (2001, February). E-learning in the United States: New directions and opportunities for university continuing education. *Global E-Journal of Open, Flexible, and Distance Education, 1*(1), 71–83.

REFERENCES

Armstrong, L. (2000). Distance Learning: An academic leader's perspective on a disruptive product. *Change, 32*(6), 20–27.

Brown, J. S., & Duguid, P. (2000). *The social life of information*. Boston: Harvard Business School Press.

Carlson, C., & Carnevale, D. (2004, October 29). Technology threatens colleges with extinction, ex-president warns. *Chronicle of Higher Education, 51*(10), A34.

Christensen, C. M. (2000). *The innovator's dilemma: When new technologies cause great firms to fail*. New York: HarperBusiness.

Dunkel, H. B., & Fay, M. A. (1978). Harper's disappointment: University extension. *Adult Education, 29*(1), 3–16.

Fitzpatrick, E. A. (1944). *McCarthy of Wisconsin*. New York: Columbia University Press.

Gleick, J. (1999). *Faster: The acceleration of just about everything*. New York: Pantheon Books.

Jenkins, T. S. (1953). Correspondence course instruction: An investigation of practices, regulations, and course syllabi as developed in state teachers colleges. Unpublished doctoral dissertation, University of Oregon.

Kett, J. F. (1994). *The pursuit of knowledge under difficulties: From self-improvement to adult education in America, 1750–1990*. Stanford, CA: Stanford University Press.

Klor de Alva, J. (1999–2000). Remaking the academy in the Age of Information. *Issues in Science and Technology, 16*(2), 52–58.

Lenzner, R., & Johnson, S. S. (1997). Seeing things as they really are. *Forbes, 159*(5), 122–128.

MacLean, A. M. (1923). Twenty years of sociology by correspondence. *American Journal of Sociology, 28*(4), 461–472.

National Center for Educational Statistics (1997). Distance learning in higher education institutions. Available at http://nces.ed.gov/pubssearch/pubinfo/asp. PublicationIDNecs9802.

National Center for Education Statistics (2003). *Distance education at degree-granting postsecondary institutions: 2000–2001*. Washington, DC: U.S. Department of Education, National Center for Education Statistics. (NCES 2003-017).

Noble, D. F. (2001). *Digital diploma mills: The automation of higher education*. New York: Monthly Review Press.

Noffsinger, J. S. (1926). *Correspondence schools, lyceums, chautauquas*. New York: Macmillan.

Ohles, J. F. (1985). The microcomputer: Don't love it to death. *T.H.E. Journal, 13*(1), 49–53.

Peters, O. (1983). Distance teaching and industrial production: A comparative interpretation. In D. Stewart, D. Keegan, & B. Homberg (Eds.), *Distance education: International perspectives* (pp. 95–113). London: Croom Helm.

Pittman, V. (1987). Correspondence study guides: An academic cottage industry. *Scholarly Publishing, 18*(3), 197–203.

Rosentreter, F. M. (1957). *The boundaries of the campus: A history of the University of Wisconsin Extension Division, 1885–1945*. Madison, WI: University of Wisconsin Press.

Russell, T. L. (1999). *The no significant difference phenomenon: As reported in 355 research reports, summaries, and papers.* Raleigh: North Carolina State University.

Toffler, A. (1970). *Future shock.* New York: Random House.

United States Department of Agriculture (1900). Farmers' reading courses. *Farmer's Bulletin, 109,* 5–19.

Vincent, J. H. (1971). *The chautauqua movement.* Freeport, New York: Books for Libraries Press. (Original published 1886)

Young, R., & Phillips, C.A. (1982). Increasing completion rates with computer-assisted instruction. In J. S. Daniel, M. A. Stroud, & J. R. Thompson (Eds.), *Learning at a distance: A world perspective.* Edmonton: Athabasca University/International Council for Correspondence Education.

6

FUNDING OF DISTANCE AND ONLINE LEARNING IN THE UNITED STATES

Mark J. Smith and William J. Bramble

University of New Mexico, USA

INTRODUCTION

Distance education has become a popular and largely effective tool worldwide for expanding education access to potential students. Institutions that offer distance education in the United States share the same basic goals as their counterparts around the world: To extend learning opportunities to larger publics, to increase their enrollments, and to do so cost-effectively. They also share many of the same concerns, including cost, organizational change, careful adoption of new teaching and learning technologies, and the quality of instruction and learning. Unique political, historical, and geographical features of the American educational enterprise, however, result in some notable differences, particularly in organizational structure and funding.

This chapter explores how distinctive features of the American system of higher education—the national interest in democratic education, the division of powers between federal, state, and private concerns, and the number, diversity, and distribution of higher education institutions—influence the structuring and financing of distance education. Based on uniquely American historical and political foundations, federal, state, local, and institutional means of funding distance and online learning are discussed, as are current and proposed funding formulas. This chapter primarily addresses formal post-secondary education; K–12 education and corporate and organizational training, meanwhile, is addressed in other chapters.

EDUCATION: A NATIONAL INTEREST

The development of America's vast educational enterprise since the seventeenth century has centered on democratized education—access to education is regarded as a right for all people, not a privilege for wealthy citizens (DeVane, 1965). Open access to schooling and its result, an educated citizenry, are seen as essential to a stable, productive, and equal society (Giamatti, 1988). A clause in the Northwest Ordinance (1787), "Religion, morality, and knowledge, being necessary to good government and the happiness of mankind, schools and the means of education shall forever be encouraged," is regarded by many as a national charter for public education (Good, 1960). Democratized education has long been more an ideal than a practice, though steady progress has been made toward realizing this goal. Distance education, in its many forms and modes of delivery, has been a major step toward extending access to formal learning opportunities.

NON-CENTRALIZED CONTROL

Immediate control of schools in the United States has never been consolidated nor standardized under a strong federal authority. Perhaps the most apparent explanation is the division of powers established in the U. S. Constitution. Education was not enumerated as a power of the federal government, so it is understood to be "reserved to the States and the people" under the Tenth Amendment to the U. S. Constitution. The federal government wields broad influence over education of the American people, through national policies and funding, but it has long managed to refrain from interfering too much in specifics. Those remain the jealously-guarded domain of the states and private interests (DeVane, 1965; Moore, 2003).

Early American Colleges

The precedent of local control of education has roots in the colonial period. Harvard College, the first colonial college, was established in 1636, only seven years after Puritans settled in Massachusetts. Several more institutions, all essentially private, were founded in the North American colonies, with the purpose to train men for the ministry and for civil leadership (Good, 1960; Marsden, 1994). A few states chartered public higher education institutions within a few years of the Revolutionary War; the University of North Carolina at Chapel Hill was first, opening its doors in 1795 (Powell, n.d.). Over the next decades, more states opened public colleges and universities. Three colonial colleges—the University of Pennsylvania,

College of William and Mary, and Rutgers University—originally private, became state-supported institutions. These early state-owned colleges and universities, so prominent in the infancy of the Union, further solidified the preeminence of state, rather than federal, governmental power in the establishment and direction of American public higher education. The idea of a national university was discussed during the Constitutional Convention in 1787 and promoted by early presidents. Yet five military service academies, a few specialized graduate schools for the nation's uniformed services, and Gallaudet University (www.gallaudet.edu)—a specialized school for the deaf and hard of hearing—are the only national public institutions of higher education in the United States (DeVane, 1965; Giamatti, 1988).

Education is considered a public good under state authority, but public ownership of higher education is not automatic. The U. S. Supreme Court found in *Dartmouth College v. Woodward* (1819) that the State of New Hampshire must honor the charter of Dartmouth, a private institution, as a binding contract that could not be unilaterally dissolved. The state government could not, by its will alone turn a private school into a public one (DeVane, 1965; Good, 1960). In the aftermath of the Dartmouth decision, states knew they would have to start their own public colleges, and private groups knew that ownership and control over their own institutions would be protected (Good, 1960).

Many more states founded public colleges and universities, helped in this effort by federal land grants. Private interests, including religious denominations and non-sectarian groups, knew they were safe to found their own institutions of higher learning. The last few decades have seen new private institutions open their doors to fill some niche. Some of the new institutions in the last three decades, such as the University of Phoenix, have been for-profit ventures.

Community and Technical Colleges

Two-year colleges are a significant, and largely unique, element in the U.S. system of higher education. According to the National Center for Education Statistics (NCES, 2006), there are 1,061 public community colleges and 622 private junior colleges in the United States. These institutions constitute 40% of the nation's degree-granting institutions, and accounted for 38% of undergraduate enrollments in the fall 2004 term (NCES, 2006).

Public community and technical colleges provide accessible options for higher education. Because community colleges often obtain some of their institutional funding through local mill levies, they have an impetus to serve and respond to needs of the local tax base. Most have open admission policies, and lower tuition is lower than for most of their four-year counterparts (American Association of Community Colleges, 2006). They offer diplomas, certificates, and associate degrees that require two years or less of full-time college-level work to complete (Good, 1960). Besides preparing many students for transfer to universities, junior colleges, and community colleges offer programs in technical, health and public safety trades that prepare students for jobs—often right in their communities (American Association of Community Colleges, 2006).

Further extending their mission of extending college accessibility, community colleges are increasingly deciding to offer distance education courses and programs. According to a Sloan Consortium report (Allen & Seaman, 2006), 67% of associate-degree granting institutions consider online learning a major long-term strategy. Major distance learning goals of two-year institutions include improving course access and affordability, increasing overall enrollments, and meeting the needs of local employers (NCES, 2003). Statistics available from the Department of Education (NCES, 2003) suggest that two-year colleges are accomplishing these goals. In 2000–2001, 90% of the 1,070 public two-year colleges offered distance education courses. These institutions offered 50,900 distance courses, twice as many as public four-year institutions (22,000 courses). They also had more than one-half of all undergraduate distance course enrollments, with nearly 1.5 million students.

Because of a prescient design in America's infancy that shared the reigns of higher education in the United States among state and private parties, there are more than 4,200 accredited degree-granting institutions and thousands of other post-secondary learning providers (NCES, 2006). From the earliest colonial colleges built to train preachers and civil leaders, to the present diversity of research universities, liberal arts colleges, local technical colleges, and various specialized institutes, America's higher education system has spread across the landscape with thousands of campuses whose infrastructure is worth trillions of dollars. Most of the higher education needs of the nation are met through these established, campus-based institutions. Neither political necessity nor shortage of infrastructure necessitates raising a national virtual or Open University to quench a burgeoning demand for education (Moore & Kearsley, 2005).

DISTANCE EDUCATION IN THE UNITED STATES

Yet as Edelson and Pittman explain in chapter 5 (this volume), distance education in the United States, especially asynchronous online learning, is growing rapidly. This growth mirrors advancements in theory and technology for education, computers, and telecommunications (Moore & Kearsley, 2005). There are a variety of political, economic, and personal motivators for the growth of distance education. States have sought to increase the number of college-educated citizens, while containing the costs of higher education. Universities and community colleges have launched distance education programs, and students have sought to advance their education in more economical and expedient ways (Epper & Garn, 2003; Moore, 2003).

Historical Considerations

Correspondence courses became successful in the 1880s, when an expanding railroad system allowed the U.S. Postal Service to expand and be more dependable. Initially geared toward vocational training or personal enrichment, college credit by correspondence was first offered by the University of Chicago in 1892—a year after its founding. The university's first president, William Rainey Harper, brought the idea from the Chautauqua Correspondence College, a significant provider of correspondence courses (Moore, 2003; Moore & Kearsley, 2005). Education by correspondence gained further ground when the U. S. Army realized its potential for providing job training to soldiers (Moore & Kearsley, 2005).

Over time, radio, television, telecommunication, and microcomputer networking technologies have largely replaced correspondence teaching. Each level of technological sophistication advanced potential course enrollments and pedagogical approaches available to designers and instructors. The growing availability of personal microcomputers in the 1980s and the development of the World Wide Web in the 1990s, added multimedia content and real-time interaction. Computing devices, including desktop and laptop computers, personal data assistants (PDAs), and iPods have ushered in an era of dramatic growth for distance learning, as the world becomes essentially a digitized, borderless educational environment (Gunawardena & McIsaac, 2003; Peters, 2003; Potashnik & Capper, 1998).

Types of U.S. Distance Learning Institutions

Modern approaches to distance learning have caught on in the United States. About 62% of American degree-granting institutions offered distance education courses in 2004–2005 (NCES, 2006a). During the 2005 fall term, nearly 3.2 million students took at least one online course (Allen & Seaman, 2006). Given the number of higher education institutions and students in the United States, it is easy to see that most of the schools offering distance learning are not online virtual universities, but those with physical campuses which also teach at a distance. It is important to consider, then, two classifications of distance learning institutions: Single-mode and dual-mode (Moore & Kearsley, 2005).

Single-Mode Institutions

Single-mode institutions only offer distance learning courses and programs; they are far less prevalent in the United States, which has no national virtual university, than in Europe, Asia, and Africa (Moore, 2003; Moore & Kearsley, 2005). A few states operate public virtual universities, such as New Jersey's Thomas Edison State College (www.tesc.

edu) and Empire State College in New York (www.esc.edu), but most single-mode institutions in the United States are privately owned. In the last few decades, especially during the "dot.com" boom of the 1990s, many small to medium virtual colleges sprang up to cater to a growing demand from busy adults for certificates and degrees that could be earned off campus.

U.S. single-mode schools often limit their curricula to several specialized areas, such as education, health care, religion, public safety, and business (Distance Education and Training Council, 2006). For example, American Public University (www.apus.edu) offers undergraduate and graduate programs in public administration, homeland security, and related subjects of interest to a market of military and civilian public officials. Concord Law School (www.concordlawschool.edu) awards standard and executive law degrees entirely online.

Dual-Mode Institutions

Single-mode upstarts in the United States are greatly outnumbered by thousands of "brick-and-mortar" institutions, which have invested significant time, money and effort in campus infrastructure over many years. They are not easily supplanted by a totally new movement, nor are they likely to radically change format to become single-mode, online learning institutions. Instead, many long-established colleges and universities have added distance education to their existing operations, making them "dual-mode" institutions (Moore, 2003; Moore & Kearsley, 2005). For example, Pennsylvania State University (www.psu.edu) offers many courses and programs to students online through its World Campus (www.worldcampus.psu.edu/).

Several dual-mode start-up institutions have opened in recent years. Like their single-mode virtual counterparts, most dual-mode start-ups are privately owned; many operate for profit. Notable among these is the University of Phoenix (www.phoenix.edu). This institution offers Associate through Doctoral degree programs to adult learners on numerous physical campuses, and through an Online Campus—which alone boasts the largest enrollment of any institution in the United States. In fact, with 115,800 students in 2005 (National Center for Education Statistics, 2006a), the University of Phoenix Online Campus is the only American institution to be considered a mega-university according to Daniel's (cited in Moore, 2003) enrollment threshold of 100,000.

Off-Campus Extension

The efforts of many institutions to extend their reach beyond their main campuses involve classroom instruction on satellite campuses, in addition to Web-based instruction. This makes greater use of extensive educational infrastructure, and allows for personal contact that many instructors and students prefer. Some universities, such as our own, The University of New Mexico (www.unm.edu), operates distance education centers on branch campuses of the institution. The courses offered through the remote centers broaden the reach of the main campus and enhance the offerings of the branch campuses. Many moderately sized institutions that do not operate branch campuses of their own, such as Appalachian State University (www.appstate.edu), arrange for use of classrooms at community colleges or partner institutions to teach classroom sections of education and business classes. Extension courses may be taught by faculty who travel from the main campus or by locally hired adjunct faculty. Although online courses are overtaking other methods, some extension courses are still taught through instructional television, which allows an instructor to teach the same class to students gathered at the same time in multiple classrooms; students at remote sites view lectures on television sets, and check in through audio-conferencing to ask or answer questions.

AMERICAN DISTANCE LEARNERS

In the United States, individuals pursuing collegiate education online are relatively likely to have computers with Internet access in their homes; this makes computer- and Web-based learning an often-practical option. According to the U. S. Census Bureau (2005), a majority of American households own computers (61.8%) and have Internet access (54.7%). These figures have increased remarkably in the past few years. Just over one-third of households owned computers, and fewer than 20% had Internet access in 1997 (U. S. Census Bureau, 1999). Decreasing technology pricing and increased marketing of less expensive computers will likely cause these numbers to continue to increase.

Given the widespread computer ownership and Internet access in U. S. households, distance education systems with higher user technical requirements and costs are probably more common here than in any other country in the world. In fact, it is often the case that learners, rather than distance learning providers, are the early adopters who promote new technologies to the other (Rogers, 1995). Molina and the 2006 EDU-CAUSE Evolving Technologies Committee (2006) suggest that ubiquitous technology in the United States has turned the tables on campus technologists. At one time, campus technologists were the knowing, professional initial adopters and advocates of new technologies; whereas now much of their work is in response to adoptions already made by the individual clients of their institutions. Many institutions are facing the need, not only to find and develop instructional uses, but also to intelligently respond to spontaneous student uses of technologies such as iPods, PDAs, and mobile phones.

LEVELS AND SOURCES OF FUNDING

We now turn to discussing the particular approaches and formulas applied to online and distance learning in the United States. As we have shown, the U.S. system of republican government, a national will for popular access to all levels of education, and the westward expansion of the national territory (and consequent land grants to education) have led to a uniquely American system of higher education. This system is characterized by a broad distribution of thousands of independent institutions, operated by states and religious and private parties. Not only is this a unique arrangement geographically and politically; it also presents a unique challenge for management and financing of new approaches to education, requiring input, and often changes at many levels. In the remainder of this chapter, we attempt to present the funding picture for distance and online learning at the federal, state, and institution levels.

Federal Influence and Funding

In the United States, the federal government has gradually increased its influence on higher education through a series of laws and policies dating back to the early nineteenth century. Most of these laws and policies are rather broad, intended to clarify and persuade movement in the direction of national hopes and goals, to support basic research, and to ensure quality of and access to education (Giamatti, 1988). The most significant federal influences on higher education, including distance education, have been through accreditation, land and financial grants, and financial aid to students.

The federal government, under the George W. Bush administration, increased its oversight of elementary and secondary education through No Child Left Behind Act of 2001(NCLB). Legislation may extend similar accountability into U. S. post-secondary education, as well. Only time will tell how the extension of the federal hand into the details of education will impact post secondary education. Secondary impacts are almost certain, as the students educated under the current system of K–12 education apply to and are admitted to colleges. It is too early to tell the extent of effects that expanding NCLB-like control will have on federal funding to higher education, but the nation has already seen Congress eliminate several types of specific funding for instructional technology and distance education in the wake of NCLB (Lorenzetti, 2006).

Regional Accreditation

The federal government's interest in educational quality is demonstrated in part through accreditation. Most colleges are accredited regionally by one of six agencies approved by the U. S. Department of Education and the Council for Higher Education Accreditation (CHEA):

- Middle States Association of Colleges and Schools
- New England Association of Schools and Colleges
- North Central Association of Colleges and Schools
- Northwest Commission on Colleges and Universities
- Southern Association of Colleges and Schools
- Western Association of Schools and Colleges

In addition to regional accreditation, units or programs may seek national accreditation from 1 of 62 specialized bodies for specific disciplines such as business, education, law, and medicine (Eaton, 2006). For instance, accreditation of a business school by the Association to Advance Collegiate Schools of Business (www.aacsb.edu) is a distinction for any university's college of business. Accrediting agencies evaluate institutions and programs through self- and peer-review of academic quality, student achievement, teaching, research, and service. Accreditation is voluntary, and meeting accreditation standards costs money, but it is regarded as a mark of a quality college or university that will ensure a worthwhile education (CHEA, 2006; Eaton, 2006). Accreditation is often required for institutional and individual federal monetary assistance.

Recognized accreditation is especially important for schools offering exclusively distance education, to distinguish themselves as legitimate, quality institutions. Unfortunately, the lack of face-to-face personal contact among instructors and learners that characterizes most distance learning can be fertile ground for fraudulent "diploma mills." These questionable institutions offer worthless certificates or degrees that represent little or no work or learning. To protect against such intrusions, the Distance Education and Training Council (DETC), a national accrediting body, specifically accredits institutions that offer career-oriented training and degrees by way of distance learning (DETC, 2004). The six regional accrediting bodies have also adopted criteria and procedures for evaluating institutions' distance education offerings (Moore & Kearsley, 2005).

Land Grant Funding

In addition, the U.S. government has used land policy to encourage and steer educational policies and practices along lines of national will. These lines have been largely utilitarian: to open access to education, to expand university curricula into vocational areas necessary for economic growth and stability, and to enhance national security (Giamatti, 1988). Federal land grants for state higher education institutions began with the Ohio Enabling Act of 1802, in which Congress granted two townships (12 sq. miles; 31.08 sq. kilometers) to each newly admitted state to endow a public university (DeVane, 1965; Giamatti, 1988). The Morrill Act of 1862 established a more significant federal land grant program. It gave about 30,000 acres of land (121.4 sq. km.) to each state to launch a college of agriculture, engineering, and other vocational disciplines to support new and growing industries. Seventy-six land-grant colleges grew up alongside existing state colleges, which offered traditional liberal arts disciplines and professional degrees in law and medicine (DeVane, 1965; Giamatti, 1988; Good, 1960; National Association of State Universities and Land-Grant Colleges, 2005).

Land-grant institutions served the needs of agrarian and industrial eras in the American economy. They provided for numerous institutions to which families could send their young men and women, often in-state, to be educated and trained for jobs and adult life. Students could spend four or so years in school, and return home during breaks and following graduation to contribute to local industries and family businesses and farms. These federal programs succeeded in opening access to higher education; they did so by adding to the wealth of higher education infrastructure in the United States during an era before today's distance education technologies were imaginable. Land-grant universities still receive significant finances to support their operations in teaching and research, but we have yet to see what role the federal government will take in electronically extending the land-grant institutions.

Direct Fiscal Assistance

The federal government has assisted higher education financially with a series of laws since the Morrill Act. These appropriations and grants have been directed more at institutions and individuals than at states, as was the case land grants (Giamatti, 1988). Some funding laws supplemented the Morrill Act. The Hatch Act of 1887, for example, established agricultural research stations to support extension education in each state. The Second Morrill Act of 1890 provided annual federal appropriations to each of the land-grant institutions. Other federal laws extended the federal government's hand into oversight; the Smith-Hughes Act of 1917 created a board to evaluate how states spent federal money on vocational training (Good, 1960).

In the twentieth century, the direction of federal involvement in higher education turned to a greater level of person- and program-specific aid. The Reserve Officer Training Corps (ROTC), for example, provides financial aid enabling many young people to attend college in exchange for a limited military commitment. The Servicemen's Readjustment Act of 1944, popularly known as the G. I. Bill, and subsequent "G. I. Bills" provided for veterans to attend college or pursue other training, during or after their military service. As a result, millions of new students have entered America's college in the decades since World War II (DeVane, 1965). The success of the G. I. Bills has led to other financial aid programs, including grants and low-interest loans to students and families which help people afford a college education. These include Pell Grants, work study, Stafford Loans, and other financial aid programs for students with demonstrated financial needs.

Other federal monies given to higher education are aimed at funding research. The National Science Foundation (NSF), founded in 1950, has greatly increased government spending on research projects in physical and behavioral sciences. The National Defense Education Act (NDEA) of 1958 provided for fellowships and scholarships that would strengthen science education, a great national priority during the Cold War and "Space Race." This act marked a change in Congress' thinking about the federal role and obligation to higher education (DeVane, 1965). As a result, more federal monies have been set aside by a wide variety of departments and agencies to fund university research in areas valuable to the nation. Among other benefits to the institutions and nation, federal funds supplement faculty salaries and provide opportunities for students to pursue graduate studies while engaging in meaningful research work.

Most federal funding specifically for distance education comes through grants to institutions, and through regulatory changes which serve to lessen barriers to education access. The Fund for the Improvement of Postsecondary Education (FIPSE; see www.ed.gov/programs/fipsecomp/awards.html) is one significant grant program that supports local efforts to improve quality and access to education, including distance and distributed instruction.

On the regulatory side, two major rule changes in the past five years have opened access to federal financial aid to fund distance learning. In 2002, the U. S. Department of Education dropped the twelve-hour rule, which required significant in-classroom contact for federal financial aid programs, including federal student loans and federal income tax credits (Carnevale, 2003; Moore & Kearsley, 2005). Further extending the availability of federal aid programs to distance learners and institutions, the Deficit Reduction Act of 2005 (Public Law 109-171, 2006) repealed the "fifty-percent rule," which prohibited schools from participating in Title IV federal aid programs if they enrolled more than half distance students or offered more than half of its courses through distance education ("How Federal Activity Will Affect Your Program" 2006; Nelnet Policy Services, 2006).

In general, U.S. government funding that supports distance education is an extension of the longstanding view that education is a power reserved to the states, and that the national government should just provide general assistance and guidance to education. Land grants helped provide geographically proximate access to quality higher education, while emphasizing agricultural and engineering subjects in which the nation needed trained workers. Federal funding was expanded in the last century to include individual financial aid with the G. I. Bills and need-based financial aid. At times, the federal hand in higher education has included laws and policies meant to remove previously imposed barriers. As a reserved power education, including post secondary education, is governed and funded far more specifically at state, local, and institutional levels.

State Governance and Financing

The states have the most authority over higher education, particularly over public institutions, within their territories. Unlike federal funding for higher education—which is principally through grants—state legislatures fund public, post secondary institutions largely through direct, recurring appropriations in state budgets. When state budgets are tight, as is increasingly the case since the turn of the century, states are often strained in their ability to fund higher education at appropriate high levels. Given the lesser emphasis of traditional institutions on fixed expenditures, in deference to variable expenditures based on student numbers, the funding of distance learning is problematic. As mentioned elsewhere in this text, the greater need for distance and online learning is for recurrent, rather than project-based funding, tends not to fit the funding priorities established for traditional institutions. At some point, states will need to revisit the balance between traditional and distance learning and reassess longstanding formulas for their higher education appropriations if state resources for higher education are to be put to their best use.

State appropriations for public colleges and universities have declined over the past decades, largely because of fiscal pressures from other funding requirements and interests. Kane and Orszag (2003) report an overall decline in state higher education budgeting between 1977–2002, from $8.50 to $7.00 per $1,000 of personal income. As a result, the state portion of many public institutions' annual budgets is surprisingly small. Total state funding at the University of Colorado at Boulder (www.colorado. edu), for example, amounts to 8.1% of the institution's fiscal year 2007 budget—compared to almost 39% from student tuition and fees, and nearly 24% from federal grants and contracts (University of Colorado at Boulder, 2006). At the University of New Mexico, the state appropriation for operating expenses and capital amounts to 18.3% of the university's 2006–2007 revenue budget (www.unm.edu/~budget).

In the last few years, there has been a slight reversal of this declining trend. Nationwide, state funding of colleges and student aid programs increased by 5.3% in 2006 (Fischer, 2006). However, these increases do not make up for enrollment increases and inflationary cost increases over the years of declining state monies. For example, Oklahoma would need to increase its annual higher education budget by an additional $70 million, just to fund increased student numbers (Walters, 2006).

State appropriations have generally not been updated to accommodate institutions' needs related to technology and distance education. The amount an institution receives in appropriations is typically calculated using funding formulas that depend on its credit hour generation. The formulas favor variable costs such as faculty salaries, and maintenance expenses for built infrastructure having a much longer durability than computer hardware and software and telecommunication channels. State legislatures tend to view technology and distance education as special initiatives, rather than as core budget items. As a result, technology is funded through mechanisms such as special grants, fees, and special appropriations, which do not adequately provide for sustainability (Distance Learning Policy Laboratory Finance Subcommittee, 2002).

State appropriations for distance education are not confined to college and university budgets. A number of states, including Michigan, North Carolina, and Florida, have begun virtual school programs at the secondary school level, that draw on distance learning research and practices in higher education and other adult learning settings. Other states are taking steps that show they recognize the need to get behind educational technology development and implementation. In 2006, for example, Virginia created an Office of Learning Technology within the State Council of Higher Education. The office is to work with public as well as private colleges and universities, to assess and address learning technology needs, including those in distance education (Virginia Joint Commission on Technology and Science, 2006).

INSTITUTIONAL STRUCTURE AND BUDGETING

In a climate of leaner higher education grants and appropriations from federal and state governments, institutions more than ever bear the ultimate responsibility for their own success or failure. This would be a sufficient challenge if higher education were "business as usual," with traditional campus-based operations as institution's sole concern. However, facing both demands for greater access and opportunities for greater reach, thousands of American institutions have added distance education to their traditional operations. As they do so, schools try to determine and adopt the most appropriate ways to organize and fund both traditional and distance education operations. Per Rogers' (1995) writing on diffusion of innovations, successful and sustained adoption of distance education approaches and technologies will be largely consistent with existing practices, and socio-cultural values in the institution and its cultural setting. In the United States, successful distance education efforts are those that fit with decentralized governance, with a system of numerous, broadly distributed education providers, and with American capitalist competitiveness for market niches and students. As a consequence, not every distance education innovation has prospered in the United States, e.g., the Open University, despite its success in many other developed and developing countries.

The structure and relationship of distance education to an institution ranges, as Curran (chapter 3, this volume) suggests, from highly integrated in, to partly or largely independent of the larger institution. Distance education in single-mode colleges is fully integrated, since that is their mission. Sometimes, enterprising professors in smaller traditional colleges take up the idea of distance education on their own, and offer individual courses using Web sites, e-mail or open source tools like Moodle. They may have some degree of department or administration backing, but may not have the assistance of a dedicated office to support (or even take over) course development and delivery (Moore & Kearsley, 2005).

Many institutions have adopted a business-like model for their distance education operations, in which distance education is managed as a separate business operation or profit center. Administrators and educators in public and private non-profit institutions, where education is seen as a service, are understandably reluctant to talk of students as "customers," or higher education as an "enterprise," but a business model goes beyond labels into ways of organizing, operating, handling finances, and interacting with distance students ("Business Model," 2006).

Under a business model, dual-mode institutions often organize and operate distance education as an auxiliary to their on-campus education through specialized offices or units. These units consolidate most of the operations and services related to distance and extension education: Everything from course development and delivery through a course management system, to admission, advisement, library services, and course registration ("Business Model," 2006; Moore, 2003; Moore & Kearsley, 2005).

In these units, faculty members' responsibilities are commonly unbundled. Rather than one person making all decisions about a course's content and delivery, staffs of instructional designers and technical specialists assist faculty in developing or converting courses for distance teaching. They also manage hardware and software, and develop media. The instructor, then, no longer holds the role of the sole creator—or owner—of a course (Howell, Williams, & Lindsay, 2003). This perspective leads to the potential for substantial changes in the roles for professors in the "university of the future."

Tuition and fees from distance courses may go directly into a special budget for the distance or extension unit, which pays for all or most of the unit's expenses. Distance education units are often expected to be at least partially self-sustaining, ideally generating profits through tuition for course enrollments that can assist with other campus programs and expenses. These profits generated may then be absorbed into the institution's general budget, rather than remaining with the distance education office to reinvest in new technologies and instructional staff. This has obvious consequences for the potential expansion and further development of distance education programs.

Some post secondary institutions do not centralize management of distance education into one office. The University of Idaho (www.uihome.uidaho.edu) offers distance education through three separate organizations: Virtual Campus, Independent Study in Idaho, and Engineering Outreach; each has separate course listings and mechanisms for student support and course registration. At Johns Hopkins University (www.jhu.edu), in Maryland, multiple schools and an outreach center all have separate distance education systems (see webapps.jhu.edu/jhuniverse/academics/distance_education/).

In some cases, distance education is separate from the parent institution, organized and operated as a subsidiary organization (see chapter 3, this volume). In some cases, these subsidiaries are for-profit companies, such as eCornell (www.ecornell.com). Cornell University (www.cornell.edu) formed this for-profit company to develop and distribute online education using its name in 2000 (Carr, 2000). Not all separate distance education operations are for-profit. UCLA Extension (www.uclaextension.edu) is connected to the University of California-Los Angeles (www.ucla.edu), but hires its own faculty and staff and offers its own courses; it does not just offer UCLA courses online, but provides lifelong continuing education, including for-credit and enrichment learning opportunities.

CONSORTIA

Another common way for educational institutions to manage their distance education efforts is through consortia and similar partnerships with other institutions. Sixty percent of degree-granting post-secondary institutions in the U. S. that offer distance education are members of distance learning consortia (NCES, 2003). Most consortia connect institutions within states, allowing them to collaboratively publish a centralized catalog of courses and programs. The Southern Regional Education Board's Electronic Campus (www.electroniccampus.org) houses a shared catalog and other basic information for prospective students. Many consortia also supply centralized library and support services to students, and provide an avenue for leaders to cooperate on decision-making and funding. These functions can save member institutions financially, through economies of scale and reduced duplication of courses and services. Distance education consortia vary in shared academic and administrative services; most enrollment, instruction and related activities remain in the hands of each member institution (Epper & Garn, 2003).

Among education consortia discussed in this volume and elsewhere, eArmyU (www.earmyu.com) stands out as a successful example in the United States. Through articulation agreements and distance learning technologies shared by eArmyU members, 27 institutions provide 145 certificate and degree programs to U. S. Army soldiers who are otherwise limited in their opportunities by frequent moves and deployments to achieve a higher education. eArmyU allows these learners to access courses from nearly any duty station, and to combine online courses from many schools into a program of studies at a selected institution. The Army and its personnel benefit from the education gained; member institutions increase enrollments that produce student credit hours and graduates. The formation of this consortium by the client with a known set of needs is probably responsible for much of its success, compared to partnerships started by distance learning providers in search of an expanded customer base.

Funding for distance education consortia presents its own set of challenges. Despite the benefits to members, consortia often do not produce measurable student credit hours, degrees, patents, and the like. Most of the partnerships studied by Epper and Garn (2003) received significant start-up appropriations ranging from less than $500,000, to $30 million. However, levels of ongoing funding are seldom as generous. Many receive no ongoing appropriations and are required to support themselves.

DISCUSSION AND CONCLUSIONS

In this chapter, we describe how organization and funding of online and distance education in the United States is a product of the nation's history and system of government. The American system of higher education is massive, diverse, and widespread, with more than 4,000 colleges and universities with billions of dollars worth of infrastructure on campuses in every state and territory. These numerous unique institutions, some dating from the seventeenth century, have no single controlling organization or agency responsible for decisions or providence in any area, particularly over finances. State and federal governments and institutions juggle separate, but connected powers and responsibilities in the education of America's people. With this established higher education infrastructure and decentralized governance of education, there has not been an obvious need, nor a political impulse, to create a national virtual university. Distance education has nevertheless become popular among institutions and learners, alike. However, U.S, distance education is most often a supplement to traditional, campus-oriented education, rather than a pioneering national effort to meet a national need to educate the masses.

Reflecting the divided control of higher and distance education, we discussed federal, state, local, and institutional levels and sources of funding separately. Federal control is very general, directed at providing access to higher education to as many Americans as possible. Federal assistance to distance education has come through specific grant programs, and through policy changes that removed barriers to using financial aid programs for distance learning. States, on the other hand, directly finance higher education through appropriations. Current appropriation formulas and legislative priorities, developed during several centuries of predominantly physical campuses and classroom contact, are not ideally suited to the cost structures of distance education and other technology initiatives. Institutions, then, are left with the ultimate responsibility for the success or failure of distance education. In most institutions, distance learning is valued, but is relegated to specialized offices, which are expected to be largely self-contained and self-supporting.

REFERENCES

Allen, I. E., & Seaman, J. (2006, November). *Making the grade: Online education in the United States, 2006.* Needham, MA: Sloan Consortium. Retrieved January 21, 2007, from http://www.sloan-c.org/publications/survey/pdf/making_the_grade.pdf.

American Association of Community Colleges (2006). *First responders: Community colleges on the front line of security.* Washington, DC: Author. Retrieved August 23, 2006, from http://www.aacc.nche.edu/Content/ContentGroups/Headline_News/March_2006/AACC_1st_Responders_web.pdf.

Business model for online offerings benefits students, program (2006, March 15). *Distance Education Report, 10(6),* 1–2, 8.

Carnevale, D. (2002, November 15). 12-hour rule, viewed as limiting distance education, expires. *Chronicle of Higher Education, 49(12),* A36.

Carr, S. (2000, March 14). A for-profit subsidiary will market Cornell's distance programs. *Chronicle of Higher Education.* Retrieved February 8, 2007, from http://chronicle.com/free/2000/03/2000031401u.htm

Council for Higher Education Accreditation (2006). *Recognition of accrediting organizations: Policies and procedures.* Washington, DC: Author.

DeVane, W. C. (1965). *Higher education in twentieth-century America.* Cambridge, MA: Harvard University Press.

Distance Education and Training Council (2004). *2004 distance education survey: A report on course structure and educational services in Distance Education and Training Council member institutions.* Washington, DC: Author.

Distance Education and Training Council (2006). *DETC 2006–2007 directory of accredited institutions.* Washington, DC: Author.

Distance Learning Policy Laboratory Finance Subcommittee. (2002, August). *Using finance policy to reduce barriers to distance learning.* Atlanta, GA: Southern Regional Education Board.

Eaton, J. S. (2006). Accreditation and recognition in the United States. Washington, DC: Council for Higher Education Accreditation. Retrieved August 11, 2006, from http://www.chea.org/pdf/AccredRecogUS_7-06.pdf.

Epper, R. M., & Garn, M. (2003). Virtual college and university consortia: A national study. Boulder, CO: State Higher Education Executive Officers and Western Cooperative for Educational Telecommunications. Retrieved August 5, 2006 from http://www.wcet.info/resources/publications/vcu.pdf.

Fischer, K. (2006, January 6). State appropriations: Still more money needed. *Chronicle of Higher Education, 52(18),* A14.

Giamatti, A. B. (1988). *A free and ordered space: The real world of the university.* New York: W. W. Norton and Company.

Good, H. G. (1960). *A history of Western education* (2nd ed.). New York: MacMillan.

Gunawardena, C. N., & McIsaac, M. S. (2003). Distance education. In D. H. Jonassen (Ed.), *Handbook of research on educational communications and technology* (pp. 355–395). Mahwah, NJ: Erlbaum.

How Federal activity will affect your program. (2006, March 15). *Distance Education Report, 10*(6), 5–6.

Howell, S. L., Williams, P. B., & Lindsay, N. K. (2003). Thirty-two trends affecting distance education: an informed foundation for strategic planning. *Online Journal of Distance Learning Administration, 6*(3). Retrieved August 15, 2006, from http://www.westga.edu/~distance/ojdla/fall63/howell63.html.

Kane, T. J., & Orszag, P. R. (2003, September). Funding restrictions at public universities: Effects and policy implications. Retrieved January 20, 2007, from http://www.sppsr.ucla.edu/ps/webfiles/faculty/kane/funding.pdf.

Lorenzetti, J. P. (2006, March 1). Federal funding for distance education initiatives. *Distance Education Report, 10*(5), 1, 2, 8.

Marsden, G. M. (1994). *The soul of the American university: From protestant establishment to established nonbelief.* New York: Oxford University Press.

Molina, P. G., & Educause Evolving Technologies Committee (2006). Pioneering new territory and technologies. *Educause Review, 41*(5), 113–134.

Moore, M. G. (2003). *From Chautauqua to the virtual university: A century of distance education in the United States.* Columbus, OH: Center on Education and Training for Employment. (ERIC Document Reproduction Service No. ED482357).

Moore, M. G. & Kearsley, G. (2005). *Distance education: A systems view* (2nd ed). Belmont, CA: Thomson Wadsworth.

National Center for Education Statistics (2003). *Distance education at degree-granting postsecondary institutions: 2000–2001.* Washington, DC: U.S. Department of Education, National Center for Education Statistics. (NCES 2003-017).

National Association of State Universities and Land-Grant Colleges. (2005). *NASULGC 2005 people and programs.* Retrieved February 7, 2007 from http://www.nasulgc.org/publications/2005%20P&P%20final.pdf.

National Center for Education Statistics (2006, June). *The condition of education: 2006.* Washington, DC: U.S. Department of Education, National Center for Education Statistics. (NCES 2006-071).

National Center for Education Statistics (2006a). Digest of education statistics, 2005. Washington, DC: U.S. Department of Education, National Center for Education Statistics. (NCES 2006-030). Retrieved August 9, 2006, from http://nces.ed.gov/programs/digest/d05_tf.asp.

Nelnet Policy Services (2006). Analysis of the higher education Reconciliation Act of 2005 (S. 1932). Retrieved October 8, 2006, from http://www.nelnet.net/media/newsletters/shoolnews/HERA_SchoolChanges.pdf.

Peters, O. (2003). Models of open and flexible learning in distance education. In S. K. Panda (Ed.). *Planning and management in distance education* (pp. 15–28). London: Kogan Page.

Potashnik, M., & Capper, J. (1998, March). Distance education: growth and diversity. *Finance and Development, 35*(1), 42–45.

106 • Mark J. Smith and William J. Bramble

Powell, W. S. (n.d.). *Carolina—a brief history*. Retrieved August 9, 2006, from http://www.unc.edu/about/history.html.
Rogers, E. M. (1995). *Diffusion of innovations* (4th ed.). New York: The Free Press.
University of Colorado at Boulder (2006, September). 2006–2007 campus management information figures and rates. Retrieved January 20, 2007, from http://www.colorado.edu/pba/budget/.
U.S. Census Bureau (1999). Computer use in the United States: October 1997. Washington, DC: Author. (P20–522). Retrieved August 15, 2006, from http://www.census.gov/prod/99pubs/p20-522.pdf.
U.S. Census Bureau (2005, October). Computer and Internet use in the United States: 2003. Washington, DC: Author. (P23–208). Retrieved August 15, 2006, from http://www.census.gov/prod/2005pubs/p23-208.pdf.
The Virginia Joint Commission on Technology and Science. (2006). Legislative review: Science and technology related legislation passed by the 2006 General Assembly. Retrieved January 26, 2007, from http://jcots.state.va.us/pdf/2006/BillsPassed.pdf.
Walters, A. K. (2006, January 6). Outlook for higher education in the state legislatures: OKLAHOMA. *Chronicle of Higher Education, 52*(18), A20.

7

FUNDING DISTANCE EDUCATION

A Regional Perspective

Santosh Panda and Ashok Gaba

Indira Gandhi National Open University, India

INTRODUCTION

Tertiary education is at the center stage of debate today, not as much for how it should be strategically planned and managed, nor even for internationalizing the curricular reforms, but as for how and from where it should be funded, and how to reduce the unit cost to break even without sacrificing quality. Privatization and/or private initiative has been one significant option, even for countries like the Peoples Republic of China (World Bank, 2002); there is increasing proliferation of for-profit institutions especially in the developed countries (Altbach, 1999); and distance and online learning is being adopted to generate resources besides providing for increasing access (Perraton & Lentell, 2004). As discussed in the first chapter, consortia and alliances including virtual university education are fast emerging in this segment. Since tertiary education is breaking the traditional and elitist ivory towers, many enterprising ventures, including the service university (Tjeldvoll, 1998–99), entrepreneurial university (Clark, 1998), McUniversity (Rinne, 1999), and virtual university (Rumble & Latchem, 2004) are taking shape. Distance education, which ranges from the traditional print-based delivery at one end to fully online delivery at the other, today occupies the centre stage in the debate on tertiary education. The preceding chapter focused on the issue of funding of distance education in the U.S. context. The present chapter takes the discussion forward to underline the practices, especially in the single mode open universities, from the Asian perspective. It focuses largely on the Indian sub-continent, which has one of the largest distance education systems in the world.

FUNDING OF HIGHER EDUCATION

It has been well established that higher education, the world over, is cash starved; and with government financial support constantly dwindling, institutions are often told to adopt alternative funding strategies for sustenance and progress. In so far as the status of state policy and funding of higher education is concerned, three aspects—gross enrolment ratio, student fees, and pattern of funding—assume considerable significance. The *gross enrolment ratios* (GERs) of a few selected countries, given in Table 7.1, indicate great disparity within both the developed and the developing countries, and also between the two worlds. Some Latin American and Southeast Asian countries are comparable to some of the developed ones, though the GER is generally low in the Asian and African nations.

The South Asian nations specifically are hard pressed to increase the GER; for instance, in India, only 11.4% of the age group of 18–23 years is in higher education; this comprises more than 12 million students, including those studying at a distance (although the off-campus students may belong to any age group above 21 years).

A comparison of fees charged to students as percentage of unit operating expenditure (Table 7.2) indicates that Chile, Jamaica, Indonesia, and the United States charge high fees—as much as 26%—while France charged 1% of the total expenditure, and Brazil, Venezuela, and Bangladesh did not charge any fees for meeting operating expenditure of higher education. Whereas there exists considerable variance in student tuition fees, the United Kingdom, for example, made provisions for larger student loans and student scholarships to facilitate higher education of the meritorious as well as disadvantaged students. Germany and France did not charge any fees to qualified students. For the United States, fee percentage was as low as 15%. Faced with the dual challenges of reduced public funding and protests against increase in student fees, universities are compelled to generate revenue from other sources.

The pattern of institutional funding is reflective of the state policy on education. The government/public expenditure on education in selected developing countries (Table 7.3) indicates that, as percentage of Gross Domestic Product (GDP), these countries spend much less on education generally, though countries like Thailand and Myanmar spent as high as 31% and 18%, respectively, of the total government expenditure on edu-

Table 7.1 Gross Enrollment Ratio in Higher Education (2001)

Country	Year	Gross enrollment ratio (%)
Developed Countries		
Total	2001	54.6
Canada	2001	59.1
USA	2001	81.4
New Zealand	2001	71.7
Australia	2001	64.6
Germany	2001	49.9
Japan	2001	49.2
U.K.	2001	63.6
Hong Kong	NA	NA
Developing Countries		
Total	2001	11.3
Asia		
Philippines	2001	31.1
Thailand	2001	36.7
Indonesia	2001	15.2
India	2001	11.4
Sri Lanka	2001	N.A
China	2001	19.0
Central Asia	2001	30.7
East Asia and the Pacific	2001	13.4
Africa		
Botswana	2001	4.4
Nigeria	2001	7.5
Sub-Saharan Africa	2001	2.5
Latin America and Caribbean		
Mexico	2001	21.5
Brazil	2001	18.2
LA&C total	2001	25.7
World Total	2001	23.2

Source: Adapted from UNESCO (2005b, Table 9)
NA= not available

cation. This, however, is not reflective of their expenditure on higher education.

Contrary to what is noted above, in some of the countries, federal and provincial governments have been giving considerable support to higher education. In Denmark, Netherlands, Canada, India, and United States, governments provided funding support to campus-based higher education to the tune of 99%, 98%, 90%, 89%, and 78%, respectively. These World Bank data further suggest that, in Norway, France, Australia, Germany, Indonesia, Kenya, and the UK, government finance for higher education was 90%, 89.5%, 88%, 68.5%, 62.8%, 62.2%, and 55%, respectively (World Bank, 1995). However, both the Organization for Economic Co-operation

Table 7.2 Higher Education Fees as a Percentage of Unit Operating Expenditure in Selected Countries

Region Nation	Year	Fees as percent of operating expenditure, per unit
Central and South America		
Brazil	1991	No Fees
Chile	1991	26.0
Jamaica	1991	25.0
Mexico	1991	No Fees
Venezuela	1991	No Fees
Asia	Mid 1980s	
Bangladesh	No fees	
China	1991	9.0
India	Mid 1980s	5.0
Indonesia	1989	25.0
Sri Lanka	Mid 1980s	3.0
Thailand	Mid 1980s	5.0
Industrial Countries		
France	1990	1.0
Japan	1991	9.0
United Kingdom (UK)	1990	No Fees
United States (US)	1985	15.0

Source: Adapted from Albrecht (1995, p. 43, Table 3.4)

and Development (OECD) countries—largely developed countries including Canada and the United States—and the World Education Indicator (WEI) countries—developing countries and Russia—spent almost a similar amount as a percentage of GDP on tertiary education (i.e., 1.4%), and some of the WEI countries, Jamaica and Malaysia, for example, spent more then the OECD countries (UNESCO, 2005a). Due to the transition of higher education from an elite system to a mass system during the last few decades in all of these countries, governments are finding it difficult to support further expansion of higher education; and the offering of higher

Table 7.3 Public Expenditure on Education (2000-01)

Country	As % of GDP	As % of total government expenditure
Myanmar	1.4	18.1
Indonesia	1.5	9.6
Pakistan	1.8	7.8
Bangladesh	2.5	15.7
Sri Lanka	3.1	-
Philippines	3.5	-
India	4.1	12.7
Thailand	5.4	31.0
Malaysia	6.2	-

Source: Adapted from UNESCO (2003, Table A5)

education to large masses has led to the proposal of cost recovery, especially from students. Some countries, however, have increased the percentage of GDP expenditure for higher education to meet the growing demand. It is therefore not surprising that most of them have resorted to distance and allied forms of delivery of education and training.

FUNDING OF DISTANCE EDUCATION

As stated in the introduction to this chapter, a regional perspective on funding of distance education shall be discussed further in a later section. Brief cases of selected single mode open universities are described to provide a context for further appreciation of patterns of funding in one of the mega distance education systems from a fast growing developing country.

British Higher Education and Funding of UKOU

Universities and polytechnics, the two institutional mechanisms of British higher and further education, were earlier funded by the University Grants Committee (UGC), during 1988–93 by the Universities Funding Council (UFC), and from 1993 by the Higher Education Funding Councils (HEFCs) for England, Wales, and Scotland separately. Establishment of the UK Open University (UKOU) in 1969 altered the perceived pattern of funding, though not to its advantage. The UKOU was funded directly by the government through the Department of Education and Science (now the Department of Education), and not by the UFC, based on the statement of its own requirements by the university. The HEFC of England is empowered to fund teaching, basic infrastructure and non-project elements of research throughout the country, while the HEFCs of Wales and Scotland fund important schemes locally. There were two kinds of awards: Mandatory (for full-time conventional university students), and discretionary (for part-time students and all OU students). More than 90% of HEFC's grants were for teaching funds, and some for research. The policy of funding of the OU has led the university to function in competition with other providers of higher education in the country. Peters and Daniel (1994) commented that

> In practice, constraints on public funding have meant that the number and size of discretionary awards have been severely limited. [The result is] that almost all the OU students meet the cost of tuition fees from their own pocket, unless their employers or the OU's own financial assistance fund are able to help. (pp. 32–33)

A core-plus-margin approach to funding of teaching was specified by the HEFC; that is, institutions have to admit a certain number of students for the stipulated level of grant in 11 academic subject categories (ASC; Daniel, Peters, & Watkinson, 1994). Within each subject, there are separate funding procedures for full-time and part-time students. Thus, an institution can get funds for 22 types—11 subject areas separately for part-time and full-time students (or modes). For any year's funding, the Council increases the grant by certain percentage for inflation, and then does a baseline adjustment for each ASC and mode on the basis of their Average Unit of Council Funding (AUCF). AUCF is obtained by dividing the grant for teaching by the total student enrolment. Student numbers for each ASC and mode have to be maintained for each year, and sometimes institutions over-admit students in some ASCs or modes to offset under-enrolment in other ASCs or modes. Further, institutions have to maintain a certain degree of quality in teaching, negligence of which would reduce the grant. There may also be a withdrawal of funded students from those ASCs with poor teaching, which can further reduce funding. Besides teaching, the HEFC also gives grants for specific purposes, like increasing access and use of new technology.

The core-plus-margin approach of HEFC has been beneficial for the OU since it has ensured stable grants for 11 subject areas. However, funding based on student enrolment has a disadvantage for the OU for subject areas with large part-time student enrolment. Areas like science, engineering and technology, and education have a higher public funding index, and the OU charges very low fees in comparison to full-time students of conventional universities. It had been found that student numbers at OU have resulted in lower public funding in comparison to full-time equivalent student places in other conventional universities. Further, in comparison to campus-based universities, the range of public funding varies widely in the OU, though the cost of teaching (for example in science subjects) has been almost equal to conventional higher education institutions. But across all the 11 subject areas, government funding of full-time equivalent study in the OU varies between 42–83% of the government funding of full-time study in conventional institutions (Peters & Daniel, 1994). Some of the programs of the OU, like the postgraduate certificate in education, are fully funded by the government (Perraton, 2004); on the other hand, since the government stopped giving credence to the idea of increasing the teaching staff, the university had to increase the length of course offer, before revision, from five to eight years to thereby offset reduction in public funding (Rumble, 2003). Daniel et al. (1994) suggested a revised policy of funding by a plan of integrated student assistance and student credit point system.

Funding of Higher Education and the Open University of Hong Kong

Higher education in Hong Kong is highly competitive, and there are thousands of international providers of cross border education to 80% of its students of the relevant age group. Nearly 30% of its institutions are privately funded. Government spending on education is also high; in 1993–94 more than 16% of total government spending was on education, one-third of which was allocated to higher education. The Universities and Polytechnics Grants Committee (UPGC) provided grants to all higher education institutions as recurrent grants, capital grants, and research grants (Hope & Dhanarajan, 1994), though the Open University of Hong Kong (OUHK, the erstwhile Open Learning Institute—OLI established in 1989) does not come under its purview. Since the government does not take much responsibility for adult higher education, the role of OUHK assumes considerable importance. The OLI, which received funding directly from the government, was to become a self-supporting institution within four years of its existence; and from 1993, as per the mandate, there was no government subsidy, and the total revenue and the total recurrent expenditure were almost equal.

The very professional approach adopted by OUHK has made this possible. Its academic decisions are sound business decisions. Besides developing learning materials in-house, very high quality course materials are purchased from overseas distance teaching institutions and adapted to local requirements. The strategies adopted towards the secondary use of materials facilitating speed, breadth, quality and cheapness have contributed to the OU's cost-effectiveness (Dhanarajan, Swift, & Hope, 1994). There is a small core of academic and administrative staff, with double the size of part-time tutors to provide student support. There has been considerable investment in information technology to support management decision-making and offset the staffing costs. Strict quality assurance protocols have been developed and applied to maintain high quality in processes and products. Students generally pay about 86% of the cost of their education, which is quite high. It has been argued that the cost of education should be shared jointly by the government, the students and the employers, as is the case of higher education in many countries of the world.

Funding of Sukhothai Thammathirat Open University (STOU)

As a government institution in Thailand, the main source of income for this first open university in Southeast Asia is the government. In 1993, STOU was among 19 institutions to receive direct funding from the Thai government. From 1989–1993, the government subsidy more than doubled, though STOU's grant was just 1% of the total budget of the Ministry of University Affairs. The grant received by the open university was the lowest of all the universities in the country. In 1993, the ratio between government allocation and STOU's self-financing for salaries and wages was 69:31, which was not favorable to the open university in comparison to funding for conventional face-to-face education. Government assistance excluded purchase of media air-time, printing supplies and fees for course writers, proctors, and tutors (Chaya-Ngam, 1994). Various other agencies, including governments of other countries, have provided donations to STOU.

Though the university is receiving a very low government subsidy, outside donations and facilities for media, tutorials, examinations, etc. have made it possible for it to manage successfully its increasing number of students and expanding activities.

Funding of Universitas Terbuka, Indonesia

For the Universitas Terbuka (UT), Indonesia's open university established in 1984 as a state university, the method of government funding is similar to other universities, except that the amount of funds allocated varies from institution to institution. While fees received from students varied from 10–20% in campus-based universities in 1991–92, student fees and sale of instructional materials accounted for 44% of UT's total revenue, and that was increasing every year (Djalil, Musa, Kesuma, & Damajanti, 1994). During the past years, however, the ratio of government grant and students fees (including scholarships) has been to the tune of 20:80 (Belawati, 2006). Universities receive three types of government grants: Routine, development, and OMF (operation, maintenance and facilities). While UT expenditures were lower than those of its counterparts, the routine grants were 2–5% higher, development grants were 3–20% higher and OMF grants were 2–4% higher than those of campus-based universities (CBUs). Staff salaries, research, and teaching operations accounted for highest budget allocations in CBUs, while these operations were at a low volume at the UT. Therefore, the UT was in an advantageous position of being more self-sufficient than its counterparts.

The unit cost of UT was less than 3% of CBUs. On the other hand, the government allocated about 0.8%, 1.3%, and 0.6% of its higher education budget for routine, development, and OMF activities, respectively, of UT. The open university earned about 56% of its income, while the government grant was about 34% in 1993–94 (17% routine, 10% development, and 7% OMF) (Djalil, et al., 1994). The allocation of funds within the university was as follows: About 70% for operational activities (including capital and recurrent costs for physical facilities, equipment, buildings, salaries, etc.); 21–27% for teaching-related activities (like program design and development, radio and TV programs, tutorials, and other academic services); and 2% for research, community services, and other student support services. In the 2006 budget, this equation was considerably altered: 61% fixed costs (45% fixed recurrent and 16% fixed capital), and 39% variable costs. In terms of cost classification by capital and operational costs, the allocation was as follows: 7% for capital, and 93% for operations (48% for administration, 42% for academic, and 3% for maintenance and utilities) (Belawati, 2006). Belawati further writes, "…As a rough comparison, the cost for studying at UT is approximately about 9–25% of that in Indonesian state face-to-face universities. This percentage will be much lower if it is compared to the cost for studying at private face-to-face universities" (p. 15).

Since the government financing policy was not going to change drastically in the near future, UT had to maintain (and even increase) its earning from students and other sources to maintain its level of activities with sufficient quality. For the open university, though the government grant was substantial, it was not proportionate to the increase in student enrolment. However, since the unit cost of the university was much lower, it had greater cost advantage in comparison to the CBUs. Further, since about 80% of the total students was comprised of in-service teacher trainers, it is to be seen in the future what pattern of funding and cost behavior will be observed when the composition of the student body drifts away from the dominant students teachers towards more diversified learners population.

Funding of The Open University of Sri Lanka (OUSL)

In Sri Lanka in the 1990s, only 3.41% of the Gross National Product (GNP) was spent on education, and expenditure on higher education was 14.22% of all educational expenditure (0.37% of GNP). The government of Sri Lanka fully funds the conventional national universities, while the OUSL—also a national university—is partly funded by the government (Wijeysekera, 1994). The government grant to OUSL increased over the years from 33% in 1982, to 56% in 1992. Since 1981, there has been considerable assistance from international donors for staff development, equipment, temporary staff salary, and consultancies. The UGC fund was available for meeting recurring expenditure other than the salary of permanent staff.

The government grant was based on the number of full-time equivalent (FTE) students of the OUSL, which should be equivalent to conventional universities. Since 1992, foundation and certificate level students are considered as one-fourth equivalent of full-time conventional university students, diploma and degree level students as fully equal, and postgraduate students as one-half of FTE.

The university was expected to generate about one-third of its expenses from student fees, though it was difficult to enhance the fee structure, keeping in view the economic difficulties faced by a large number of students. Survey data showed that nearly 45% of drop-outs do so because of the burden of course fees. To reduce the burden on students, the UGC had to reconsider the formula for FTE for allocation of funds. The OUSL's involvement in the distance education modernization project, initiated in 2005 and supported by the Asian Development Bank, shall further reform its technology-enabled educational delivery, though the post-reform costing needs are worth observing.

FUNDING OF HIGHER EDUCATION IN INDIA

India, which we analyze here as a case study, was under British rule until 1947. The post-colonial expansion of education, and more particularly higher education, has been tremendous. From just 590 colleges and 27 universities in 1947, the number had grown to 13,500 and 304, respectively, in 2004, with 10.5 million students and 450,000 teachers (Government of India, 2006; Panda, Venkaiah, Garg, & Puranik, 2006). The organizational structure for higher education includes four types of institutions:

1. central/federal universities, fully funded by the federal government;
2. state/provincial universities, largely funded by the state governments, with some development grants received from the federal University Grants Commission (UGC);
3. deemed-to-be universities, generally funded by private initiatives;
4. institutes of national importance, fully supported by the federal government.

Colleges either are affiliated with a parent university (sometimes more than 300 colleges are attached to one university), or act as constituent colleges or, as happened in the recent past, some have been declared as autonomous colleges fully empowered to award their own degrees. The system as a whole enrolls about 6% of the relevant age group of 17–23 years; and the rate of growth has stabilized at about 5% per annum.

For central universities, the entire development and maintenance expenditure is met by the central government. For maintenance, the government provides grants minus the income received from other sources. For the state universities, the maintenance expenditure is met by the concerned state governments, and, in some cases,the universities are running with huge deficits. For development expenditures, both the UGC and state governments share the cost.

The Education Commission of 1964–66, the most comprehensive education policy statement so far, recommended that the government should endeavor to progressively increase its expenditure on education to reach the level of 6% of national income (i.e., GNP) over a twenty-year time frame. Though the time has elapsed, the federal government of today is seriously considering doing so. The trends show that the expenditure on education in India increased two-fold over the period 1966–86 (from 1.8 % of GNP in 1965-66, to 3.7 % in 1985–86; see Table 7.4). The highest that it reached in the successive years was 4.4 % in 2000–01, whereupon there is a visible declining trend. The decadal growth rate in average per capita real expenditure on education suggests that while there was an increase from 5.7% in the 1970s to 6.4% in the 1980s, it declined to 4.1% during the 1990s. This is largely attributed to the efforts of the government to withdraw from the education sector—particularly the higher education sector—during the 1990s. By comparison, it has been pointed out that in countries like India and Chile, expenditure has increased faster than the

Table 7.4 Indian Expenditure on Education as a Percentage of GNP: 1951–2005

Year	Expenditure as a percent of GNP
1951–52	0.67
1965–66	1.82
1985–86	3.71
1989–90	4.21
1999–2000	4.30
2000–01	4.40
2001–02	3.90
2002–03	3.83
2003–04 (RE)	3.81
2004–05 (BE)	3.54

Source: Adapted from Tilak (2006, p. 613, Table 1)
RE: revised estimates
BE: budget estimates

increase in student enrolment. The reverse is the case for countries like Brazil and Philippines (UNESCO, 2005a).

In the Indian constitution, education is on the concurrent list; therefore, the central and state governments share the expenditure on education. For higher education, in the year 1995–96, while the central government shared 51.51% of plan expenditure, its share was only 11.46% for non-plan expenditure (Table 7.5). Over the years, the share of non-plan expenditure by the central government has been marginally reduced. In comparison to the total educational expenditure, the share of higher education (plan) was about 6%, and non-plan about 11.5%, while both taken together it

Table 7.5 Plan and Non-Plan Expenditure on Higher Education (1995–96): Share of Central and State Governments

Agency	Expenditure (million rupees)	Percentage of subtotal	As percent of total expenditure
Plan			
States	2,306.2	48.49	6.32
Centre	2,450.5	51.51	6.72
Subtotal	4,756.7	100.00	13.04
Non-Plan			
States	28,090.2	88.54	76.99
Centre	3,639.1	11.46	9.97
Subtotal	31,729.3	100.00	86.96
Plan+Non-Plan			
States	30,396.4	83.31	83.31
Centre	6,089.6	16.69	16.69
Total	36,486.0	100.00	100.00

Source: Government of India (1997)

Table 7.6 Sources of Funds (Recurring) for Education in India: 1992–93 (%)

Level/Source	Government	Local bodies	Fees	Other (e.g. endowments)	Total
Primary	91.1	7.5	0.0	1.4	100.0
Middle	88.6	8.0	0.0	3.3	100.0
Secondary	93.2	3.0	2.9	1.0	100.0
Higher secondary	84.4	3.6	10.2	1.8	100.0
Intermediate	18.2	0.8	58.8	22.2	100.0
Total school sector	89.5	5.0	2.9	2.6	100.0
Higher education (1986–87)	75.9	0.0	12.6	11.5	100.0

Source: Adapted from Tilak (2004)

was about 10%. Comparison between 1994–95 and 1995–96 suggested that plan expenditure was reduced by 4.66% and non-plan expenditure by 4.11% (Powar, 1998). The trend has continued over the past years.

Analysis of recurring (non-plan) expenditure by level (i.e., from primary schooling to higher education) shows that 94.5% of the expenditure on school education was met by government sources. The corresponding proportion for higher education (in 1986–87) was 76%, and "fees" and "endowments" accounted for the rest (12% each; see Table 7.6). Privatization of higher education, which was encouraged as a matter of government policy during the 1990s, and the impact of which is not fully reflected in the data presented for 1992–93 in Table 7.6, is expected to increase the share of the component to a much higher level.

A commonly suggested cost recovery method, therefore, was to increase student fees. However, the share of fees in the total expenditure in higher education has declined over time (Table 7.7). This has happened because fees for courses in higher education were kept constant for a long time, even though the cost of providing education increased. In the Indian context, alternative ways of increasing the fees have been suggested in the past: (1) a uniform increase for graduate and post-graduate courses, (2) increasing the fees based on the cost of provision of courses, (3) giving autonomy to colleges for deciding on the fees to be charged for courses offered, among

Table 7.7 Funding for Higher Education by Source (percent)

Year/Source	Government	Local bodies	Fees	Others	Total
1950–51	49.1	0.3	36.8	13.8	100.0
1960–61	53.1	0.4	34.8	11.7	100.0
1970–71	60.4	0.5	25.5	13.5	100.0
1980–81	72.0	0.8	17.4	10.8	100.0
1985–86	79.7	1.4	14.4	4.5	100.0
1986–87	75.9	0.0	12.6	11.5*	100.0

Source: Adapted from Tilak (2004)
includes local bodies.

others (Tilak, 2004). In most colleges and universities, over 90% of the expenditure goes towards paying salaries of teachers and staff. Therefore, it is not surprising that many dual mode universities have resorted to distance education, especially during the past five years.

FUNDING OF DISTANCE EDUCATION IN INDIA

Distance education in India was initiated in 1962, in the form of undergraduate level correspondence courses offered by a dual mode university distance education centre/institute (DEI)—the central University of Delhi. The courses initially enrolled 1,111 arts students. This initiation was as much to provide opportunities to those who otherwise could not access campus-based education as it was to offset escalating unit cost of education. Though initially fully subsidized, at later stages two developments distinguish it from its earlier form: One, that distance education (DE) offered as off-campus program was compelled to earn its own revenue; and two, that DE programs were rather considered as revenue earning mechanism to support many developmental activities on campus, sometimes even to support the salaries of the parent conventional university teachers and others. The first provincial open university was established in 1982, and the national open university in 1985. By that time, 9% of the total students of higher education were studying at a distance.

The present scenario of distance higher education in India is quantitatively depicted in Table 7.8. DE is offered by dual mode university distance education institutes (DEIs), single mode state open universities (SOUs), and the national open university (Indira Gandhi National Open University; IGNOU), which has additional mandates to fund and accredit DE programs in the country, and to offer its programs overseas.

Dual Mode University Distance Education

The initiation of dual mode university DEIs was intended to both provide for increasing educational access and to generate additional financial resources to support campus based education. Though such programs, which follow the curricula and evaluation mechanisms of the parent university, were fully supported by government funding, in subsequent years

Table 7.8 Status of Distance Higher Education in India (2006)

Indicators	Number
Institutions	14 OUs, 106 IDTIs
Students	2.87 million (about 28.3% of all students)
Programs	441 (certificate, diploma, degree)
Courses	3,863
Counselors	64,838 (counselors, tutors, instructors)
Regional centers	111 (only open universities)
Study centers	4,388 (only open universities)

internal resources were invested to initiate and expand such programs by many universities. Today, there are 106 university Distance Teaching Institutes (DTIs) in India, some with an annual student intake of more than 100,000 and some others with as low as 1000—and, therefore, economically non-viable. In the initial years, these institutions were given developmental grants from the University Grants Commission (UGC), a task which the Distance Education Council (DEC) of IGNOU has undertaken to perform from 1999. The DTIs, since they have little freedom in financial decision making of their own, function within and under the control of the mainstream university in which they are located. They show considerable variance in student fees as a source of income. While the DTI of Madurai Kamraj University received a public subsidy of up to 52% (student fees being 48%), SNDT Women's University generated 92% from student fees. Universities like Sri Venkateswara and Kerala met all their expenses from the contribution made by students (Pillai & Naidu, 1998).

On the basis of a nationwide study, Datt (1991) reported that there were two kinds of DTIs: Those generating surplus, and those incurring deficit (Table 7.9). His analysis showed that DTIs of universities of Annamalai, Allahabad, Madras, Patna, and SNDT Women's were surplus generating

Table 7.9 Sources of Funding in Selected DTIs (INRs. at current prices)

Institute	Year	Cost per student	Fee income per student	Surplus per student	State subsidy per student
SCC & CE, Delhi University	1988–89	584 (100)	320 (54.8)	–	264 (45.2)
DCC, Punjab University	1988–89	1832 (100)	601 (32.8)	–	1231 (67.2)
DCC, HP University	1988–89	620 (100)	404 (65.2)	–	216 (34.8
ICE, Madras University	1988–89	472 (100)	794 (167.9)	321 (67.9)	–
DCC Patna University	1988–89	368 (100)	447 (121.4)	79 (21.4)	–
SNDT Women's University	1988–89	242 (100)	341 (140.8)	99 (40.8)	–
ICC & CE, Allahabad University	1988–89	495 (100)	435 (88)	60 (12)	–
DCC, Annamalai University	1985–86	132 (100)	590 (447)	458 (347)	–

Source: Datt (1991)
Note: Figures in parentheses are percentages; DTI= distance teaching institutes

institutions; and their surplus money was being utilized for either augmenting the resources of the parent university or creating infrastructure for the distance education delivery.

Skeleton academic and other staff, economic models of course design and development, and absence of any significant media input were responsible for generating surpluses for them. Most DTIs spend little on student support services, library facilities, and audio-video programs. Datt (1991) pointed out that some DTIs generating huge income on their own were deliberately depressing costs so as to generate surpluses. Those which incurred deficits (like Delhi, Panjab, and HPU) were subsidized either by the UGC or the concerned state government. At the University of Delhi, the fee income per student was almost 55% lower than the unit cost. Though the unit cost was very high at Panjab University, this was largely due to the low level of enrolment and higher student-teacher ratio (63:1). Further, the non-teaching staff-student ratio was 1:297 in case of Madras University, and 1:35 in case of Panjab University. The School of Correspondence Courses and Continuing Education (SCC&CE) of Delhi University fell in between these two extremes, where the student-teacher ratio was 360:1, and the student-non-teaching staff ratio was 139:1. The results of coefficient of correlation suggested a strong negative relationship between enrolment and cost per student in the cases of Bombay, Patna, Delhi, Madras, and Punjab universities. The author emphasized that the DTIs must have core teaching and supporting staff; enrolments should increase in undergraduate courses; and, there should be increase in state support to DE (Datt, 1991).

State Open Universities

Development of single-mode state-supported state open universities in India—one established before the IGNOU was established, and 12 after— was a conscious decision of many state governments in pursuance with the federal government policy to provide greater access to education and training, especially to the disadvantaged sections of their communities. This was over and above what IGNOU and dual mode DEIs have been doing so that the gross enrolment ratio in higher and further education moves forward. Unlike the DTIs, the SOUs are autonomous in their decision making including curricular innovations. Though many of them have been adopting learning materials developed by IGNOU, their mandate is to offer innovative academic programs in regional language of the state and as per the regional and local needs of its people.

The state open universities in India generate resources from four sources:

1. state government grants;
2. central government grants (through UGC/IGNOU);

3. grants from private sources; and
4. student fees.

Some of the open universities also receive developmental grants from the IGNOU-DEC. Dr. B. R. Ambedkar Open University (BRAOU), which received only state grants in 1982–83 (without any internally generated funds), received Rs.23.90 million from state grants and generated Rs.30.80 million internally in 1992–93. The university generated about four-fifths of its income from student fees, and the state government grant was reduced to 22%. The university spent more than 20% more on students than what it received. On the other hand, the Yashwantrao Chavan Maharashtra Open University (YCMOU) received state subsidy in the form of block grants every year. The grants were to be reviewed after three years. Block grants were given for meeting development costs and the university was expected to meet all operational costs on its own. The state government also granted money for site development and construction work on the campus. As per agreement that the open university shall meet its recurring expenses on its own after five years of its existence, the university now does so. The contrast between two SOUs is presented in Table 7.10. While BRAOU received about 18–19% in grant (non-plan) from the state government (without any plan grant support) and generated about 80% from student fees, YCMOU—which largely focuses on agricultural and teacher training programs—did not receive any grant (plan or non-plan) from the state government and had to meet more than 98% of its expenses from student fees (though the Indian Council for Agricultural Research provides a meager plan grant for its agricultural programs, including establishment of agri-informatic centers; Naidu, 2005).

Latest data for the financial year 2003–04 (Table 7.11) suggest that except for the University of Delhi, no DTI from the sampled institutes (Datt & Gaba, 2006) had been supported by the government grant—either federal or state. Some of the DTIs accrued their full income from only student fees, and a state open university like YCMOU, which focuses heavily on its agricultural programs, meets above 90% of its expenditure from student fees. Further, the subsidy from the Distance Education Council for development expenditure relating to learning material development, staff training, media development, research, and learner support services, had been negligible, and its impact is yet to be properly studied and documented.

Also from the 2003–04 financial year, the unit cost of education, the fee charged per student, and the fee as percentage of unit cost for selected OUs and DEIs are presented in Table 7.12. Except for the University of Mumbai, where the fee charged by its DEI was 464% of its institutional expenditure per student, the two SOUs charged students more than they spent on them. These data clearly show that the level of the student fee is not as important as how much the institution is spending on each student, indicating

Table 7.10 Sources of Funds: SOUs: BRAOU and YCMOU (INRs)

Institution	Year	Plan/Non-Plan	State Government		DECa/ICARb		Fees and other internal sources		Total	
			Rs.c	%	Rs.c	%	Rs.	%	Rs.	%
BRAOU	2001–02	Plan	–	–	5.0a	100.00	–	–	5.0	100.00
		Non-Plan	40.5	18.12	–	–	183.0	81.88	223.5	100.00
		Total	40.5	17.72	5.0a	2.19	183.0	80.09	228.5	100.00
	2002–03	Plan	–	–	–	–	–	–	–	–
		Non-Plan	50.0	19.36	–	–	208.2	80.64	258.2	100.00
		Total	50.0	19.36	–	–	208.2	80.64	258.2	100.00
YCMOU	2001–02	Plan	–	–	2.6b	100.00	–	–	2.6	100.00
		Non-Plan	–	–	–	––	134.0	100.00	134.0	100.00
		Total	–	–	2.6b	1.90	134.0	98.10	136.6	100.00

Source: Naidu (2005)
[a] *Distance Education Council*
[b] *Indian Council of Agricultural Research*
[c] *Millions*

Table 7.11 Sources of Income of Selected OUs and DTIs, 2003–04 (estimates) (INRs. in million)

Institution	Government	DEC	Fees & others	Total
OUs				
IGNOU[a]	853*	0	2120	2973
	(28.69)	(0.00)	(71.31)	(100.00)
BRAOU	59	0	273	332
	(17.77)	(0.00)	(82.23)	(100.00)
YCMOU	20	7	246	273
	(7.33)	(2.56)	(90.11)	(100.00)
UPRTOU	8	2	25	35
	(22.86)	(5.71)	(71.43)	(100.00)
DTIs				
Andhra University	0	1	153	154
	(0.00)	(0.65)	(99.35)	(100.00)
University of Delhi	50	0	134	184
	(27.17)	(0.00)	(72.83)	(100.00)
University of Mumbai	0	0	132	132
	(0.00)	(0.00)	(100.00)	(100.00)
Annamali University	0	0	366	366
	(0.00)	(0.00)	(100.00)	(100.00)

Source: Datt and Gaba (2006)
Note: Figures in the brackets are percentage to total
* *Includes Rs. 813 million plan grant*
[a] *Data of IGNOU is related to year 2004–05 (budget estimates)*

thereby the level of quality of teaching at a distance. For instance, even if the University of Mumbai is charging reasonably from its distance students and saving the surplus, it spends the least on its students. On the other hand, the University of Delhi charges the lowest fees to its distance students and spends reasonably on them—this is so because, like its parent university, the DEI is also highly supported by the federal government's UGC. Similarly, even if the student unit fees for IGNOU are a little higher than others, it spends three to four times more on each student than what other institutions do. In summary, there is a need to better balance student fees, unit cost, and quality of instruction.

Funding Policy: IGNOU Case

The Indira Gandhi National Open University was established by an Act of Indian Parliament in 1985 in response to long-standing policy deliberations to have a national open university in India in the pattern of and with similar objectives to the open university in the UK. Unlike the UKOU, IGNOU was made directly responsible to the Indian Parliament and, therefore, did not come under the purview of the UGC. This was deliberately done to keep in view full institutional freedom for innovations and

Table 7.12 Student Fee as Percentage of Unit Cost for Open Universities and Dual Mode Universities (DTIs) (2003–04)

Institutions	Unit cost (in INRs)	Fee per student (in INRs)	Fee as % of unit cost(in INRs)
Open Universities			
BRAOU	1,745	1,435	82.23
IGNOU	8,118	5,790	71.32
YCMOU	2,323	2,397	103.19
UPRTOU	2,527	3,115	123.27
University DTIs			
Andhra University	2,080	2,070	99.52
Annamalai University	3,824	3,698	96.71
University of Delhi	1,641	946	57.65
University of Mumbai	512	2,376	464.06

Source: Datt & Gaba (2006)

reforms in all aspects of education and training. IGNOU was also given the unique additional responsibility of funding, maintaining quality, and accrediting the distance education programs and systems in the country through the Distance Education Council, created as a statutory body under IGNOU Act. As a special provision approved by the Indian Parliament, the national open university was allowed international jurisdiction for offering its programs and services overseas. As another unique provision, the Indian government allowed IGNOU to uplink educational television and teleconferencing programs from its own campus (since no agency other than the government is allowed to uplink from the Indian soil). Basically mandated to provide educational access to all the disadvantaged sections of Indian society, the national open university has grown in size in the last twenty years from two programs with 4,381 registered students, to the second largest university in the world (Panda, 2005; see Table 7.13).

As a national open university created by the Indian Parliament, the federal government was fully committed to fund both the capital and operating expenditure of the university. The government's concern was expressed by the university's second vice chancellor:

Table 7.13 IGNOU—Second Largest Mega University in the World (2006)

Indicators	Number
Student enrollment	1.43 million (14% of total higher education; 50% of total distance education)
Graduates	311,575
Programs	125 (certificate, diploma, degree, non-credit)
Courses	1000 (modular, credit-based)
Regional centers	58+ 6 sub-regional centres
Study centers	1409 (including 22 telelearning centres)
Counselors	48,000
Coverage	32 countries, 37 partner centres

When the University was established in 1985, one of the major considerations that the government had in view was the cost-effectiveness of the open university system without sacrificing standards. It was envisaged that although the initial cost especially on capital was likely to be substantial, the per student operating cost would be a modest fraction of the expenditure incurred by the conventional university. (Kulandai Swamy, 2002, p. 64)

As seen in Table 7.14, the federal government fully subsidized the university in the first year, and there was substantial federal government financial support till 1990–91. Subsequently, the university increased its revenue from student fees, other sources, bank deposits, sale of publications—in that

Table 7.14 TheSources of Finance for IGNOU (1985–2006) (INRs. in millions)

Year	Grants from Govt. of India	Grants from state govt.	Student fee	Receipts from publications	Interest on bank deposits	Other sources	Total
1985–86	29.29 (100.00)	0 (0.00)	0 (0.00)	0 (0.00)	0 (0.00)	0 (0.00)	29.29 (100.00)
1986–87	75.21 (97.54)	0 (0.00)	1.86 (2.41)	0.06 (0.08)	0 (0.00)	0.13 (0.17)	77.27 (100.00)
1990–91	133.71 (80.28)	0.37 (0.22)	27.50 (16.51)	1.23 (0.74)	2.83 (1.70)	0.91 (0.55)	166.55 (100.00)
1995–96[a]	178.42 (45.02)	0.67 (0.17)	174.99 (44.15)	4.10 (1.03)	17.32 (4.37)	20.84 (5.26)	396.34 (100.00)
2000–01[c]	457.50 (28.13)	0.82 (0.05)	1075.70 (66.13)	10.00 (0.61)	40.16 (2.48)	42.37 (2.60)	1626.55 (100.00)
2001–02	540.60 (27.89)	(0.00)	1317.63 (67.97)	6.3 (0.33)	59.47 (3.07)	14.43 (0.74)	1938.43 (100.00)
2002–03	100.00 (5.77)	0.20 (0.01)	1410.91 (84.91)	18.5 (1.07)	95.12 (5.49)	47.52 (2.74)	1732.25 (100.00)
2003–04	219.90 (14.36)	0.40 (0.03)	1156.25 (75.50)	15.84 (1.03)	83.76 (5.47)	55.35 (3.61)	1531.50 (100.00)
2004–05	294.75 (16.05)	0 (0.00)	1354.70 (73.76)	32.32 (1.76)	42.66 (2.32)	112.28 (6.11)	1836.71 (100.00)
2005–06 [p]	370.51 (15.52)	0 (0.00)	1775.16 (74.37)	26.77 (1.12)	36.55 (1.53)	117.93 (7.45)	2386.92 (100.00)

Source: Kulandai Swamy (2002); Data compiled from the Annual Accounts, IGNOU.
[a] *Does not include JICA Grant of Rs. 680.00 Millions for construction of building and installation of equipment in EMPC.*
[c] *Does not include Grant of Rs. 80.00 Millions for North East Project.*
[p] *provisional*
Grants from both central and state governments.
**Includes all internal resources including student fees.*
Figures in parentheses are percentages to total in the respective years.

order—and the federal grant in 2005–06 has been reduced to about 16% of its total income. It is therefore presumed that while the university shall continue to generate resources from student fees, national and international collaborative contributions, and sale of its learning materials, the grant from the federal government shall continue to decrease, and the grants from state governments in forms of rent/land cost of its regional centers will still be negligible. It is therefore not surprising that the income from student fees as percentage of its gross operating costs has gone up from 17.29% in 1986–87 to 69% in 2003–04 (Gaba & Bhusan, 2004). But, as a limitation of the economy of scale in general, the national open university will ultimately have to consider options other than student fees to break even.

Analysis of its operating costs provides further insight to the financial behavior of the national open university (Table 7.15).

The initial significant operating cost center was the institutional overheads, followed by development and production of learning material, and provision of student support services. Subsequently, until 1994–95, the university spent the greatest proportion of its budget on developing multiple-media learning materials. After this time, the institutional overhead was drastically reduced and expenses on student support services were substantially increased. It would be wrong to presume that the university is spending less on overhead, including its general administration, common services, campus maintenance, and others. As a percentage, it was 15.5. However, in real terms, the amount was a whopping INRs 129.87 million in 2000–01. While during the past decade the number of study centers has doubled, the real expenses have increased almost six times. Further, the salary and non-salary components of the operating costs have been maintained at a proportion of 23:77 over the past years.

CONCLUSION

As observed from the above analysis, funding of distance education in India is not to the same as that for conventional campus-based universities. The difference is reflective of the very distinct nature of distance teaching and learning. In India, the campus-based dual mode university distance education institutes are the most disadvantaged in this regard. The situation is similar to that of OUHK in Hong Kong and YCMOU in India where they have to generate most of their resources rather than rely on subsidies/grants from the government. It may be observed that funding policies of governments in the Asian region in general had been influenced by the stage of growth of the institution, the specialized client focus (for instance, disadvantaged sections of the society), the institution's ability to generate and mobilize resources, and the subsidy policy of the governments themselves. Even if campus-based education and distance education could be distinctly viewed as different, one may argue that unit cost of education

Table 7.15 Operating Costs of IGNOU (1985–2006) (INRs. in millions)

Year	Material development and production	Student support services	Institutional overheads	Total
1985–86	0.31	0	2.68	2.99
	(10.52)	(0.00)	(89.48)	(100.00)
1986–87	3.23	0.37	7.18	10.78
	(29.99)	(3.48)	(66.53)	(100.00)
1990–91	43.68	32.39	36.47	112.54
	(38.81)	(28.79)	(32.40)	(100.00)
1995–96	60.93	77.56	79.53	218.02
	(27.95)	(35.57)	(36.48)	(100.00)
2000–01	226.54	481.90	129.87	838.31
	(27.02)	(57.48)	(15.50)	(100.00)
2001–02	192.04	510.41	320.86	1023.31
	(18.77)	(49.89)	(31.36)	(100.03)
2002–03	165.04	500.1	469.09	1134.23
	(14.55)	(44.09)	(41.36)	(100.00)
2003–04	208.26	474.9	526.31	1209.47
	(17.22)	(39.27)	(43.52)	(100.00)
2004–05	133.89	391.2	844.35	1369.44
	(9.78)	(28.57)	(61.66)	(100.00)
2005–06 [P]	129.43	378.16	1038.35	1545.94
	(8.37)	(24.46)	(67.17)	(100.00)

Source: Kulandai Swamy (2002); Data compiled from the Annual Accounts, IGNOU.
Note: Figures in parentheses are percentages to total in the respective years.
[P] *provisional*

(both actual and optimum) may be an important guiding principle for funding. There is a misplaced perception by both governments and common citizens that distance education is economically cheaper to administer than other forms of education due to economy of scale. However, there is a limit to economy of scale. In India,

> Either at the time of establishing the IGNOU or later, the Government of India has not articulated a unique funding policy for the open university as such, distinct from the policy followed in funding conventional universities. Generally, the analysis of costs and benefits of university education has not been attempted. Education at all levels has been treated as part of social service. It is only in recent years that economics of higher education has come to be discussed and the universities are asked to generate funds. (Kulandai Swamy, 2002, p. 64)

Neither the federal government nor the Distance Education Council has a consistent and fully implemented policy for funding respectively the national open university and the SOUs and DEIs.

While considering the issue of funding the institutions themselves, care must be taken to also look into the funding of their various sub-systems and functions (Rumble & Litto, 2005). The development of distance education in the Asian region has different missions—besides continuing professional/human resources development in a variety of professions, it has a social purpose: To serve those at the margins. Therefore, the funding of distance education should be seen as a unique entity of its own.

REFERENCES

Albrecht, D. (1995). *Financing universities in developing countries.* London: Falmer.

Altbach, P.G. (1999). The logic of mass higher education. In I. Fagerlind, I. Holmesland, & G. Stromqvist (Eds.), *Higher education at the crossroads: Tradition or transformation?* Stockholm: Stockholm University Institute of International Education.

Belawati, T. (2006). Financial management system in open and distance learning: An example at Universitas Terbuka. *EduComm Asia, 12*(1), 2–6.

Chaya-Ngam, I. (1994). The funding of open universities: The case of STOU. In I. Mugridge (Ed.), *The funding of open universities* (pp. 53–66). Vancouver: The Commonwealth of Learning.

Clark, B. (1998). *Creating entrepreneurial universities: organizational pathways of transformation.* Oxford/Paris: Pergamon and IAU Press.

Daniel, J., Peters, G., & Watkinson, M. (1994). The funding of the United Kingdon Open University. In I. Mugridge (Ed.), *The funding of open universities* (pp.13–20). Vancouver: The Commonwealth of Learning.

Datt, R. (1991). *Study of cost of distance education institutes with different size classes in India* [Research report]. New Delhi: National Institute of Education Planning and Administration.

Datt, R., & Gaba, A. (2006). Cost of dual mode and single mode distance education. In S. Garg, V. Venkaiah, C. Puranik, & S. Panda (Eds.), *Four decades of distance education in India: Reflections on policy and practice* (pp. 380–391). New Delhi: Viva Books.

Dhanarajan, G., Swift, D. F., & Hope, A. (1994). Planning for self-financing at the Open Learning Institute of Hong Kong. In G. Dhanarajan, P. K. Ip, K. S. Yuen, & C. Swales (Eds.), *Economics of distance education: Recent experiences* (pp. 171–183). Hong Kong: Open Learning Institute Press.

Djalil, A., Musa, I., Kesuma, R., & Damajanti, N. S. (1994). The financing system of the Universitas Terbuka. In I. Mugridge (Ed.), *The funding of open universities* (pp. 21–38). Vancouver: The Commonwealth of Learning.

Gaba, A., & Bhusan, B. (2004, February 23–29). Funding of open and distance higher education in India: Quality and policy issues. *University News.* New Delhi: AIU.

Government of India (1997). *Analysis of budgeted expenditure on education 1993–94 to 1995–96.* New Delhi: MHRD.

Government of India (2006). *Higher education in India.* Retrieved August 31, 2006, from http://www.education.nic.in/higedu.asp.

Hope, A., & Dhanarajan, G. (1994). Adult learning and the self-financing imperative—Funding the Open Learning Institute of Hong Kong. In I. Mugridge (Ed.),

The funding of open universities (pp. 39–51). Vancouver: The Commonwealth of Learning.

Kulandai Swamy, V. C. (2002). *Education for knowledge era.* New Delhi: Kogan Page.

Naidu, C. G. (2005). Case study: Funding and financial management at the Indira Gandhi National Open University. In A. Hope & P. Guiton (Eds.*), Strategies for sustainable open and distance learning* (pp. 158–176). London: RoutledgeFalmer.

Panda, S. (2005). Higher education at a distance and national development: Reflections on the Indian experience. *Distance Education, 26*(2), 205–225.

Panda, S., Venkaiah, V., Garg, S., & Puranik, C. (2006). Tracing the historical developments in open and distance education. In S. Garg., V. Venkaiah, C. Puranik, & S. Panda (Eds.), *Four decades of distance education in India: Reflections on policy and practice* (pp. 3–23). New Delhi: Viva Books.

Perraton, H. (2004). Resources. In H. Perraton & H. Lentell (Eds.), *Policy for open and distance learning* (pp. 100–115). London/New York: RoutledgeFalmer.

Perraton, H., & Lentell, H. (Eds.) (2004). *Policy open and distance learning.* London: RoutledgeFalmer.

Peters, G., & Daniel, J. S. (1994). Comparison of public funding of distance education and other modes of higher education in England. In G. Dhanarajan, P. K. Ip, K. S. Yuen, & C. Swales (Eds.), *Economics of distance education: Recent experience* (pp. 31–41). Hong Kong: Open Learning Institute Press.

Pillai, C. R., & Naidu, C. G. (1998). *Cost analysis of distance education: IGNOU.* New Delhi: IGNOU.

Powar, K. B. (Ed.) (1998). *State funding of higher education.* New Delhi: Association of Indian Universities.

Rinne, R. (1999). The rise of the McUniversity. In I. Fagerlind, I. Holmesland, & G. Stromqvist (Eds.), *Higher education at the crossroads: Tradition or transformation?* (pp. 157–169). Stockholm: Stockholm Institute of International Education.

Rumble, G. (2003). Management of resources. In S. Panda (Ed.), *Planning and management in distance education* (pp. 109–118). London/New York: RoutledgeFalmer.

Rumble, G., & Latchem, C. (2004). Organisational models for open and distance learning. In H. Perraton & H. Lentell (Eds.), *Policy for open and distance learning* (pp. 117–140). London/New York: RoutledgeFalmer.

Rumble, G., & Litto, F. M. (2005). Approaches to funding. In C. McIntosh & Z. Varoglu (Eds.), *Lifelong learning & distance higher education* (pp. 33–49). Vancouver: Commonwealth of Learning, and Paris: UNESCO Publishing.

Tilak, J. B. G. (2004, February 14). Free and compulsory education: Legislative intervention. *Economic and Political Weekly, 39*(7), 618–620.

Tilak, J. B. G. (2006). On allocating 6% of GDP to education. *Economic and Political Weekly, 41*(7), 613–618.

Tjeldvoll, A. (1998–1999, Winter). The service university. *European Education, 30*(4), 5–19.

UNESCO (2003) *South and East Asia: Regional report.* Montreal: UNESCO Institute for Statistics.

UNESCO (2005a). *Education trends in perspective: Analysis of the world education indictors.* Paris: UNESCO-UIS/OECD.

UNESCO (2005b). *EFA global monitoring report.* Retrieved August 11, 2006 from http://portal.unesco.org.

World Bank (1995). *Profiles and strategies for education: World Bank review.* Washington DC: The World Bank.

World Bank (2002). *Higher education in developing countries: Peril and promise.* Washington DC: World Bank/IBRAD.

Wijeysekera, D. (1994). Funding of open universities: The Sri Lankan context. In I. Mugridge (Ed.), *The funding of open universities* (pp. 103–116). Vancouver: The Commonwealth of Learning.

8

COSTS AND QUALITY OF ONLINE LEARNING

Alistair Inglis

Victoria University, Australia

INTRODUCTION

The past ten years have seen a massive shift towards online learning—not just in institutions involved in distance education, but also in institutions involved in mainstream education. While the shift has been afforded by advances in information and communications technology (ICT), what seems more than anything to have been responsible for the shift has been a belief on the part of senior managers that moving to online learning offered a way of reducing costs. It is now realised that this belief was misplaced and that the relationship between costs and quality is far more complicated than was originally believed.

What led to the misconception that moving from face-to-face to online delivery would save costs was a failure to understand the economics of distance education. The economics of online learning are quite similar to the economics of distance education (Inglis, 1999). Those who already had a good grasp of the economics of distance education were well placed to understand the economics of online learning. These people realised that savings could only be achieved through economies of scale. However, economies of scale needed to be achieved under conditions that protected the quality of students' learning experience.

Institutions are still interested in the potential that online learning offers for reducing costs. However, they are much more realistic as to what can be achieved. They recognise that costs can escalate just as easily as they can be reduced and that what online learning offers, more than savings in costs, is the potential to achieve an improvement in the quality of students' learning.

For educational managers, managing costs within an institution that is delivering courses online effectively does not necessarily require a complete grasp all the subtleties of the relationships between costs and quality. What is necessary is to be able to appreciate the ways in which the key factors interact.

WHAT DO WE MEAN BY "ONLINE LEARNING"?

The term "online learning" carries different meanings for different people. The way in which the term is interpreted has an important bearing on what can be said about the relationships between costs and quality. It is therefore important to be clear on how that term is being used here.

A common sense meaning of the term is that it is learning that takes place via a computer attached to an intranet or the Internet. Leaving aside the question of whether online learning also includes learning mediated via CD-ROM or other local storage media, defining the "online learning" in these terms allows for a wide range of possibilities. The learner might be studying off-campus or on-campus, completely online, or only partly online, and if partly online, may be using the online medium as a central component of the course or simply to augment learning in a course that is otherwise being taught face-to-face.

Taking into account the various combinations of mode and relationship to face-to-face teaching six possible ways in which a student may engage in online learning can be identified (see Table 8.1). The number increases to nine if the institution offers courses on more than one campus and uses online learning to support teaching across campuses.

Each of the options shown in Table 8.1 carries different cost implications. Each also has different implications for the quality of a student's learning experience. Asking whether the drive to reduce or at least contain costs in online learning has affected the quality of the student's learning experience is not particularly meaningful unless one takes into account how online learning is being used. To provide an authoritative answer to such a question, one would need to consider all the possible ways in which online learning is used across a range of education and training providers. One would also need to take into account the variation in the capabilities of teachers and institutions in taking advantage of the potential of online learning.

Table 8.1 Incorporation of Online Learning into Courses Delivered On- and Off-Campus

	On-campus	Off-campus
Augmentation	Online course outlines and/or learning resources supporting classroom-based teaching	Print-based learning packages + online discussion
Face-to-face + online	Online resources and/or discussion + tutorials	Online learning resources + local tutors
Fully online	Computer-based learning in computer access laboratories	Online learning resources + online discussion

TWO BASIC MODELS OF ONLINE LEARNING

There is also a much more fundamental difference that can be discerned between different examples of use of online learning. If one looks across the field of online learning, it is possible to discern two quite distinct approaches to delivery (Inglis, 2003a; Inglis, Ling, & Joosten, 2002). One approach relies on the use of self-instructional materials. The other approach relies on either synchronous or asynchronous online discussion.

In the approach that is based on use of self-instructional materials, such materials may include text, interactive multimedia resources, streaming video or streaming audio, or other types of materials. Inglis et al. (2002) referred to this as the *resource-based learning* (RBL) model. Inglis et al. refer to the alternative approach as the *virtual classroom* model. (It should be pointed out that the term "virtual classroom" is sometimes used to refer specifically to interaction involving synchronous communication. However, as the term is being used here, it refers to asynchronous as well as synchronous communication.)

Most examples of use of online learning involve the use a mix of self-instructional materials, or at least learning resource materials and online discussion. However, what distinguishes the models is the relative importance given to each. In courses that conform to the resource-based learning model, such discussion as occurs serves the purpose mainly of enabling learners to clarify misunderstandings. In courses that conform to the virtual classroom model resources may be used to provide the basis of discussion.

THE INEXTRICABLE RELATIONSHIP BETWEEN COST AND QUALITY

The adage that "one gets what one pays for" is meant to convey the idea that cost and quality are inextricably related. As a general rule, increasing the quality of a product or service involves increasing its cost. This principle applies to online learning as much as it does to other areas of human activity. However, other factors also need to be taken into account.

Over time, the cost of producing a product or providing a service is likely to decrease as a result of recovery of the initial development costs, improvements in the efficiency of production, or invention of new production methods. In recent times, technology has played an important role in reducing costs by taking over functions that were previously performed by people.

The costs involved in supporting online learning ought always, therefore, to be considered in relation to quality. While costs may be reduced by performing functions more efficiently, costs may also be reduced by allowing a slippage in quality or by cutting back on richness of the learning experience.

Just as it has now been accepted that there is little point in asking whether distance education is less or more effective than face-to-face teaching, there is little point in trying to establish whether online learning is less or more effective than print-based distance education. The quality of online teaching is determined by a combination of factors that may vary more or less independently of each other. For example, quality may be thought of in terms of the authoritativeness of the subject matter that is presented, the way in which information is presented, the authenticity of the learning activities that are supported, the degree to which students engage in interaction, or the extent and nature of support that is provided to students. All of these factors contribute to the overall quality of a student's learning experience and these are not all.

THE CRITICAL ROLE OF ECONOMIES OF SCALE

Central to an understanding of the economics of online learning is having an appreciation of the part that economies of scale play in managing costs. The key factor that accounted for the success of the United Kingdom Open University was the realisation by the University's planners that the way to secure the funds needed to develop the high quality materials needed for effective resource-based learning, is by exploiting the potential that exists in this mode for obtaining economies of scale.

Economies of scale are obtained by increasing the number of students over which the fixed costs incurred in teaching at a distance are spread. The way in which economies of scale impact costs in distance education has been extensively analysed in the literature (Bates, 1995; Inglis et al., 2002; Rumble, 1997). However, Ashenden (1987) pointed out that the economies of scale are obtainable at two levels within an institution. At the course level, economies of scale may be obtained by spreading the costs of development of the course materials across larger cohorts of students. Meanwhile at the institutional level, economies of scale of a different kind can be obtained by spreading the costs of institutional infrastructure across all the students studying via this mode.

THE ECONOMICS OF ONLINE LEARNING

While the costs involved in delivering courses online are often of a different magnitude from those involved in print-based distance education, and while not all forms of online learning involve teaching at a distance, the ways in which costs vary with changes in student intakes follow the same principles (Inglis, 2003a). Print-based distance education requires a substantial infrastructure for printing, collating, binding, packaging, and despatching of learning packages. Online delivery also requires a heavy investment in infrastructure. However, the components of infrastructure are different. This includes servers, gateways, networking, and learning management systems.

The development of courseware is another major component of costs in print-based distance education. It is also a major component of costs in the case of courses offered online that conform to the resource-based learning model. The cost of design and development of similar types of courseware is much the same, irrespective of whether the courseware is developed for distribution in print or online. The reason for this is that the largest portion of the cost of development is accounted for the time taken by teachers and instructional designers to design the learning activities, write the materials, and develop the assessment.

Where substantial differences occur between the costs of print and online delivery is where a course exploits some of the more advanced capabilities of the online medium. One of the major advantages of delivering courses online is that doing so offers possibilities that are not available in print. For example, it offers a richer array of presentation options, including use of illustrations without a premium for colour, animation, audio, video, and interactive multimedia; it offers the possibility of asynchronous and synchronous student-student and tutor-student interaction; and it offers the possibility of computer-marked testing. There would be little advantage in shifting from print-based to online delivery if some of these options were not going to be used. Print-based delivery is both effective and well understood. Yet taking advantage of most of these options for enhancing the experience of the learner involves additional cost. Using any of these options generally demands a greater investment in time, greater technical know-how, greater attention to detail, and consequently greater cost. Thus to take advantage of the special attributes of the online environment, it may be necessary to make a more substantial investment in both courseware and infrastructure development than would be required to offer the same course in print. The levels of costs involved will also be much higher if high production values are adhered to. If courseware is delivered using the tools provided with a learning management system such as WebCT, Blackboard, or Angel, the costs involved in the production of courseware can be quite modest. However, if courseware includes lavish use of graphics and animation, the costs of production will be greatly increased. The way in which it is anticipated such costs can eventually be recouped will be discussed later.

Another major strength of online learning is that it permits much more frequent and extensive interaction between teacher and student, and between student and student. Indeed, the learning networks model of online learning assumes a model of delivery based on this type of interaction (Harasim, Hiltz, Teles, & Turoff, 1995). However, the more dependent that interaction is on the participation of teaching staff, the more that the balance between fixed and variable costs is tipped in the direction of an increase in variable costs, and the less scope there is to obtain economies of scale. The additional costs imposed on teaching staff by the need to participate in online discussions and respond to email are amongst the hidden costs that Bacsich and Ash (1999) have identified in online learning.

Hidden costs are coming to be considered an important issue in relation to online learning because they seem to be higher compared with known costs than for other modes of delivery. Also, they seem to fall more on staff and students as individuals than on institutions (Bascich & Ash, 1999). Hidden costs make the costs of delivery (in the case of the institution) or of completing a program (in the case of the student) appear less than, in fact, they are. Such hidden costs will not enter into cost-benefit comparisons. Yet they have the potential to drain the resources available to support a program, and may therefore jeopardise the long-term viability of a program. Another effect of the existence of substantial hidden costs is to bring about cost shifting away from the provider and onto the learner. However, probably the most important effect of hidden costs is that they prevent individuals and institutions from making expenditure decisions rationally. If a learner, teacher, or institution is not aware of all costs their decisions, then their actions, will be based on the perceived costs rather than on the actual costs. Were they not hidden, institutions, staff and students would all act in ways that took into account these costs.

The Relationship Between Costs and Quality in Online Learning

Economies are not worth chasing if they are going to affect quality to the extent of making the product unacceptable. If reducing the quality of an offering results in an increase in attrition and failure rates, the viability of an offering may be put at risk. However, the question that then arises is: In terms of which factors should quality be measured?

In trying to evaluate the quality of a course, it is necessary to consider the spectrum of factors that can impact the student's learning experience. If one is, therefore, to avoid the risk of overlooking one or more of the factors impacting the quality of a student's learning experience, what is needed is a conceptual framework that ensures that all factors relevant to a student's learning experience have been considered. The Quality Framework presented by Inglis and colleagues (2002) offers ways of ensuring that all the important aspects of course delivery are taken into account. The Framework identifies a range of factors that have the capacity to impact the quality of students' learning experience. A methodology for using the Framework for managing quality improvement is also provided. The Framework is constructed in a way that assumes that the functions of an educational provider will be distributed across different organisational units, and that the priorities of an organisational unit with respects to these functions will change with time.

Interaction has long been recognised as a factor critical to students' success in distance learning. However, it is also recognised that interaction may take different forms. Moore (1989) subdivided the different types of interaction into tutor-student, student-student, and student-materials interaction. The relative importance one places on each of these types of interaction depends on the model of online learning to which one subscribes. When it comes to considering the issue of quality, therefore, the type of judgements one is likely to make about the design of online learning will depend on the view one has on the importance of different types of interaction. The types of interaction that are supported in an online environment and the ways in which they are supported have a critical bearing on the costs of delivery because of the ways in which they impact the potential to obtain economies of scale.

One of the basic principles that most contributors to the literature of the economics of online distance learning (ODL) have recognised is that one of the most important aspects of quality is the time invested by the subject matter expert in the design of the course materials. Much of this investment is independent of the medium of delivery. It is time spent in analysing the intended learning outcomes, designing learning activities. This time can be quite substantial. Yet the benefits to learners can be quite profound.

ONLINE LEARNING IN DIFFERENT CONTEXTS

The factors that affect the relationship between cost and quality differ between different contexts. The ways in which individual providers respond to the issue of cost vary considerably. Looking at the responses can offer a better understanding of the relationship.

Single Mode Distance Education Providers

The transformation of distance education in the 1970s and 1980s was achieved largely through the establishment of the large national single mode distance education providers modelled on the UK Open University. Single mode distance education providers are very efficient. They need to be in order to obtain the economies of scale that make them economically viable. However, the efficiency of their operations confers on these institutions a degree of inertia when it comes to implementation of new technologies and new methods of delivery. Such institutions have a substantial investment in their existing systems. Retooling for new methods of delivery involves considerable investment, and the investment needs to be justified in terms of the return it is likely to generate over time. If an institution is already operating efficiently, the scope for generating a greater return may be small.

Single mode distance education providers that were originally leaders in innovation tend, paradoxically, to be somewhat slower to embrace new learning technologies than some more traditional institutions. Major distance education providers have recognised that that print still offers many advantages. The approach they have generally adopted to online learning up to now is to integrate it into their existing delivery systems.

Many single mode distance education providers are located in developing countries; for example the Indhira Ghandi Open University (IGNOU) in India. For these institutions, there is another very practical reason why print is still the preferred medium of delivery. The nations they serve do not yet have an adequate telecommunications infrastructure to support online learning into students' homes or places of work.

It is not be surprising, therefore, to find single mode institutions often lagging behind the leaders in the adoption of new learning technologies. However, one would also expect to find these institutions moving much more purposefully and decisively once the case for change has been made. The challenge for institutions of this type is to develop strategies for innovating that don't threaten the fundamental soundness of their basic delivery model. The way forward for them is likely to lie in adopting the types of strategies employed in industry for promoting research and development—developing a culture of "backroom" research and development to test out new concepts. There is some evidence that single mode institutions are already following this track. The UK Open University was one of the first institutions to make use of online learning. Its use of the conferencing system FirstClass predated the establishment of the World Wide Web by many years. Yet the University is still heavily committed to print.

Sukhothai Thammathirat Open University (STOU) in Thailand is an example of a national open university, modelled on the UK Open University, that still has not yet made a substantial investment to online delivery. STOU makes use of a variety of media, including print and broadcast television. However, it is only recently that the University has started to embrace online delivery. STOU's approach, as described in its STOU Plan 2000 (Brahmawong, nd), is to develop print and online streams in parallel—using print for the majority of its courses, and computer-based delivery for students who have access to the Internet. The University's strategy recognises the limited penetration for the Internet into Thailand's rural communities. Approximately 90% of Thailand's population live in rural areas (Brahmawong, nd).

For single mode institutions, the economies of scale that enabled them to be successful in distance education also give them a distinct advantage when it comes to delivering programs online. These institutions are in a position to obtain maximum economies of scale at both the institutional and the course level. Such institutions achieve economies of scale by adopting the RBL model. It is therefore to be expected that they will continue to use the RBL model in teaching online.

Dual Mode Institutions

Some of the most interesting developments in online learning at the present time are to be found in dual mode institutions. However, before elaborating on that point, it is necessary to consider what is signified today by a "dual mode" provider. The term "dual mode" first came into common use following the establishment of a succession of single-mode national distance education providers, to describe institutions that deliver programs in both on- and off-campus. With the advent of online learning, the boundary between on-campus and off-campus delivery started to become blurred. A growing number of institutions that had no previous history of off-campus provision were attracted into delivering courses off-campus. Today, virtually all institutions teach online to some extent, and by virtue of teaching online, allow students to study off-campus. Dual mode institutions now include amongst their number, institutions that have been major distance education providers—institutions such as Penn State University in the United States, the University of British Columbia in Canada, Deakin University and the University of South Queensland in Australia, the University of South Africa, and countless institutions for which off-campus (or fully online) delivery is, and is likely to remain, minor components of their programs.

It is for the latter institutions that the issues of balancing costs and quality are proving to be most challenging. These institutions have not developed the culture of off-campus providers; they do not possess the infrastructure for off-campus delivery; they have not established the student support services that are needed; and their delivery systems are not designed to operate at the level of efficiency required.

The ways in which dual mode institutions are approaching the task of delivering courses online appears to reflect, to some extent, their previous involvement in distance education. This is possibly most evident in Australia. Australia stands out as one of the few countries of those that have had a long record of participation in distance education that has not established a national single mode distance education provider. Australia's Open Learning Agency is a brokering organization that neither offers nor accredits its own courses, but registers students in courses offered by a range of participating universities. On the other hand, Australia has a dozen or so major distance education providers, all of which are dual mode; it also has a dozen or so universities that have had little experience at delivering at a distance. Looking across the university sector, it becomes evident that the universities with previous experience in distance education have been finding it relatively easier to migrate to delivering programs online. The University of Southern Queensland, which has won a number of awards for its approach to distance education, went on to become a pioneer in online learning (Naidu, 1997). Similarly, the University of South Australia and Charles Sturt University have gone a long way towards establishing the sort of robust infrastructure for teaching online that previously they provided for print-based distance education.

Yet the handicap under which the more traditional dual mode institutions operate can sometimes be turned to advantage, as such institutions wrestle with the exigencies of their situations that force them into trying out refreshingly new solutions to managing costs.

Collaborative Ventures

One way of achieving greater economies of scale that becomes very practicable when teaching online is to collaborate with other providers (Bates, 2001). This strategy offers the advantages of, on the one hand, increasing the sizes of student intakes, while on the other, of reducing the costs to the individual providers. Collaborative ventures may be restricted to individual programs, or they may involve whole institutions. They may even involve the establishment of new organizations.

The collaboration between the University of British Columbia (UBC) and the Monterrey Institute of Technology (ITESM) in the development of a Masters degree in Educational Technology is one example that has already been described in some detail in the literature (Bartolic-Zlomislic, & Bates, 1999a, 1999b). In this example, development of the program was undertaken by one institution (UBC), while the funds for the project were provided by the other (ITESM). The program has been made available to students of both institutions. For UBC, undertaking the project enabled the University to extend its program without incurring the full development costs. For ITESM, it enabled a program to be provided in an area where it lacked staff with the necessary expertise.

A more recent example of collaboration of institutions across national borders can be found at Victoria University in Australia. Staff who teach the Sports Administration program there have joined with faculty teaching sports administration at the Georgia Southern University in the United States, and the University of Ontario in Canada, to develop a shared course on International Issues in Sport. Each of the three partners has contributed a case study around which student activities are based. The course is offered by all three universities and staff members of all three universities take part in teaching the course. The quality of this course was enhanced by virtue of the closer engagement that could be offered to students with international issues as a result of the participation by teachers from three different countries. The sharing of responsibility for development of the resource materials reduced the cost of development to each institution, while sharing the teaching responsibilities reduced the staff cost of offering the course. It is not difficult to imagine how this model might be adapted to a range of fields of study where it is important for students to acquire an international perspective.

After the World Wide Web became established, a number of attempts were made to establish consortia of universities to offer degree courses online. Amongst the best known of these are California Virtual University and the Western Governors University (Marginson, 2004). Most of these consortia were established with very large initial capital investments, based on business plans that in many cases had not been adequately researched. Most have since failed. Cardean University, based in the U.S. state of Illinois, and established by Carnegie Mellon, Stanford, Columbia, Chicago, and the London School of Economics, was initiated with an investment of U.S.$100 million and offered its first online courses in 2000. However, by late 2001 it had laid off half of its staff and was failing (Marginson, 2004). The UK e-University, established with UK67 million pounds of public funding and involving British Universities, collapsed by April 2004 (Garrett, 2004). The magnitude of the initial capital investment necessitated the recruitment of large numbers of students for these ventures to reach the breakeven point before the initial investment ran out; but the students did not materialise, so the programs could not be maintained.

What appears to be one of the more successful consortia—although success here is relative—is the distance education arm of Universitas 21 (http://www.universitas21.com/). This is a worldwide partnership of 16 prominent universities including such respected institutions as the University of Virginia, University of British Columbia, the University of Hong Kong, the University of Edinburgh, and the University of Melbourne. The consortium has been established to support a range of collaborative activities, of which the delivery programs online is one. Universitas 21 Global, the distance education operation, is based in Singapore. It has been established in partnership with Thompson Learning. The operation has a small full-time staff and a larger number of adjunct staff from around the world. The quality of the programs being offered by Universitas21 is being monitored by a separate organization, 21pedagogica Ltd. This organization, which has also been set up by Universitas 21, is responsible for reviewing faculty appointments, subjects, and degree programs of Universitas 21 Global. Currently, Universitas 21 Global offers one program—a Masters in Business Administration—but more are planned. The way that Universitas 21 has gone about establishing Universitas 21 Global gives it prospects of greater success than some of the earlier attempts at establishing consortia. Entering the market with a high-value postgraduate award puts Universitas 21 in a comparatively strong position. Its position is further enhanced by the reputations of the universities that stand behind the award. However, the future for Universitas 21 Global is by no means assured. As Marginson (2004) points out, the numbers of students that it has been able to attract into its initial program are much less than was anticipated. Therefore, once again the question must be asked whether the sponsor institutions will have the patience to wait while the numbers build up.

Industrial Training Providers

Industrial training is provided in a variety of ways. It can be delivered in-house by the training departments of businesses and government organisations, or it can be delivered by publicly funded and private technical and vocational education training providers. The ways in which online learning is used in these different contexts varies considerably, and it is not possible to examine the variety of scenarios here. Two will have to suffice.

In Australia, the Australian National Training Authority (ANTA) was responsible for a major national initiative to build a collection of online courseware matched to the national curricula (in 2005, ANTA was absorbed by the Department of Education, Science and Technology). This project began in 1999 with funding provided by the Australian Government and is now managed as the Australian Flexible Learning Framework (http://flexiblelearning.net.au/toolbox/index.htm), a range of strategies that has been adopted to foster uptake of flexible and online learning through collaborative projects. So-called toolboxes, comprising learning activities, resources and user guides, are developed under contract following a tender process. Copyright of the completed toolboxes is retained by the Australian Government, and providers pay a modest fee (currently AU$400) for use of the toolboxes. The quality of the toolboxes is independently evaluated, and the whole project has been subject to ongoing study. In the state of Victoria, further economies of scale have been obtained in use of the toolboxes by making them available to all training providers online through the TAFE Virtual Campus—an online delivery platform using WebCT as its learning management system (LMS). The flexible learning toolboxes exemplify how economies of scale can be obtained on a national scale. However, the success of the initiative is accounted for in part by the fact that providers in the vocational education and training sector in Australia teach to national curricula.

An interesting development that is emerging in in-house training is that e-learning is beginning to converge with knowledge management (Inglis, 2003b; Lytras, Pouloudi, & Poulymenakou, 2002). The main drivers for this convergence are the savings that can be achieved from combining the two functions which in any case make use of the same technologies.

A NEW APPROACH TO INCREASING COURSEWARE REUSE

If improving the quality of online learning depends on taking advantage of the more advanced capabilities that are available when delivering courses online, then the levels of investment in courseware development and production will need to be much higher than distance education providers have been accustomed to making in the past (Dearing, 1997, Appendix 2). The way in which it is envisaged, such investments can be recouped is through achieving even greater economies of scale through even greater reuse.

Distance educators are already accustomed to the idea of reuse of courseware. It is partly by this means that economies of scale are obtained in print-based distance education. Distance education packages typically undergo major revision every five to seven years. However, reuse in distance education has been mainly practiced within institutions, and then mainly within faculties. What is now proposed is that reuse be practiced amongst providers. In order to achieve the economies of scale needed to bring the cost-per-student of interactive multimedia courseware down to the level of print-based courseware, the extent of reuse needs to be increased beyond that which can be achieved within individual institutions. It is believed that the way in which this can be achieved is by shifting the focus of development and production from the creation of whole courses to the creation of portions of courses, and by changing the orientation of course development from a design-development-production model to an assembly model.

According to this view of the future, courseware will be developed in the form of learning objects (LOs)—small self-contained components, designed in most cases to facilitate the attainment of a single learning outcome and capable of being combined in different sequences for different purposes (Wiley, 2000). However, moving to a model of courseware development based on the use of LOs will involve further cost before it yields the promised savings. Constructing courses by assembling them from LOs will require additional infrastructure (IMS, 2003). Existing LMSs are not capable of managing LOs, copyright and royalty payments. The way in which the capabilities are acquired is through the pairing of an LMS with a Learning Content Management System (LCMS) designed to interoperate with the LMS. Collections of LOs will be stored in digital repositories. LOs suitable for a particular task will be retrieved through the use of associated metadata (IEEE, 2002).

Adding metadata to a LO will involve significant additional cost. Building LOs into a particular curriculum may require their customisation. The more that a learning object is customised, the higher the fixed costs associated with its use in a particular situation. Transformation of existing courseware into LOs constitutes a different form of reuse (Doorten, Giesbers, Janssen, Daniels, & Koper, 2004). This type of reuse eliminates a major portion of the cost of development. However, if it is, the process of decomposition and of applying metadata to the resulting LOs will still incur a cost. Whether or not existing courseware is suitable for conversion into LOs will depend on whether it is capable of being decomposed into self-contained "chunks".

Adoption of this model should enable much larger investments to be made in the design and development of courseware, and this offers the prospect of an improvement in quality. However, it doesn't guarantee such an outcome. Institutions are apt to take savings when they are available, rather than reinvest them in the further improvement. Therefore, the opportunity to achieve economies through the use of LOs may result in a lowering of costs rather than an improvement in quality. The future success of the LO model, then, depends on the development of an LO economy—trade in learning objects that will stimulate the type of competition between courseware developers that will in turn drive up quality.

Anecdotal evidence suggests that there is not as yet a great deal of reuse of LOs. This may be because of the range of LOs available for use and it may be because of the difficulty of contextualisation of LOs for use in a particular situation (Robson, 2004). The reason for believing this is that we already have an analogue in the use of textbooks in academic programs. While many students may complain about the price of textbooks, the reason why textbooks cost as little as they do is that they are adopted so widely across different institutions. The ability to gain access to low-cost but high-quality courseware is what will eventually bring about the acceptance of some variant of the LO model.

CONCLUSION

The shift to online learning may not offer a guarantee of a reduction in delivery costs. However, neither need it result in an escalation in costs. Being able to deliver courses online at a level of cost that is commensurate with alternative forms of delivery depends on the attention given to the management of costs.

One of the major reasons for the unrealistic expectations displayed earlier was that the shift to online learning brought many institutions that had no prior experience in distance education into the field of online learning. Many of these institutions initially entered the field believing that online learning offered the opportunity to expand their markets without correspondingly increasing costs. It was this belief that led to a number of failed attempts to establish virtual universities. With the benefit of experience the proponents of these initiatives have learnt that achieving cost savings through moving online is not as easy as it initially seemed. Those virtual institutions that have stayed in the field have moved to more sustainable models.

However, managing costs successfully also depends on having a comprehensive understanding of the factors that contribute to the quality of a student's learning experience. Managing costs with a view only to performing functions in the most economical way possible may very well result in a return to the high attrition, high failure rate patterns that were characteristic of the early days of distance education. Sensitively tuning the delivery system so that the full range of learning needs are met will enable providers to build sustainable operations.

REFERENCES

Ashenden, D. (1987). *Costs and costs structure in external studies. Evaluations and investigations program.* Canberra, Australia: Commonwealth Tertiary Education Commission.

Bacsich, P., & Ash, C. (1999). The hidden costs of networked learning—The impact of a costing framework on educational practice. Proceedings of ASCILITE 99, Queensland University of Technology, Brisbane, Australia. Retrieved October 5, 2004, from http://www.ascilite.org.au/conferences/brisbane99/papers/papers.htm.

Bartolic-Zlomislic, S., & Bates, A.W. (1999a). Assessing the costs and benefits of telelearning: A case study from the University of British Columbia, Canada. Retrieved from http://research.cstudies.ubc.ca/.

Bartolic-Zlomislic, S., & Bates, A.W. (1999b). Investing in online learning: Potential benefits and limitations. *Canadian Journal of Communication, 24*(3), 349–366.

Bates, A. W. (1995). *Technology, open learning and distance education.* London: Routledge.

Bates, A. W. (2001). National strategies for e-learning in post-secondary education and training (Fundamentals in Education Planning No. 70) Paris: UNESCO, International Institute for Education Planning. Retrieved January 12, 2005, from http://unesdoc.unesco.org/images/0012/001262/126230e.pdf.

Brahmawong, C. (nd). STOU Plan 2000: Distance educational system of Sukkothai Thammathirat Open University. Retrieved February 27, 2005, from http://asia-pacific-odl.oum.edu.my/doc/chaiyong-STOU-DE.doc.

Dearing, R. (Ed.) (1997). *Higher education in the learning society.* Hayes, Middlesex, UK: National Committee of Inquiry into Higher Education. Retrieved from http://www.leads.ac.uk/educol/nci ncihe/docsinde.htm.

Doorten, M., Giesbers, B., Janssen, J., Daniels, J., & Koper, R. (2004). Transforming existing content into reusable learning objects. In R. McGreal (Ed.), *Online Education Using Learning Objects* (pp. 116–127). London: RoutledgeFalmer.

Garrett, R. (2004). The real story behind the failure of UK eUniversity. *Educause Quarterly, 27*(4), 4–6.

Harasim, L., Hiltz, S. R., Teles, L., & Turoff, M. (1995). *Learning networks: A field guide to teaching and learning online.* Cambridge, MA: MIT Press.

IEEE (2002). Draft standard for learning object metadata (LOM), Learning Technology Standards Committee (LTSC). Retrieved from http://ltsc.ieee.org/doc/wg12/LOM_WD6_4.pdf.

IMS (2003). IMS learning design specification. Retrieved from http://imsglobal.org/learningdesign/index.cfm.

Inglis, A. (1999). Is online delivery less costly than print and is it meaningful to ask? *Distance Education, 20*(2), 220–239.

Inglis, A. (2003a). A comparison of online delivery costs with some alternative distance education methods. In M. G. Moore & W. G. Anderson (Eds.), *Handbook of distance education* (pp. 727–740). Mahwah, NJ: Erlbaum.

Inglis, A. (2003b). Will Knowledge Management Technologies be behind the Next Generation of E-learning Systems? Proceedings of the Forum of the Open and Distance Learning Association of Australia, Canberra.

Inglis, A., Ling, P., & Joosten, V. (2002). *Delivering digitally: Managing the transition to the knowledge media* (2nd ed.). London: RoutledgeFalmer.

Lytras, M. D., Pouloudi, A., & Poulymenakou, A. (2002). A framework for technology convergence in learning and work. *Educational Technology and Society, 5*(2), 99–106.

Marginson, S. (2004). Don't leave me hanging in the Anglophone: The potential for online distance higher education in the Asia-Pacific Region. *Higher Education Quarterly, 58*(2/3), 74–113.

Moore, M. G. (1989). Three types of interaction. *The American Journal of Distance Education, 3*(2), 1–6.

Naidu, S. (1997). Collaborative reflective practice: An instructional design architecture for the Internet. *Distance Education, 18*(2), 257–283.

Robson, R. (2004). Context and the role of standards in increasing the value of learning objects. In R. McGreal (Ed.), *Online education using learning objects* (pp. 159–167). London: RoutledgeFalmer.

Rumble, G. (1997). *The costs and economics of open and distance learning*. London: RoutledgeFalmer.

Wiley, D. (2000). Learning objects and instructional design theory. Retrieved June 7, 2007, from http://wiley.ed.usu.edu/docs/astd.pdf.

9

COSTING VIRTUAL UNIVERSITY EDUCATION

Insung Jung

International Christian University, Japan

INTRODUCTION

As a result of the exponential growth in information and communication technology (ICT), many new forms of educational systems have been experimented with over the years. ICT has made education more affordable, flexible, and effective, especially for adult learners. Particularly with the Internet and the Web as technologies commonly available to education since the middle 1990s, higher education institutions have focused on how to make use of the Internet and the Web in their teaching and management. Most of those institutions have integrated the Internet and the Web into their courses and created totally online courses. Some have expanded their services to working adults through online courses or programs.

New types of higher education institutions have emerged as well. A virtual university is one of those types. The virtual university can be defined as "a metaphor for the electronic, teaching, learning, and research environment created by the convergence of several relatively new technologies including, but not restricted to, the Internet, World Wide Web, computer mediated communication..." (Van Dusen, 1997). Virtual universities have exploited the use of ICT, usually to extend their provision locally or internationally to new educational markets. For virtual universities, ICT has been seen as the way to increase access and student numbers and reduce costs. There is research evidence indicating that even though its fixed costs are higher than classroom-based programs, a virtual program can be cost-effective due to increased enrollments, increased student access to quality programs and resources, and other benefits (Jung, 2003a; Jung & Rha, 2000). And for virtual universities starting from scratch, cost savings may be much easier to make than for conventional universities adding virtual programs to existing systems (Mason, 2006). But there are also cautions, primarily due to the initial fixed costs to install the infrastructure, develop virtual courses, and purchase equipment; providing continuous student services, hiring new staff, maintaining virtual systems, and offering new training also add substantial costs to the virtual university.

This chapter will analyze major internal and external factors that explain what drives costs in a virtual university, and address issues associated with cost saving strategies. As applicable, cases will be presented as well. Finally the chapter will highlight the implications of this costing and the economics of a virtual university education for its planners and managers.

COSTS IN VIRTUAL EDUCATION

Costs in virtual university education can be analyzed in different ways. For example, the two case studies conducted by Bartolic-Zlomislic and Bates (1999), and Bartolic-Zlomislic and Brett (1999), used costing measures such as (1) capital and recurrent costs, (2) production and delivery costs, and (3) fixed and variable costs. The cost structure of each technology was analyzed and the unit cost per learner was measured in these studies. But the costs assessed in Bartolic-Zlomislic and Brett's study did not include overhead costs, as these were unknown.

A more detailed costing methodology, especially for a virtual training approach in a corporate context, was provided by the study done by Whalen and Wright (1999). Acknowledging the lack of comprehensive, tested costing methodologies, they divided the costs into fixed capital costs and variable operating costs. Capital costs represent the server platform and the cost of the content development. The costs for the content development include items such as instructional and multimedia design; production of digital materials; software development; content integration; and modification, training, and testing. Operating costs include the costs for the time that students and trainers spend using the courses.

Whalen and Wright analyzed the costs per course, the costs per phase of development, the costs per student, and the costs per mode of delivery. In general, Web-based training was more cost-effective than classroom teaching, mainly due to the reduction in course delivery time and the potential to deliver courses to a larger number of students in Web-based training. Asynchronous teaching on the Web was shown to be cost-effective compared with synchronous teaching on the Web, because of the cost of having a live instructor due to the extra time required to deliver the course. Also, the online education platform costs affected cost per course, due to the different license fees and upgrading costs across the platforms. The amount of multimedia content in the courses was another significant factor in costs.

It is also indicated that in measuring costs in virtual education, life span and duration of courses, travel expenses, and opportunity costs should be considered (Rosenberg, 2001). Similarly, Jung and Leem (2000) developed a cost structure of a virtual program, including development costs (direct and indirect), operating and delivery costs.

More comprehensive models of costing distance education are discussed by Rumble (2003). Those models suggest different methods of measuring total costs and average costs. Moreover, Rumble categorizes factors driving costs in distance education. Those factors include technology choice, course development, organizational structure, the curriculum, and the number of learners.

In general, key costs in virtual education can be divided into fixed costs, variable costs, and learner's opportunity costs (Jung, 2003b). Fixed costs, the costs that are unaffected by variations in the number of students, include costs for technologies and facilities. These fixed costs are spread out over all the students enrolled in a virtual university. Thus, the fixed cost per student drops rapidly as more students are served, because of economies of scale (Puryear, 1999). Variable costs, those that vary with the number of students, include the costs for developing and delivering courses, maintenance costs, and staff salaries in conventional universities; whereas in virtual universities, costs for developing courses become fixed costs, since those costs do not change with the increase in the number of students. Learners' opportunity costs, the notional costs of undertaking one activity rather than another, include learner salary and travel costs during the education period. To see the cost structure of a virtual university education, the composition of fixed and variable costs needs to be calculated in the total and average cost equation.

INTERNAL FACTORS DRIVING COSTS IN VIRTUAL UNIVERSITY EDUCATION

There is reasonably extensive literature concerning factors affecting the costs and benefits of virtual education. Among those factors are numbers of students and courses offered, interactive features of courses, employment scheme, technology, development approaches and types of virtual courses, student supports, and ratio between fixed and variable costs.

Number of Students and Courses

The literature has shown that distance education, in general, can be more cost-effective than conventional education, and that cost-effectiveness of distance education increases as the number of students increase and the number of courses declines (Jung, 2003a). Since the cost of developing a course is one of the major expenses in distance education, the most cost-efficient approach is to offer fewer courses for larger numbers of students. In fact, many educators and policy makers believe that the primary benefit of virtual education is that costs can be distributed over a large number of students, resulting in economies of scale for educational institutions (Kearsley, 2000; Inglis, 2003; Whalen & Wright, 1999). It is assumed that large student enrollment would increase revenue and lower the cost per student and operating expenses. The concepts of total and average costs show this point clearly.

The total costs are the sum of the fixed and variable costs, variable costs being variable cost per student multiplied by the number of students: Total Costs = Fixed Costs + Variable Costs = Fixed Costs + (Variable Cost per student x Number of students). Whereas, average costs per student are total costs divided by the number of students: Average costs per student = Total Costs / Number of students = (Fixed Costs + Variable Costs) / Number of students = Fixed Costs / Number of students + Variable Costs / Number of students. In the end, we have an equation of: Average costs per student = Fixed Costs / Number of students + Variable Cost per student. As seen in this equation, as number of students increases, average costs decrease and higher fixed costs in virtual education are spread over more students.

Interactive Features of Courses

While the possibility of reducing the costs appears to be one of the main factors that motivate decision makers to adopt virtual education, two other factors also seem to be important: Improving the quality of students' learning experience through various types of online interaction, and increasing access (Inglis, 1999). From the student's perspective, virtual education means increased opportunities for interaction with other students and instructors, and for wider access to a variety of multimedia resources and experts worldwide. These two factors, in fact, add costs to virtual education. A case study presented below illustrates this point.

Case study

A case study by Bartolic-Zlomislic and Brett (1999) analyzed costs and benefits of an entirely online graduate course in changing the software from a UNIX-based mail and conferencing software, to a Web-based software. The result of the study projected that their online program will make a small notional profit per year during five years, and 19 students will be needed to break-even. The study concluded that it was possible to develop highly cost-effective online courses within a niche market, at relatively moderate cost to learners. And the greatest cost of the online course was tutoring and marking time spent by the instructors, due to the nature of the course, which emphasized active online discussions. These costs could be lowered if the format of the course was changed to a less constructivistic environment. Other studies also confirm that interactive features, such as amount of instructor-led interaction (Inglis, 1999; Whalen & Wright, 1999), and choice of synchronous versus asynchronous online interaction (Whalen & Wright, 1999), are important cost factors in virtual education.

Employment Scheme

In conventional public and private four-year universities in the United States, the major internal factors that contribute to over 60% of total expenditures include instructional costs, student services, academic support, plant operations and facilities, and research (Brown & Gamber, 2002; Chronicle of Higher Education Almanac, 2004). Especially instructional costs that include the salaries of full-time and contractual faculty, fringe benefits, and graduate assistance funding, which represents more than 30% of total expenditures at higher education institutions. In virtual universities, a significant portion of instructional costs is shifted to costs for course development.

The case of NKI, one of the largest distance education institutions in Norway, provides an evidence of this shift (Paulsen & Rekkedal, 2001). The NKI allocated 23% of its budgets to salaries for faculty and staff, and 14% to material development (if its budgets included costs for technology purchase and management, these figures would be even smaller). The University of Phoenix Online provides another example of minimizing instructional costs by hiring part-time instructors whose responsibility is exclusively to teach and make heavy use of technologies in teaching and student support (Jackson, 2000).

It is important to note that instructional costs are recurrent operating costs, whereas costs for material development in virtual universities are non-recurrent capital costs. That is, online materials in virtual universities will have a useful lifetime that extends beyond the time of development. Salary costs for faculty and staff, on the other hand, will be incurred in each financial period.

In virtual universities, content providers, course developers, and tutors are more likely to be hired on short-term or piece-work contracts. As Rumble (2003) mentions, the employment scheme in an institution is a critical factor in determining costs. In conventional universities, one full-time or part-time faculty has played several roles of content providers, course developers, and tutors. And now in virtual universities, each of those roles has been assigned to different part-time or piece-work faculty scattered all over the world. In this case, costs for office space or facilities may be saved as well.

Technology

Costs for plant operations and facilities, which represent about 6% of conventional university total expenditures (Chronicle of Higher Education Amanac, 2004) can be saved in virtual universities. With limited numbers of physical plants and facilities, the costs for services and maintenance of grounds and facilities, utility bills, property insurance, and other items can be saved in virtual universities. However, technology costs would be higher in virtual universities compared with conventional higher education institutions, despite a continuing decrease in costs related to the technologies, particularly computer hardware.

In a study that attempted to examine the costs of shifting from a print-based course to an online course (Inglis, 1999), technology costs such as Internet service provider (ISP) charges and individual support for online courses represent a major component of overall costs. After analyzing previous studies on cost-effectiveness of ICT in higher education, Bakia (2000) concluded that "the most obvious obstacles (in implementing online education in developing countries) include prohibitive Internet connection costs and inadequate technical infrastructures. Several factors suggest that the use of ICT in education, at least in the short-term, will be relatively more costly in developing countries, even if Internet access were readily available and affordable" (p. 52).

Technologies involve both fixed costs and variable costs. Fixed costs are the up-front investments needed to put in place the necessary technical infrastructure and software for making the technology available. Variable costs are the costs of serving additional students. Regarding technologies in virtual education, variable costs include those of providing and maintaining additional computers or virtual learning platforms, training staff and students, providing electricity, and perhaps telephone service. The variable costs of advanced technologies tend to be higher than other media because of high purchase and maintenance costs. But the variable cost of conventional university education can be even higher, because you need additional faculty salaries for a certain number of students. Several studies report that virtual education has higher fixed costs than classroom-based education, but these higher costs for technology and course development can be offset by lower variable costs in course delivery (Jung, 2003a; Puryear, 1999; Whalen & Wright, 1999).

Course Development

Like technology costs, course development costs in virtual education are also fixed costs. The costs for virtual course development include costs for instructional and multimedia design, production of digital materials, software development, content integration and modification, training, and testing. These costs depend on approaches to course development and types of virtual courses. When a course team approach is adopted, and several experts in course design and development are involved, the costs will be higher compared to a situation where one faculty develops his or her own virtual course. Shifting print-based courses to online courses or using existing online materials will be cheaper, compared to new course development. As pointed out previously, a constructivistic course design and development will increase fixed costs. Moreover, learning objects databases will likely drive these fixed costs higher. The amount of multimedia in virtual courses is also another cost factor. In a case of virtual courses with high fixed costs, large numbers of students are needed to achieve economies of scale to bring average costs down to an acceptable and affordable level.

A virtual course can be developed in such a way that it has low fixed costs and high variable costs. If the course is implemented based on virtual seminars or debates, the variable costs will become higher than other types of courses. To successfully implement the virtual seminars or debates, one moderator should be assigned to a small number of students. Virtual courses that emphasize the value of interactivity over mass information distribution, demonstrate improved learner satisfaction and higher-order cognitive and collaborative development, but they require higher variable costs.

Generally, the fixed costs in a virtual university education are related to technology sophistication, such as multimedia or learning objects inclusion. Variable costs are strongly influenced by the level of interactivity in a virtual course.

Student Support

Costs for student support are important for both types of universities. In conventional universities, these costs represent 5% of their expenditures. Anderson (2004) points out that "a continuing and expensive problem in distance education is the provision of effective and cost-efficient student support services" (p. 68). The costs for student support will depend on types and degrees of services provided. Usually, if a service is more individualized and involves a human tutor or expert, it costs more. One way to reduce the costs is to automate most of the student services, including registration, payments, information search, financial aid application, access to library resources, career development, and counseling. There is a case where call centers at Athabasca University, Canada's Open University, operated on an information database, with a limited number of trained call center advisors playing the role of traditional tutors to provide student supports. The call center approach, in general, showed cost savings without decreasing student satisfaction (Anderson, 2004).

Fixed Costs versus Variable Costs

As implicated in discussions above, in general, virtual university education has high fixed costs and low variable costs, whereas conventional education has low fixed costs and high variable costs. Assuming all costs can be classified as either fixed or variable, the total costs are the sum of the fixed and variable costs: Total costs = Fixed costs + Variable costs (variable cost per student × number of students). We see here that in order to reduce costs of virtual education, it is necessary to lower variable costs.

In practice, however, there are several cases where virtual institutions operate on a similar cost structure with conventional campus-based ones. One example is shown in a cost-effectiveness study of online teacher training (Jung, 2003b). This study, entitled "ICT Integration in School Curriculum," compared the cost-effectiveness of an online teacher training method with a face-to-face training method in teaching. The results of the study showed that the online teacher training was more cost-effective than the face-to-face teacher training, mainly due to lower opportunity cost of the participants. The total costs of the online training were approximately 59% of those of the face-to-face training when learners' opportunity costs were included. The cost per enrolled student of the online training was approximately 43% of that of the face-to-face training. The average cost per completed student was calculated by dividing the total costs by the number of students who completed the training course. The cost per completed student of the online training was approximately 56% of that of the face-to-face training. However, if the learners' opportunity costs were excluded from the analysis, the face-to-face training was superior in reducing the costs than the online training, which is contradictory to the results of other cost-effectiveness studies (Inglis, 1999; Jung & Rha, 2000; Whalen & Wright, 1999). It is possible that in this study, the student population in the online training was not large enough to achieve economies of scale. The online program, with 108 enrolled students, integrated a face-to-face test session conducted in several different locations, with supplementary printed materials mailed to each student.

It should be noted that the cost structure of the two teaching training modes in this study is quite different from that found in other studies (Capper & Fletcher, 1996; Rumble, 1997, 2003). In this case, the fixed costs of the face-to-face training were higher (19.5%) than the variable costs (7.3%), whereas in the online training the fixed costs were much lower (10.8%) than the variable costs (85.3%). These figures indicate that the costs for hardware and network infrastructure were shared with the costs for non-training activities in calculating the fixed capital costs of the online training, and enough investment was not made in developing the online training course. And they also suggest that without containing or reducing costs involved in producing and delivering supplementary materials, offering face-to-face sessions, and thus hiring more staff, variable costs cannot be lowered. A long-term cost-effectiveness of virtual education is not likely to be achieved, or it takes more time to be achieved, even with a large number of students.

EXTERNAL FACTORS DRIVING COSTS IN VIRTUAL UNIVERSITY EDUCATION

External factors have also had impact on costs in virtual university education. These external factors would vary depending on the context where a virtual university is mainly operated. However, in general, three external factors have been discussed in various occasions: Public funding policy, quality assurance (QA), and culture.

Public Funding Policy

The public funding policy has a direct impact on cost containment efforts at virtual universities. One example case can be found in Korea. Since 2001, a total of 17 single-mode virtual universities providing bachelor's degree programs to adult learners have been established in Korea. Those virtual universities did not receive any initial funding from the government, and thus had to provide their own grants to establish the virtual programs (Jung, 2004b). To reduce the financial burden, these institutions formed consortia or developed partnerships with other institutions—including the private sector—to reduce investment risks by sharing resources in providing virtual programs. The government, instead of providing direct funds to those virtual universities, initiated policies that provided incentives for private participation and investment in virtual education programs. More recently, several e-learning support centers have been established by the government to provide developmental supports, including multimedia production facilities, instructional design services, and online course development to those virtual universities. Even though the government provides legal support and indirect funding to the virtual universities, those universities are operated mostly based on students' tuitions and fees. Thus they have to make every effort to contain costs. Such efforts include forming a variety of partnerships, increasing number of enrolled students, revising existing online materials instead of creating new ones, keeping the number of full-time staff minimum, utilizing high quality part-time academics, and automating all administrative processes.

Even in other countries where public funding has been provided to virtual universities, competition for public resources has been stiff over the recent years. Higher education institutions in most parts of the world have been experiencing serious budget cuts from central or local governments. Virtual universities have not been immune to this trend.

Quality

Quality Assurance (QA) is another external factor affecting costs in virtual universities. Over the past years, developing and implementing policies to assure quality has become a priority of distance education (including virtual education) and for higher education (Jung, 2004a). We have begun to observe the development and implementation of QA and accreditation policies for virtual education that are different from those for on-campus education in some countries.

High fixed costs, especially for course development, are often seen as an indicator for high quality virtual education. According to a survey on QA systems in mega-universities (a mega-university is defined as "a distance teaching institution with over 100,000 active students in degree-level courses" (Daniel, 1996, p. 29) and selected distance teaching institutions, the internal QA system during the development of courses/programs and materials is well integrated into the whole operations of most distance teaching universities surveyed (Jung, 2004c). Most of the mega-universities follow a standardized QA process to ensure quality. A separate QA system for e-learning or virtual courses has not been developed in most of the institutions investigated in this survey. Instead, in most cases, they adopted the same QA criteria as they use in QA for conventional distance education to assess and manage the quality of virtual programs or courses. The internal QA systems of most of the institutions surveyed have been linked to the national QA framework, either for distance education or for higher education in general. No national level QA system for virtual education has been reported in the survey. In the mega-universities, the higher costs involved in the QA system for course development can be spread across many learners. On the other hand, in smaller institutions, including more recent virtual universities, it will not be easy to reduce costs while at the same time assuring high quality.

Culture

Another possible external factor affecting costs of virtual university education seems to be related to culture in a society. One example can be found in virtual education in Japan. More than any other country, Japan values synchronous modes of education and face-to-face interaction over asynchronous interaction (Jung & Suzuki, 2004). The Japanese government used to allow only synchronous modes of interaction in distance education until 2001. That is, until recently, distance education institutions in Japan could not offer their courses at a distance, without adding face-to-face components or real-time interactions. Given the heavy uses of the asynchronous features of Internet technology, virtual education could not easily proliferate in Japanese culture. And in virtual courses, synchronous features such as occasional face-to-face schoolings and video conferences need to be incorporated in order to attract attention of Japanese learners. We can clearly see how learning culture is related to costs in virtual education through this case.

CONCLUSIONS AND RECOMMENDATIONS

Since the mid-1990s, many conventional distance education institutions have begun to introduce ICT mainly as supplementary modes of instruction. But some institutions have created Internet-based virtual programs. Examples include the online MBA program of the Athabasca University in Canada, and the online Lifelong Education Graduate School at the Korea National Open University. Conventional, campus-based universities have been also attracted to ICT and have begun to introduce virtual programs to expand their educational services to adult learners. In China, for example, more than 50 conventional universities have created online graduate programs with government support. In Japan, at least two conventional universities have begun to offer graduate programs via the Internet. More than 60% of the conventional universities in United States have been offering virtual courses or programs. Universities in Australia and the UK have also created e-learning programs within their conventional distance education units or as separate services (Jung, 2004a). Totally virtual institutions have appeared in the higher education market, as well, to respond to new challenges, which include the globalization of knowledge and education, the emergence of the Internet, limited government funding, the development of lifelong learning society, and the demand for flexible learning (Mason, 2006). Virtual university cases can be found in several publications and portal sites, including the UNESCO's recent online publication: *The Virtual University: Models and Messages, Lessons from Case Studies* (D'Antoni, 2006).

One strong force on the development of a virtual university was that the application of digital technologies to higher education would reduce costs and lead to the increase in student numbers (Farrell, 2001). Experience to date with virtual university education shows that cost-effectiveness of virtual education is difficult to achieve (Jung, 2003a, 2003b), and "the size and the profitability of the international market for online learning and e-education is more limited, and much more competitive, than originally perceived" (Farrell, 2001, p. 145).

This chapter has analyzed the internal and external factors driving costs in virtual university education, and highlighted the need for more attention to the costs incurred by those factors to reduce the costs and possibly increase effectiveness. It has also made it clear that more empirical research will be needed to evaluate cost-effectiveness of virtual university education and suggest any proven cost saving strategies to its planners and managers. Nonetheless, the various reports and cases introduced in this chapter have suggested cost-efficient or cost-effective strategies for virtual university education that can be tailored to specific virtual education settings.

Above all, institutional partnerships are important for virtual universities, in that they reduce the cost of introducing new technologies and perhaps improve the quality of developing programs. Partnerships with business sectors may help reduce investment costs in hardware systems (such as a computer network), recruit students, and obtain advanced technical skills. Partnerships with other conventional or virtual universities may contribute to reducing costs in course development and student supports. However, careful attention needs to be paid "to the initial construction and to the continual maintenance of relationship" (Mason, 2006, p. 12) among the institutions involved in a partnership.

Second, various models of virtual education discussed so far suggest that a high level of fixed costs for course development is needed to safeguard the quality of virtual courses, and those fixed costs should be spread over a large number of students. It is generally suggested that a virtual institution should lower variable costs and offer a minimum number of best-selling courses. However, drawing large students with fewer courses is not an easy task. The danger with this is that "an institution may fail in its social remit of expanding the world of knowledge" through virtual education and "too limited a range of courses may damage the prestige of an institution, and may prove to be counterproductive" (Hülsmann, 2004, p. 27).

Third, virtual universities need to find ways to reduce the costs for student services, even though they are the key to the survival of the virtual institutions. As indicated above, using ICT in providing student supports is one way to reduce the costs for student services personnel, such as tutors. Another way is to collaborate with conventional campus-based universities, where face-to-face supports, laboratory sessions, or skill training opportunities can be provided.

Fourth, virtual universities should pay more attention to improving reusability and reducing redundancy of course materials. Learning objects databases, even though they may require more initial investments, can be developed following an international technical standard to promote the sharing of course materials, and thus achieve long-term cost-benefits. Using open sources and open courseware is another possible way to achieve cost-efficiency of virtual education.

Finally, virtual universities also need to find ways of reducing the cost per graduate by improving the graduation/course completion rate. Several cases show that per-student costs in distance teaching institutions were lower than in campus-based institutions (Perraton, 1994). Yet, per-graduate costs were not necessarily lower because of the lower graduation rate in distance teaching institutions. More detailed discussions on this issue are presented in chapter 10 of this volume.

REFERENCES

Anderson, T. (2004). Design-based research and its application to a call center innovation in distance education. *Proceedings of the NIME International Symposium on e-Learning in Higher Education; Conditions for Success* (pp.64–73). Chiba, Japan: National Institute of Multimedia Education.

Bakia, M. (2000). Costs of ICT use in higher education: What little we know. *TechKnowLogia, 2*(1), 49–52. Retrieved February 28, 2007, from http://www.techknowlogia.org/TKL_active_pages2/CurrentArticles/main.asp?IssueNumber=3&FileType=PDF&ArticleID=71.

Bartolic-Zlomislic, S., & Bates, A.W. (1999). Assessing the costs and benefits of tele-learning: A case study from the University of British Columbia. Retrieved, October 28, 2004, from http://research.cstudies.ubc.ca/.

Bartolic-Zlomislic, S., & Brett, C. (1999). Assessing the costs and benefits of telelearning: A case study from the Ontario Institute for Studies in Education of the University of Toronto. Retrieved, October 28, 2004, from http://research.cstudies.ubc.ca/.

Brown, W. A., & Gamber, C. (2002). *Cost containment in higher education: issues and recommendations.* ASHE-ERIC higher education report, v. 28, no. 5. San Francisco, CA: Jossey-Bass, in cooperation with ERIC Clearinghouse on Higher Education, the George Washington University, Association for the Study of Higher Education, Graduate School of Education and Human Development, the George Washington University.

Capper, J., & Fletcher, D. (1996). Effectiveness and cost-effectiveness of print-based correspondence study. A paper prepared for the Institute for Defense Analyses, Alexandria, VA.

Chronicle of Higher Education Almanac (2004). Finances of colleges and universities, fiscal year 2001. Retrieved, November 15, 2004, from http://chronicle.com/prm/weekly/almanac/2004/nation/0103001.htm.

D'Antoni, S. (Ed.) (2006). *The virtual university: Models and messages, lessons from case studies.* Paris: UNESCO. Retrieved February 28, 2007, from http://www.unesco.org/iiep/virtualuniversity/home.php.

Daniel, J. (1996). *Mega universities and knowledge media: Technology strategies for higher education.* London: Kogan Page.

Farrell, G. M. (Ed.) (2001). *The changing faces of virtual education.* Vancouver, BC, Canada: The Commonwealth of Learning. Retrieved March 5, 2007, from http://www.col.org/colweb/webdav/site/myjahiasite/shared/ docs/Virtual2_complete.pdf.

Hülsmann, T. (2004). Costing open and distance learning. Retrieved November 16, 2004, from http://www.col.org/TrainingResources/CostingODL/institutionsl.htm.

Inglis, A. (1999). Is online delivery less costly than print and is it meaningful to ask? *Distance Education, 20*(2), 220–239.

Inglis, A. (2003). A comparison of online delivery costs with some alternative distance delivery methods. In M. G. Moore & W. G. Anderson (Eds.), *Handbook of distance education* (pp. 727–740). Mahwah, NJ: Erlbaum.

Jackson, G. (2000, January/February). University of Phoenix: A new model for tertiary education in developing countries? *TechKnowLogia, 2*(1), 34–37. Retrieved November 18, 2004, from http://www.techknowlogia.org/.

Jung, I. S. (2003a). Cost-effectiveness of online education. In M.G. Moore, & W. G. Anderson (Eds.), *Handbook of distance education* (pp. 717–726). Mahwah, NJ: Erlbaum.

Jung, I. S. (2003b). A comparative study on the cost-effectiveness of three approaches to ICT teacher training. *Journal of Korean Association of Educational Information and Broadcasting, 9*(2), 39–70.

Jung, I. S. (2004a, March). *Quality assurance and accreditation mechanisms of distance education for higher education in the Asia-Pacific region: Five selected cases.* Paper presented at UNESCO Workshop on Exporters and Importers of Cross-Border Higher Education. Beijing, China.

Jung, I. S. (2004b). Review of policy and practice in virtual education: in the context of higher education in S. Korea. *Educational Studies,* 48.

Jung, I. S. (2004c). Convergence and diversity of quality assurance systems in distance education. *The SNU Journal of Educational Research, 13,* 75–106.

Jung, I. S., & Leem, J. H. (2000). *Cost effectiveness analysis of web-based virtual course* [Policy paper]. Korea: Korean National Open University.

Jung, I. S., & Rha, I. (2000, July-August). Effectiveness and cost-effectiveness of online education: A review of literature. *Educational Technology, 40*(4), 57–60.

Kearsley, G. (2000). *Online education: Learning and teaching in cyberspace.* Belmont, CA: Wadsworth.

Mason, R. (2006). The university: current challenges and opportunities. In S. D'Antoni (Ed.), The virtual university: Models and messages, lessons from case studies. Retrieved March 5, 2007, from http://www.unesco.org/iiep/virtualuniversity/files/chap2.pdf.

Paulsen, M. & Rekkedal, T. (2001). The NKI Internet College: A review of 15 years delivery of 10,000 online courses. *International Review of Research in Open and Distance Learning, 1*(2). Retrieved March 1, 2007, from http://www.irrodl.org/index.php/irrodl/article/view/17/46.

Perraton, H. (1994). Comparative cost of distance teaching in higher education: scale and quality. In G. Dhanarajan, P. K. Ip, K. S. Yuen, & C. Swales (Eds.), *Economics of Distance Education: Recent Experiences.* Hong Kong: Open Learning Institute Press.

Puryear, J. (1999, September/October). The economics of educational technology. *TechKnowLogia, 1*(1). Retrieved November 18, 2004, from http://www.techknowlogia.org.

Rosenberg, M. (2001). *E-Learning: Strategies for delivering knowledge in the digital age.* New York: McGraw-Hill.

Rumble, G. (1997). *The costs and economics of open and distance learning.* London: Kogan Page.

Rumble, G. (2003). Modeling the costs and economics of distance education. In M. G. Moore & W. G. Anderson (Eds.), *Handbook of distance education* (pp. 703–716). Mahwah, NJ: Erlbaum.

Van Dusen, G. C. (1997). *The virtual campus : technology and reform in higher education.* ASHE-ERIC higher education report, v. 25, no. 5. Washington, DC: Graduate School of Education and Human Development, George Washington University.

Whalen, T., & Wright, D. (1999). Methodology for cost-benefit analysis of Web-based telelearning: Case study of the Bell Online Institute. *American Journal of Distance Education, 13*(1), 23–44.

10

COST-BENEFIT OF STUDENT RETENTION POLICIES AND PRACTICES

Ormond Simpson

Open University, UK

INTRODUCTION

It is a truism that education is a social investment for both the individual and society as a whole. But increasingly as the field of education matures, it becomes more widespread and thus more expensive. It has become increasingly important to examine its economic consequences. Gradually the investors in education (who are the consumers as well)—governments, students, employers, parents, and society—will be asking what they are getting for the investment they are making in this business.

But treated in purely economic terms, education is a strange kind of product. What manufacturer would run a production line with a consistent failure rate of 20–40% on the way to the finished article—and perversely take pride in that failure rate on the grounds that it must indicate the high quality of the final product? As the manager of a small manufacturing enterprise remarked to me, "You people in universities astonish me. You seem perfectly happy with a failure rate of up to 40%. If I manufactured a product with that kind of failure rate I'd have to change my production processes or my suppliers or I'd be out of business in weeks."

In other words, student retention in higher education is a critical concept when considering the economic impact and implications of education. At one level of analysis, student dropouts could just be seen as a form of wastage which it is necessary to live with. But taking the economic view leads to questions about that wastage: How necessary it is, what can be done about it, and what are the financial consequences of living with it?

This chapter will suggest that the economics of distance and online learning are very strongly affected by the financial aspects of student retention in distance and online education—which in turn are different from the finances of student retention in conventional education.

But taking an economic view is not a simple matter. There are a number of related economic concepts that must be taken into account when discussing student retention, including:

- Returns on investment (and profit) to students, institutions, governments, and society;
- The "resale value" of an education;
- The "willing to pay" concept ;
- And finally, and very importantly, the existence of "educational investment risk."

RETURN ON INVESTMENT (ROI)

At its simplest, a return on investment in education (ROI) can be defined as the ratio of the financial benefits of an education, to the investment in that education needed to obtain those benefits, expressed as a percentage. Thus a ROI of (say) 150% means that for every $1 invested, there will be a return of $1.50. The ROI is of course closely related to profit, which is simply the benefit less the cost—in this example 50 cents. There will be individual ROIs for every element in the education process—for students, institutions, and government.

This purely economic argument ignores the considerable evidence of the social and physical benefits of higher education—for example in terms of increased health and lifespan and higher levels of happiness (however defined). There is also evidence that graduates make fewer calls on societies' resources such as social welfare benefits and medical care, and also contribute more in the form of voluntary work (Henderson, 2004). These features will have financial implications for both graduates and governments, which will increase their returns on investment, although such returns will be very difficult to quantify.

However, this chapter is concerned only with the financial implications of higher education investments; the consequent returns on those investments for students, institutions, and governments; and how further investment in retention strategies may increase those returns. Its argument is that investment in higher education has returns of greater than 100% for all three areas and consequently for society as a whole. In other words, all areas involved in higher education make a profit on their investment. The chapter will also argue that the returns on investment for all three are actually greater—sometimes considerably greater—in distance and online learning (DOL) than for conventional education, but that those returns are reduced by the lower retention rates in DOL. There is therefore a substantial case for investment in student retention in DOL, insofar as that investment can itself be shown to increase student retention in a cost-effective way.

Making these cases, of course, is a considerable challenge since it requires forecasting the lifetime increases in income in a situation where the variables are likely to be changing very considerably. For example, in both the United States and United Kingdom, where participation rates in higher education are increasing, it is not clear how far graduates will continue to command an increase in earnings over non-graduates when they are a more substantial proportion of the workforce. (This phenomenon is known as the "graduate premium.") However, a recent Organisation for Economic Co-operation and Development (OECD) report (2004) finds that the graduate premium exists amongst most countries despite the dramatic global rise in graduate numbers over the last few years. Even with higher education participation levels of 70% or more in countries like Australia and Sweden, graduate salaries are holding steady or increasing.

Returns on Investment to Full-Time Students

There have been many attempts to quantify the financial aspects of student investment in their conventional education. For example, in the UK, researchers Walker and Zhu (2003) at the University of Warwick have suggested that graduates from conventional UK universities receive a total increased income—a premium over their working lifetimes—of an average of £200,000 ($395,000 or €268,000 at exchange rates as of 5 January 2008). Grugulis (2003) estimates a similar figure. Setting such figures against the investment they have to make to get that return—mostly tuition fees—suggests that graduates will receive a lifetime ROI of around 600%. This will change in the UK when a higher level of tuition fee is introduced in 2006 and the average ROI is likely to drop. But the average conceals a very wide range (see "Resale Value," below). The total annual graduate premium for the UK's annual 300,000 graduates will be of the order of £1.5 billion per year ($2.96 billion or €2.01 billion), assuming a working life of 40 years.

If withdrawn students do not benefit from any such graduate premium, then a 20% dropout rate amongst an annual intake of 300,000 suggests a forgone lifetime increase in income of £0.3 billion per year ($0.59 billion or €0.40 billion)—a measure of the cost of dropout from UK higher education. Countries with higher levels of dropout (the US, most of Europe and Asia except Japan) will experience higher levels of dropout cost.

Returns on Investment to Educational Institutions

Very little work has been done in full-time institutions in the UK on the returns to institutions of investing in retention activities. Whilst there have been retention projects which have had clear success—Napier University in Scotland increased its retention rates by 6% through a set of student support strategies, for example (Johnston, 2002)—there do not seem to have been any attempts to calculate returns on investment in any systematic way. More work has been done in the United States, such as that reported by the Noel-Levitz organisation (www.noellevitz.com), which supplies charts to facilitate the calculation of ROIs (i.e., the "Retention Revenue Estimator," Noel-Levitz, 2005). Mager (2003), at the Noel-Levitz sponsored U.S. National Student Retention conference, reported on a study at Ohio State University that claimed a retention increase of 5% with an investment of $345,000 in proactive retention contacts, giving an increase in tuition revenue of $2.25 million. This represents an ROI of 652%. But it is not clear how common this approach is.

Returns to Government

Finally, the returns to society as a whole are difficult to evaluate. The simplest return to calculate is the increased taxes paid by graduates. In the example quoted above, increased earnings of £200,000 ($395,000 or €268,000) would result in the UK of increased tax payments to the government of about £80,000 ($158,000 or €107,000) per graduate over a working lifetime. Assuming a total of 300,000 graduates a year in the UK with working lifetimes of 40 years, this would represent an annual tax income to the government of around £600m ($1.18b or €803,000) a year. This would need to be compared to the government's original investment in the student's education in terms of direct public subsidies to higher education, currently approximately £6b ($11.8b or €8b) a year. The shortfall may be made up by the increased gross national product due to graduates as distinct from the increased earnings of graduates. This is currently estimated at £35b ($69.1b or €46.8) per year in the UK (Universities UK, 2002) which would suggest a total return on investment to the government of around 500%. But there are far too many approximations in these estimates to make them anything other than order of magnitude figures.

"RESALE VALUE" OF QUALIFICATIONS

Another concept taken from investment economics is the resale value of an education—in other words, what an employer might be prepared to pay a person with a particular qualification or what a self-employed person with that qualification might hope to earn. Of course, what an employer is willing to pay will not depend solely on a qualification but on the personal qualities of the applicant. Nevertheless, this is a useful concept, as it can take into account the varying value of any qualification over a lifetime. For example, it seems likely that this author's own qualification—a second-class degree in theoretical physics, circa 1965—probably now has a resale value of close to zero and indeed may never have had much value in the first place, except as an initial entry to the world of higher education employment.

The resale value of an education is related to the ROI in that education which varies very greatly according to the subject of the degree. The researchers at the University of Warwick, for instance, suggest that degrees in arts subjects tend to have a lower return in increased income than degrees in numerate subjects and law. Indeed for some subjects, there are indications that returns might well be less than 100%. In other words, a graduate may never recover the full cost of their education, and their qualification will have a resale value of less than they paid for it. In addition, currently in the UK, tuition fees do not vary according to the degree subject, although the costs to universities for different subjects vary—a degree in chemistry costs considerably more for a university to present than a degree in English literature. Once tuition fees rise and start to reflect actual costs more closely, then it may well be that returns will diverge even further. If students behave like rational economic creatures, then certain high cost subjects with low returns may begin to disappear from the curriculum. Whilst society may react to labour shortages in a particular area by changing the resale value of qualifications in that area, this is not likely to be a sensitive process, and it may take a number of years for such changes to be reflected in students' subject choices.

In addition, the resale value of a qualification will depend on the awarding institution. An institution whose qualifications are thought to have low resale values for any reason is likely to have difficulties recruiting students. It is also clear that online learning presents a different problem with the recent rapid growth on the Internet of fake universities (Hansson & Johanssen, 2005). Some of these are increasingly convincing in their appearance, making it hard for employers to assess competing qualifications.

THE "WILLING TO PAY" CONCEPT

The resale value of a qualification also relates to the "Willing to Pay" (WTP) price. WTP is a relatively recent concept but is proving of interest particularly in analysing the value of things that are otherwise difficult to put a price on. For example, the value of the environment can be assessed to some extent by attempting to estimate what a person would be prepared to pay for clean air or uncontaminated water. In the case of education, the WTP price of a qualification is what a prospective student is willing to pay in financial terms for that qualification. WTP clearly depends on a number of variables, including a prospective student's current financial position. A student who does not have much capital or who is unwilling to contemplate starting a career burdened by considerable debt, will have a low WTP price and may not embark on education at all. Indeed for such a student, a more applicable concept may be "Able to Pay."

Both these concepts are important when it comes to consider education as a risk investment.

EDUCATION AS A RISK INVESTMENT—
THE RETENTION ISSUE

The discussion above assumes a clear relationship between a student's original investment and an ultimate return on that investment. But of course, investment in education is actually a high risk activity, as students can, and do, drop out and fail to attain the qualification for which they have registered. As noted earlier, dropout rates from full-time higher education in the UK average about 20% each year. Dropout rates in the United States are higher at around 30–40%, probably because of higher participation rates. Education, then, is a risky investment—the student investor has a 20–30% chance of losing their stake.

It is important to enter a caveat here. We do not know enough about what happens to student investors who drop out. Clearly, some re-invest in a different education then or later, and will go on to succeed, having only lost their opening stake. Equally clearly, some turn their energies to other investments which can pay off handsomely. It is not difficult to produce a list of failed educational investors for whom that failure has had little effect, such as Bill Gates who dropped out of college, as did Steve Jobs, the founder of Apple; Albert Einstein dropped out of high school and studied on his own; Walt Disney only received his (honorary) high school diploma at the age of 58; Mick Jagger dropped out of university to help start a band which has done moderately well; and so on (Simpson, 2003). How far educational failure translates into a subsequent loss in income to the ex-student would need long term longitudinal research, which apparently remains to be undertaken on any scale.

However, it seems likely that in the majority of cases, dropout means a financial loss to the student, the institution, and society as a whole, even if that loss is difficult to quantify. If that is so, then student retention becomes a financial as well as a social issue, and it will be important to analyze student retention activities from a financial as well as an educational background. For example, a student thinking of embarking on a course known to have high dropout rates may well have a lower willing to pay a high price, given the greater likelihood of losing his or her investment. If such a course loses recruitment as a result, then it may have too low an enrolment to be financially viable.

DISTANCE AND ONLINE LEARNING (DOL)—
ECONOMICS AND RETENTION

How then do the concepts of return on investment, resale value, willing to pay the price, and education as a risk investment apply to distance and online learning? And how do those concepts relate to retention issues in DOL? As might be expected, there is not a great deal of data as yet, but what there is suggests that DOL compares quite well with conventional education, at least on return on investment.

Return on Investment in DOL for Students

Woodley and Simpson (2001), in a survey of graduates of the United Kingdom Open University (UKOU), found that they increased their earnings from 15% above average earnings to 22% above on graduation, although this figure varied a great deal by the individual's degree topic and personal characteristics. On the face of it, this figure is a lower increase in earnings than that gained by conventional graduates, and given that many DOL students are older than their full-time equivalents, this increase is actually earned for a shorter working life.

However, a different perspective is given by an analysis of the return on investment into DOL. As the researchers from the University of Warwick point out, the biggest cost of conventional education is not tuition fees or costs of maintenance during a course, but the loss of earnings whilst studying. Since many students using DOL continue to work whilst they are studying, this cost is minimized. In addition, fees for DOL are generally lower than for conventional education—for example, the total fees for UKOU degree may amount to £2,400 ($4,738 or €3,211) against the fees for a similar full-time course of around £9,000 ($17,766 or €12,042). Thus the return on investment in DOL can compare very favourably against the returns in conventional education. Using the Woodley and Simpson figures, the returns average around 2,200%, compared with around 600% for conventional graduates.

As noted before, we do not have sufficient information on what happens to dropout students to be sure that they do not experience similar increases in earnings, but it seems reasonable to assume that such increases are unlikely.

Return on Investment for DOL Institutions

The return on investment for DOL institutions depends critically on their retention rates. For reasons outlined below, much of the work on investment in retention in DOL institutions has been concentrated on proactive support. There is quite a long history in DOL of proactive contacts being successful in promoting retention. Reports include Rekkedahl (1982), who used postcards to encourage students in Norway to complete assignments and found that submission rates rose by 46%; Visser (1998) who used a motivational messaging system in the UK and found an increase in retention from 34–61% (but in a small sample); and Chyung (2001), who used the same theory in an online learning situation in the U.S. and reported successive reductions in dropout from 44–22%, and ultimately to 15%. In the face-to-face situation Case and Elliot (1997) of the United States, reported on a number of studies of increased retention, quoting in particular a study from Rio Salado College in Arizona which used a systematic phone contact with selected students and found an increase in retention of around 15%.

Such findings encouraged Seidmann (2005) to announce a formula for retention:

(10.1) $R = EId + (E + I + C)PaC$

Where R = Retention,

E = Early,
Id = Identification of vulnerable students,
I = Intensive
C = Continuous
PaC = Proactive Contact—which had the merit of stating the case for proactive contact simply.

However, none of these studies was subject to a cost-benefit analysis. The most comprehensive cost-benefit analysis of the retention effects of proactive contact may be at the UKOU (Simpson, 2003). The UKOU is a distance education university which has the advantage of large student numbers (some 160,000 undergraduates, with 35,000 new entrants each year), so that relatively large scale research can be undertaken. New students were divided into two groups with same educational characteristics. Entrants in one group were then contacted by phone shortly before course start. The contact was simply aimed at addressing the student's motivation and trying to integrate them with the university (Tinto, 1993).

Funding for the project ran out after around 900 students had been contacted. Nevertheless, there was an increase in retention of around 4% in the contacted group over the control group. This seems rather small, but it must be remembered the UKOU is an "open entry" institution which requires no entry qualifications for its students, and that the overwhelming majority of its students are studying part-time whilst holding down full-time jobs or undertaking child care. Its students are therefore particularly vulnerable to personal domestic and professional interruptions of their studies. From personal data on its students, it was estimated that the maximum possible increase in retention that the University could achieve would be of the order of 7–10% (Simpson, 2003). Thus a 4% increase in retention was anything between one-third to one-half of that maximum, which was an impressive result for one phone call, no matter how well-timed or carefully constructed.

The key characteristic of this project is that it was costed. The length of each phone call averaged about 30 minutes, including time spent in repeating unanswered calls, recording data, and training. At staff rates of pay, this worked out at about £8 ($15.79 or €10.70) per call or student contacted.

It can be shown that if an activity costing £c per student is applied to N students then the total cost of the activity is £cN. If that activity produces an increase of n% in retention then the total number of extra students retained is nN/100. Thus the cost per extra student retained is cN/(nN/100) = 100c/n. In this case, the cost per student retained is therefore 100×12/4 = £300 ($592 or €401).

Calculating the benefits of this investment is rather more difficult and will depend on the income and expenditure system of the institution concerned.

Income

In the case of the UKOU, the income stream is from students' fees and government grants.

Student fees are probably largely neutral with respect to retention. This is because the university has a partial fee waiver system based on a student's date of withdrawal (the later the withdrawal date, the smaller the waiver). This system is based on the level of costs incurred by the university on behalf of the student at that date so the university only covers its costs and makes neither a profit nor a loss from students withdrawing.

UK government grants are related in complex ways to the university's student population at various points during the year, in particular to the number of students who sit the exam. Making very substantial simplifying assumptions, it is estimated that this figure is about £1,100 ($2,171 or €1,472) per student sitting the exam.

Expenditure

In addition to income there may be savings due to decreased expenditure, especially in recruitment, an area where costs appear to be rising for many institutions. For example, in the UKOU it is estimated that the cost of recruiting new students to course start is of the order of £500 ($987 or €669) per head. Clearly some recruitment expenditure is needed to replace students who graduate—some 12,000 a year in the UKOU. But since in the UKOU more students drop out each year than graduate—perhaps around 20,000—a substantial proportion of the recruitment budget is being used to replace dropout students, in order to keep students numbers stable overall. It is very difficult to put an accurate figure on the proportion of the marketing budget used in this way, and of course the budget has fixed overheads. However, it may not be unreasonable to assume that around one-half the budget is needed to replace dropout students. Thus the potential savings to the UKOU in recruitment could be of the order of £250 ($494 or €334) per head.

Thus the total financial benefit of increasing retention will be the sum of the income generated and the savings made. In the case of the UKOU, that total is £1,350 ($2,665 or €1,806) per student retained. Since the expenditure required to realize this benefit (the "cost per student retained," estimated previously) is £300 ($592 or €401); this represents a return on investment of 1,350/300 = 450% and a 'profit' of £(1,350-540) = £810 ($1,599 or €1,084) per student retained.

If that increase in retention could be applied to all the 35,000 new UKOU students annually, then the total increase in retention would be 4% of 35,000 = 1,400 students giving a total net profit to the institution of (£810 × 1,400) = £1.1m ($2.17m or €1.47m).

This calculation involves many assumptions and approximations and is unique to the UKOU. Nevertheless, it seems clear that, depending on their financial structures, there can be substantial benefits to institutions from investing in retention. It is interesting, in that respect, that the study already cited from Ohio State University claims figures (an ROI of 625%) that are not very different from those for the UKOU (450%). In addition, it appears likely that the U.S. government will increasingly wish to tie government aid to institutions more tightly to their graduation rates (Marcus, 2004). If that is the case, then the U.S. funding model may more closely resemble the British, and the analysis here will become more appropriate.

RESALE VALUE OF DOL QUALIFICATIONS

Again, it is difficult to estimate the resale value of DOL qualifications compared with those from conventional institutions. Clearly graduates from highly prestigious institutions (Oxford, Cambridge, Harvard, Yale, and others) are likely to be able to command a premium for their qualification in the market place. The real comparators for "pure" DOL institutions are going to be with more conventional institutions who are increasingly in competition with them. As Rumble (1992) has pointed out, it is relatively easy for conventional institutions to adapt their courses to distance and online delivery and compete with DOL institutions which seldom have the campuses with full-time student facilities to compete. If pure DOL institutions are seen to have lower retention rates than such institutions, then that may well be an additional competitive edge for those institutions.

At the same time, it is important to remember that the resale value of a qualification will depend critically on its content. As noted earlier, evidence suggests that law and numerate qualifications in the UK have a higher value to employers than, say, art history degrees. Another recent report suggested that graduates in numerical disciplines were most likely to earn the highest salaries at least directly after graduation (Thomson, 2004).

But the most substantial factor affecting a qualification's resale value may be employers' perceptions of the awarding institutions. Many institutions undertake surveys to assess these perceptions, but such surveys are often perceived as marketing tools and are kept confidential to the institutions concerned. However there is no evidence in the UK that DOL qualifications are necessarily seen as inferior to those offered by conventional institutions. On the contrary, it is often realized by employers that much determination and organisational skill is involved in studying part-time, and that such qualities will be useful in the work place. Thus it is likely that employers will treat a qualification on its institutional origin rather than its mode of study, so that it is unlikely that there will be prejudice against the DOL qualifications on those grounds alone.

WILLING TO PAY PRICE FOR DOL QUALIFICATIONS

Student fees are generally much lower in DOL institutions with students usually able to continue to earn whilst studying. Clearly, the lower initial investment figure required of students for DOL may well encourage the recruitment of students with a low WTP price. It is not yet clear how price-sensitive education really is, but with rising costs at all levels it seems likely that price will become an increasingly competitive selling point for DOL as long as retention rates are also competitive.

Investment Risk

Finally, there is the issue of investment risks in DOL. The risk of dropping out of DOL courses appears to be much higher than from conventional institutions. Figures are difficult to compare, but, for example, the UKOU has dropout rates of 40–50% compared with the 20% for conventional UK courses. In the United States, a survey has found dropout rates from e-learning courses of around 70% (http://www.corpu.com/) compared with dropout rates from U.S. conventional education of around 30–40%. Thus a student choosing to enter DOL has a higher chance of losing their investment—perhaps up to twice the probability in conventional education. How far this is offset in potential students' minds by the lower initial investment is not clear—educational investors probably behave no more rationally than small financial investors. Indeed, it is only fair to note that there is little evidence as yet that students see themselves as investors in education—a recent report found that in a UK sample only 0.7% of individuals who were saving were doing so specifically for their own education (Learning and Skills Research Centre, 2004).

Student Retention Policies and Practices

Given the arguments above it is clear that student retention policies and practices can have substantial financial implications for DOL institutions. Institutions which can increase their student retention will increase the benefits to their students and hence to government and society at large. However there are a number of caveats to enter:

- Increasing student retention will require investment in various resources. It will be important for research to show that such investment has returns of greater than 100% for the institution whatever the returns elsewhere.
- Clearly for that to be possible it is also essential that research allows retention activities to be costed and their outcomes measured.
- Increased student retention must demonstrably not be at the expense of the standards of the institution's qualifications. If a perception appears amongst consumers (students and employers) that there is a loss of qualification standards as a consequence of increased retention, then that will affect the resale value of those qualifications. That of course will have serious consequences for recruitment and the willing to pay variable.

RESEARCHING RETENTION

There are a number of difficulties surrounding retention research. Among these are funding, self-selection, and control groups.

Funding

Educational research is poorly funded in comparison with research in other areas. For example, Anderson (2004) quotes figures suggesting that educational research attracts funding at the rate of 0.01% of total expenditure, whereas medical research is of the order of 3% of total health spending.

Self-selection

Even where research is undertaken, there are problems with self-selection. Institutions can offer retention-promoting activities to students, such as learning skills workshops, and it is often not difficult to demonstrate increased retention amongst those participating as against non-participants. But those participating are a self-selected group and so may well be those who would have a higher retention rate anyway. That is not to say that such activities are not worthwhile; only that it is difficult to draw firm conclusions from the data about their cost-benefits.

Control Groups

Problems of self-selection can be overcome by using control groups who do not receive the particular retention activity under evaluation. But this introduces both ethical issues and problems of comparison. Unless groups are selected to be as close as possible in constitution, then small changes in retention may well be masked. This will apply both to groups selected from within one year's cohort or from successive years. In any case, it may be difficult to detect significant changes in retention where group sizes are small.

REACTIVE VERSUS PROACTIVE RETENTION PRACTICES

This all means that there are many retention-focused practices which will be very difficult to evaluate with any degree of certainty. In general these will be "reactive" practices which require students to recognize some need and to seek out appropriate support through such activities as working through preparatory materials, attending skills developments workshops, using online learning development materials, visiting selected websites, and so on. It is relatively easy for an DOL institution to offer such self-help materials to its students and feel that it has done its best to ensure increased retention as a result, recognising that it will never be clear whether that is really the case.

However, the situation becomes clearer when we look at proactive retention practices, where an institution takes the initiative to contact its students in some active way. Here it may be possible to intervene with some students and not others in a relatively controlled way that may establish clear retention effects that can be costed, and benefits calculated.

Retention Activity Costs

Whilst the cost-benefits of retention activities may be positive, research will also be needed to explore ways in which the costs can be driven down or the retention benefits increased to increase the returns to both the institution and the student. There are various ways in which that might be possible.

Targeting Students for Retention Activities

For most institutions it should not be difficult to predict individual new students' chances of success from their personal characteristics—such as age, gender, previous educational level, and other factors—using a logistic regression analysis of previous students' success rates, and applying that to the new students. In the particular circumstances of the UKOU, for example, such a process can attach a "predicted probability of success" (PPS) percentage to a individual new student, which ranges from 83% chance of passing to a 9% chance of passing (the majority of student are in the 40–60% PPS band), although the accuracy of prediction is only 65% overall. In theory it should then be possible to selectively target students who have a low PPS with proactive support to increase their chances of passing. This of course assumes that students with a high PPS are less likely to have their chances of passing increased by such contact. However there is some limited evidence that all students, whatever their PPS, have their chances of passing increased by contact, and by roughly the same amount (Simpson, 2004). If true, then targeting may be important for political reasons but may not be justifiable on cost-benefit grounds.

Increased Proactive Contact

Increasing the number of proactive contacts undertaken is likely to increase retention rates. Case and Elliot's (1997, op. cit.) study of retention found that the optimum number of contacts to increase retention was between two and five. However, given that increasing the number of contacts obviously increases the cost, there must come a point at which there will be diminishing returns on the investment. Unfortunately, there is not enough data in their report to estimate when that point might occur. But in any case, the point is likely to be different for different institutions.

Retrieval of Withdrawn Students

The analyses outlined above are all aimed at keeping current students in the institution. But strategies aimed at retrieving students who have just withdrawn from their course or withdrew in some previous year may be equally effective. There is limited data on the costs and effectiveness of such strategies, although one report quoted in Simpson (1982, cited in Simpson, 2003) suggested a retrieval rate of around 10% for one exercise which simply contacted all newly withdrawn students immediately after that withdrawal. No figures for the cost of contact are given in this study, but if the cost was of the same order as the proactive contact cost estimated earlier in this chapter, then it would be likely to have at least the same level of cost-benefit.

POSTSCRIPTS

Finally, three postscripts.

Online Versus Distance Education

I have not distinguished between online learning and conventional distance learning (DL) in this chapter. One important area for research will be into the comparative financial advantages of online and DL, including the issue of comparative retention rates. Many institutions have seen entering the online learning field as a way of going for growth whilst cutting delivery costs. However both Rumble (2004) and Hulsmann (2000) suggest that the costs of online learning are probably higher than conventional DL. If, as suggested earlier, the dropout rates in online learning have hitherto also been higher than in DL, then the overall ROI for students, institutions, and governments will certainly be less.

The Effects of Paying Students Fees on Retention

There has been little work on the retention effects on students whose tuition fees are paid for them. There is very clear evidence from the UKOU that students who qualify for tuition fee bursaries have markedly higher drop-out rates than other students. But such students are predominantly drawn from groups who are educationally disadvantaged and whose retention would probably be lower in any case. Zajkowski (1997) in New Zealand found a modest retention effect where students' fees were paid by employers—particularly if they were contingent on passing a course:

- Fees paid by students themselves—pass rate 40%
- Fees paid by employer—pass rate 57%
- Fees paid by employer if students passes course—pass rate 64%

But these findings have not been replicated elsewhere as yet.

Other Retention Strategies

There are a number of retention strategies which have not been mentioned as they are both difficult to cost and evaluate for retention effects. For example, effort put into getting students onto the most appropriate course for them is likely to have a retention effect (Yorke, 1999; Simpson, 2004), as will enhancing external sources of support from outside the institution, such as family and other student and employer support (Asbee & Simpson, 1998). Indeed I would suggest that the Seidman formula (op cit) could usefully be amended to

$$(10.2) \qquad R = ACC + EId + (E + I + C)PaC + ExS$$

where R = Retention,

E = Early,
Id = Identification of vulnerable students,
I = Intensive
C = Continuous
PaC = Proactive Contact
ACC = Accurate Course Choice
ExS = External support.

It will need sophisticated research to determine any cost-benefits arising from such strategies. However if such strategies are low cost (as seems likely) and result in any retention increase at all, there is an excellent chance of them having cost-benefits greater than 100%.

CONCLUSIONS

It appears, then, that distance and online learning institutions may already have advantages in their basic return on investment for both students and themselves, and probably for government. But equally, the main weakness of DOL is its low retention rates (particularly in online learning), which reduces their return on investment and means that study at such institutions involves a high level of risk and may effect students' willing-to-pay level. Thus for both reasons, it appears that investing in student retention is an excellent strategy for DOL institutions. It is likely that such investment will be more effective for open entry institutions that will be starting from a lower base of retention.

There may therefore be a competitive advantage for DOL institutions over conventional higher education, or at least for those which are prepared to invest in retention research to find the most cost-effective ways to increase retention and stay ahead of the conventional competition.

REFERENCES

Anderson, T. (2004). Keynote address at the European Distance Education Network Research Conference, Oldenburg, Germany.

Asbee, S., & Simpson, O. (1998). Partners, families and friends: Student support of the closest kind. *Open Learning, 13*(3), 56–59.

Case, P., & Elliot, B. (1997). Attrition and retention in distance learning programs: Problems strategies and solutions. *Open Praxis, 1*, 30–33.

Chyung, S. Y. (2001). Systematic and systemic approaches to reducing attrition rates in online higher education. *The American Journal of Distance Education, 15*(3), 36–49.

Grugulis, I. (2003, September). The contribution of national vocational qualifications to the growth of skills in the UK. *British Journal of Industrial Relations, 41*(3), 457–475.

Hansson, H., & Johanssen, E. (2005). Fake online universities and fake degrees—International and Swedish trends. *Proceedings of the EDEN 2005 Annual Conference: Lifelong E-Learning—Bringing e-learning close to lifelong learning and working life: a new period of uptake* (pp. 532–536). Budapest: European Distance and E-Learning Network.

Henderson, G. (2004). Opening address. *Retention Conference 2004:* Staying power: Supporting student retention and success. Middlesbrough, UK: University of Teesside.

Hulsmann, T. (2000). *Costs of open learning: A handbook.* Oldenburg, Germany: Bibliotheks und Informations system der Carl von Ossietsky Universitat.

Johnston, V. (2002). Presentation at conference. Holistic student support. Preston, UK: University of Central Lancashire.

Learning and Skills Research Centre. (2004). Saving for learning: An empirical study of household behaviour in relation to saving and investment in learning. Somerset, UK: Author. Retrieved March 20, 2007, from http://www.lsneducation. org.uk/pubs/.

Mager, J. (2003). Report at the National Student Retention Conference. San Diego, CA.

Marcus, J. (2004, July 23). Republicans want proof that universities are worth funding. *The Times Higher Education Supplement, 1650*, 12.

Noel-Levitz (2005). Retention Revenue Estimator [Calculating worksheet]. Centennial, CO: Author. Retrieved March 27, 2007, from https://www.noellevitz.com/ Papers+and+Research/ Retention+Calculator/.

Organisation for Economic Co-operation and Development, Centre for Educational Research and Innovation. (2004). *Education at a glance 2004: OECD indicators.* Paris: Author.

Rekkedahl, T. (1982). The dropout problem and what to do about it. In J. S. Daniel, M. Stroud, & J. Thompson (Eds.), *Twelfth World Conference of the International Council for Correspondence Education: Learning at a distance: A world perspective* (pp. 118–121). Edmonton, Canada: International Council for Correspondence Education.

Rumble, G. (1992). The competitive vulnerability of distance teaching universities. *Open Learning, 4*(2), 28–37.

Rumble, G. (2004). E-Education—Whose benefits, whose costs? In G. Rumble (Ed.), *Studien und Berichte der Arbeitsstelle Fernstudienforschung der Carl von Ossietsky Universitat, Oldenburg: Vol 7. Papers and debates on the economics and costs of distance and online learning.* Oldenburg, Germany: Bibliotheks- und Informationssystem der Universität Oldenburg.

Seidman, A. (2005). *College student retention: Formula for student success.* Westport, CT: Praeger Publishers.

Simpson, O. (2003). *Student retention in online, open, and distance learning.* London: RoutledgeFalmer.

Simpson, O. (2004, February). The impact on retention of interventions to support distance students. *Open Learning, 19*(1), 79–95.

Simpson, O. (2004, September). Student retention and the course choice process: The UK Open University experience. *Journal of Access Policy and Practice, 2*(1), 44–58.

Thomson, A. (2004, July 9). Graduates who can figure it out land highest-paid jobs. *Times Higher Education Supplement,* 1648, 7.

Tinto, V. (1993). *Leaving college: Rethinking the causes and cures of student attrition* (2nd ed.). Chicago: University of Chicago Press.

Universities UK. (2002, June 18). Higher education contributes £35bn to the UK economy each year, says new report [Media release]. Retrieved July 1, 2005, from http://www.universitiesuk.ac.uk/mediareleases/ Default.asp?sortByYear=2002.

Visser, L. (1998). *The development of motivational communication in distance education support.* Enschede, Netherlands: University of Twente.

Walker, I., & Zhu, Y. (2003). Education, earnings and productivity: Recent UK evidence. *Labour Market Trends, 3*(3), 145–152.

Woodley, A., & Simpson, C. (2001). Learning and earning: Measuring 'rates of return' among mature graduates from part-time distance courses. *Higher Education Quarterly, 55*(1), 28–41.

Yorke, M. (1999). *Leaving early.* London: Falmer Press.

Zajkowski, M. (1997). Price and persistence in distance education. *Open Learning, 12*(1), 12–23.

11

COST-BENEFIT OF ONLINE LEARNING

Zane L. Berge

University of Maryland, Baltimore County, USA

Charlotte Donaldson

Booz Allen Hamilton, USA

INTRODUCTION

When a quality classroom learning program is compared to a quality online learning program, most of the literature and the experience of many instructors has demonstrated that people learn equally well regardless of the delivery systems used. Therefore, the goal in many organizations becomes learning effectiveness at less cost (Rosenberg, 2001). It is important in any cost-related analysis of online learning that the practitioner is confident of the viability of online learning, with a firm realization that it is not a bargain basement or second-class alternative. Fully understanding how to evaluate and communicate not only the cost-savings, but also the cost-benefits and cost-efficiencies of online learning, is a powerful tool the learning practitioner can use to garner support from his or her organization's decision makers, including those whose leadership specialty is finance.

Otto Peters (2000) affirms that online learning points towards the future of an information and learning society, and that distance education "has the power to alter traditional teaching and learning systems structurally, and to accelerate the change" (p. 246). In other words, those involved in training and education will help themselves and their respective learners experience new opportunities and benefits found only in learning at a distance—profound opportunities and benefits not present in the traditional classroom.

This chapter introduces a framework to position online learning as a cost-efficient, sound alternative and complement to traditional classroom learning. For purposes of this chapter, e-learning, online learning, distance learning, and distance education will be treated as essentially the same concept, with the exception that the term "training" is typically used in the workplace, and the term "education" is typically used in academia. Workplace training is typically narrower and less lengthy, and it usually does not provide academic credentials. Additionally, there will be some discussions that are clearly related to workplace training, and others specific to academic education.

COST EFFICIENCY OF ONLINE LEARNING

The goal to reduce learning costs and make learning ever more cost-efficient is nothing new, and in fact was in full execution prior to online learning becoming a major player in the field of education and training. The period of the 1960s and 1970s was particularly active in economic and practical evaluation of new and different educational technologies (Rumble, 1997). Cost-efficiency in online learning programs is difficult to speak of holistically, since there are so many variables (e.g., technology investments, media mix, practices, numbers of students, curriculum, course design efforts, etc.), making virtually every learning system and its measurement unique to some degree. A learning system is then cost-efficient if output per unit is greater than input per-unit costs, relative to other systems. A learning system increases its cost-efficiency over time when the output is sustained and the input does not increase.

In any analysis of costs and benefits of traditional face-to-face learning in business and in academe, it quickly becomes obvious that business organizations expect a return on investment (ROI) beyond the cost savings of the learning program (or event) itself. A key difference in measuring cost-benefit analysis is that businesses (including government, military, corporations, and non-profits) expect measurable performance improvement in the workplace after the learning has occurred. Academic education is more broad and theoretically-based. It is often perceived as learning for learning's sake, and therefore may demonstrate less focus on shorter-term expectations of changed behavior resulting from learning. To some degree, both academe and business must remain focused on cost savings of any learning program, ostensibly to remain in business.

In general, there are two separate approaches to this subject, each with its own literature, analytical tools, and standards for judging quality of results: The business practitioner [sic] approach, and an academic approach, which stems from human capital theory in economics. The business practitioner [sic] approach to this subject emphasizes logic, simplicity, transparency, and practicality. By contrast, academics emphasize scientific rigor and replicatability [sic] (Glover, Long, Hass, & Alemany, 1999).

Perhaps there is a recurring theme in all online learning: While the bottom line is always critical in program sustainment, it is important to look beyond the dollars and cents cost savings to what benefits are to be derived by all involved, immediately and in future. Traditional financial metrics to evaluate online learning are old news, and many organizations have started non-traditional measurement programs to show e-learning's positive impact on customer service, productivity, and sales (Berry, 2000). E-learning will continue its growth because it is an important driver in transforming the business enterprise into an e-business. Therefore, it seems only prudent and future-focused to track revenues and market share generated because of new job competencies, which were acquired via online learning.

TRAINING EMPLOYEES IN THE WORKPLACE

Workers both deserve and seek training in a rapidly changing and highly technical workplace environment. This current digital age is a time of online infrastructure in the workplace—where employees communicate through email, access knowledge management systems online, and file expense reports via a corporate intranet. E-learning uses specific technology in many cases that is not new, does not have to be taught, and is already a part of the workers' toolkit.

Not only has research indicated that workplace learning is important in determining the future earnings capacity of workers, but also, it is generally believed to impact the business bottom line positively. Bassi and McMurrer (2001) contend that a variety of organizations across industries, selected because they invest an above-average amount on training, would have returned an average of 45% more than the S&P 500 index annually in recent years. In fact, these authors implore the United States Securities and Exchange Commission (SEC) to require publicly held companies to report training investments as an indicator of financial performance, as the SEC does currently with other key indicators, such as purchase of capital and research and development investments.

HISTORY OF ROI

Developed by DuPont in Wilmington, Delaware, to help make business more manageable, ROI may be a poor fit for the digital age in many areas—in particular in the area of learning measurement. ROI is a measure of benefit versus cost, and "while a long-established business practice, ROI analysis remains on the frontier in measuring the impact of training"

(Glover, Long, Haas, & Alemany, 1999, p. 1). While ROI is a familiar term (i.e., some consider it to be the financial holy grail), a more thorough consideration of ROI may yield some doubts as to its complete applicability in the modern age.

Originally developed over a century ago, there are many different formulas for calculating ROI. A basic formula that is conceptually easy to understand is:

(11.1) % ROI = (benefits / costs) × 100

While it may take an accountant to help calculate traditional ROI with any precision, the reader can review several worksheets and descriptions that have been published (e.g., Shepherd, 1999). "It's a fast, convenient financial measure that helps executives understand the relationships among profit, sales, and total assets. In particular, the model shows how businesses generate profit and how well a company uses assets to generate sales" (Sommer, 2002). While determining ROI on learning programs can be a difficult process, it is generally accepted that senior management wants to realize business value on its investments and expects to reach this value conclusion, at least in part through an expression of ROI.

It is obvious that the model in Figure 11.1 is more complex than is generally contemplated when references are made to ROI. An important point is that ROI was a measure of return on the total investment in the entire business originally, not for any isolated aspect of a business, such as a project, a product, or a training course (Nickols, 2000). The formula was: Net Income / Book Value of Assets = ROI. ROI as an analysis tool works best for cost-benefit analysis of physical capital and equipment, but falls short in analyzing human capital. According to Glover et al. (1999), "Three central problems are [1] obtaining accurate measures of the full costs, [2] measuring benefits without relying on subjective estimates, and perhaps most difficult, [3] isolating the impact of the training on changes in performance" (p. i). It can be argued this human capital investment approach is a more comprehensive assessment and predictor of the business value.

Guesses are commonly a part of all financial decision making. For example, how many years will a personal computer (PC) be operable and current, so that an accurate rate of amortization may be applied? Or, how much good will does hiring a former football star add to the balance sheet? One could argue that an educated best guess from the learning professionals, in conjunction with the financial professionals, is standard operational procedure throughout business and academe. Cross (2001) contends that since e-learning is a continuous process across the enterprise, it changes all the rules, where training in the past tended to be a one-shot deal for an individual business unit. E-learning generally requires a more strategic initiative and investment, as it parallels e-business initiatives.

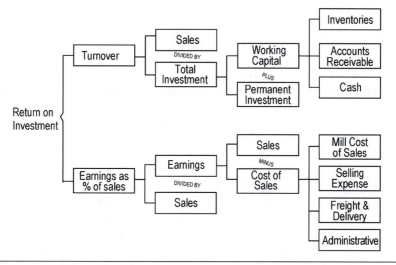

Figure 11.1 DuPont Return on Investment Model
Source: Financial Management Series by Davis, T. C. Copyright 1950 by AMACOM Books. Reproduced with permission of AMACOM Books via Copyright Clearance Center.

CRITICISMS OF ROI FOR MEASURING TRAINING IMPACT

Throughout the literature, a recurring theme in references to ROI is that it is a measure of the past instead of an indicator of the future.

> Today's accounting systems and reporting requirements are still firmly rooted in the industrial era, even though we are now squarely in the midst of the knowledge age. This results in the investor equivalent of "driving your car by looking in the rear view mirror." (Bassi & McMurrer, 2001, para. 2)

Conner (n.d., para. 3) provided the following answer to the question of "What is ROI?":

- Return on Investment (ROI) is a traditional financial measure based on historic data.
- ROI is a backward-looking metric that yields no insights into how to improve business results in the future.
- In education organizations, ROI has been used primarily for self-justification rather than continuous improvement.

It is obvious that measuring training impact, whether online or traditional, is puzzling and daunting at best. One reason human capital development is so difficult to measure is that fully trained and competent employees can be a fleeting asset, one which can leave the organization at any moment, unlike an investment in inventory or buildings. This challenge of volatility is perhaps a reason that senior management relentlessly seeks a comfort level of training ROI feedback, although they are certainly aware that terminations and resignations change the entire picture of the perceived investment, benefit, and value proposition of delivered training. In fact, there are no accounting standards related to training and education investment or reporting. Those organizations bold enough to report training statistics risk speaking in an unknown language to investors.

TRAINING IS TRADITIONALLY A GOOD INVESTMENT

Bassi and McMurrer (2001) conducted a study of organizations that spend an above average amount on training and development, and found remarkable evidence that showed improved business performance and shareholder return the following year. In other words, investments in training are reliable predictors of improved financial performance. Although admittedly an imperfect measure, it can be argued this observation is worthy of consideration. Bassi and McMurrer (2001) state that

> After controlling for all available information on the firm, this variable [employee training expenditures] is far more important in determining return than capital investments or research and development expenditures, for example. (para. 7)

The truly difficult part of calculating ROI is to identify the total financial benefit the entire organization realizes, before the total financial cost of designing, developing, producing, delivering, and maintaining that program is deducted. Looking beyond a total financial benefit is important, too (Conner, n.d.). For example, a reputation of a better-trained workforce could be viewed as a draw in recruiting top talent—how can that benefit be properly expressed on the balance sheet or income statement? It has been said that good training and failed training are booked the same way in the accounting department.

Still, it can be vigorously argued that it would be a mistake to attempt to sell a large online learning project to senior management without speaking of ROI, and without comparing online to traditional. To convince someone of a project or idea, the speaker must speak in the listener's language. The key is to speak enough ROI to convince decision makers that the online learning project is a healthy investment, instead of a detrimental cost. It is therefore critical to expand and connect the long-term benefits of the investment to those important intangibles of satisfied customers, increased revenue, lowered expenses, reduced turnover, improved employee morale, and other valuable benefits.

ALIGNING TRAINING WITH BUSINESS OBJECTIVES

As one might expect, aligning training initiatives with strategic business initiatives is imperative. This alignment ostensibly implies an understanding of what senior management is thinking and what they are seeking for the organization, as they attempt to manage a balancing act and choose between many attractive and potentially important and profitable projects and investments.

My experience has shown that most senior executives have more faith in "gut feeling" than in numbers. The numbers are input, but the decision is broader than that. Results from an *Information Week* survey reveal that "More companies are justifying their e-business ventures not in terms of ROI but in terms of strategic goals. Creating or maintaining a competitive edge was cited most often as the reason for deploying an application" (Cross, 2001, para. 49).

Aurum Technology Inc., for example, was a financial services vendor for banks and credit unions. Before merging with Fidelity Information Services in 2003, Aurum received a 2001 United States Distance Learning Association Award (USDLA) for its online learning initiative. Aurum's product was a full-functioned and competitive banking software system, marketed to banks and credit unions in the United States. However, many of Aurum's customers had discontinued attending traditional classroom software release training, because it required a group of their managers and subject matter experts to journey to Aurum's office at least twice yearly to learn of new enhancements. While these new enhancements would, without question, help them differentiate themselves in their local markets, hearing complaints about the product's perceived narrowness was something senior management battled more often than they would have liked. When the customer training department wanted to add an e-learning program (e.g., live, synchronous video-conferencing via FedEx Kinko's video-conference centers), the learning group approached senior management with a business plan that would increase customer attendance at release training, and therefore make the customers more aware of the product's robustness. In other words, the learning group aligned a training goal with a business need. In a very short time, customer attendance at training increased 900%, providing customers with extensive product knowledge they needed to differentiate their financial offerings in their markets. This online learning program became a source of income that (1) allowed the training department to fund a full-blown e-learning program, and (2) provided additional funds available for other training department expenditures.

While the focus of this chapter is cost-efficiency for online learning, one could easily conclude that measuring the benefit of training is similar, whether the learning program is traditional, online, or some combination (blended). What may be different is more leadership and financial focus on online learning investments, which is not as familiar in a more competitive economy and marketplace.

Measuring the benefit of online learning so that it can be cost-justified can be approached from many legitimate perspectives. For example, the Chief Learning Officer (CLO) will likely consider e-learning costs (i.e., design, development, delivery, administration, and sustainment) to be justified if, over time, more learners can successfully complete training courses for improved performance in the workplace, at a cost less than to travel to and from a face-to-face session. This type of cost-justification is most often referred to as cost savings. However, the business manager evaluates business metrics and expects to see a discernible difference of improved performance in the workplace by those who have completed training programs. The business manager most likely can feel justified in approving training expenditures when individual performance in the workplace can be measured as a gain. The corporation, moreover, expects to see improvements in business—increased sales, reduced costs, higher levels of customer satisfaction, etc.—which can be directly related to shareholder value.

To Cross (2001), all these measures are complementary and are valid. Hopefully, each group understands each other's goals well enough that the entire organization benefits from a well-thought-out mutually derived and mutually beneficial decision.

HOW TO TRACK BUSINESS RESULTS

Training for training's sake is not part of the current business environment, where downsizing, competition, and global impact require financial agility and precision, along with optimum worker productivity. Therefore, it is important that there is consensus among learning professionals and the line of business on the value proposition related to solving the business problem—with training, or with other performance improvement interventions (e.g., incentives, leadership, motivation, tools, and systems). The tried and true gap analysis—what is the current situation, what does the situation need to be, and what would happen if we did nothing—can be valuable in establishing current and desired performance metrics, so that the organizations know when they have succeeded, and exactly how well, in solving the business problem. Obviously, the next step after gap analysis is to identify the content and learning objectives to eliminate identified gaps. Attaching an expected dollar value to the elimination of the deficiencies is one method to establish agreed upon tangible projections and outcomes (Cross, 2001).

In the current business climate, senior management is demanding cost justification more than ever. Human resource directors want to comply, but they are faced with two unpopular choices: Invest time and energy into learning how to scientifically analyze training return on investment (a daunting task involving mathematical calculations, gathering significant amounts of data and statistical analysis), or hiring an outside firm to generate ROI reports (Taylor, n.d.).

Taylor further advocates a process undertaken with students, themselves, to set after-training goals and quantify benefits and impact of training. First, he asks his students to set their goals, and then enumerate the personal benefits they expect to receive from the training once their goals are achieved. He contends that this sets the motivation to achieve benefit goals. Next, he boldly immerses the students into ROI, by asking students to calculate the financial impact that reaching their goal will have on their organizations, since he believes goals can absolutely be translated to hard numbers. Here is a list of the type of questions Taylor poses:

- How much time will this save?
- How much inventory will be reduced?
- By streamlining this area, what additional projects will there be time to accomplish?
- How much more efficient will I be? (n.d., para. 5)

There are many ways to turn these questions into hard line numbers, but it can be argued the easiest and most familiar is employee compensation. Next, the projected savings are extrapolated over a year to predict costs savings per annum. Taylor wisely adds two more steps, which hopefully lead to action: (1) list the daily tasks required to achieve the goals, and (2) share results with managers, for validation and support.

WHY THE FOCUS ON ONLINE LEARNING ROI?

Conner (n.d.) states that any effective learning programs that could be done for a cost savings and with less travel would have a propensity to increase over time, all other things being equal.

For the past 20 years, there has been a kind of "hope and a prayer" attitude about learning. Companies would look at a program, see the possible value, and try it. They were willing to take chances. That trial and error era is over. Now, companies want to see results. Measuring value and return on investment for training and e-learning dollars has always been important, but now organizations want to be assured that the training they're spending money on actually works (Conner, n.d.).

Perhaps the most obvious argument for the cost benefit of online learning, over traditional learning, is that the organization can add value via online learning in fresh, new, and innovative ways—where opportunity and benefit were previously unavailable in traditional learning. For example, how does one place a predictable dollar value on an online learning module, which the employee can take just-in-time—as driven by need—

and learn "just enough," with a just-for-me approach? This benefit becomes particularly valuable when the learning place is flexible, the learning time is decreased, and significant absences from the workplace are minimized by avoiding attendance at multiple-day courses. How does one evaluate the opportunity and usefulness of a learner re-taking the training if certain elements are yet to be mastered, or skipping what is known; and all this learning is accomplished without abandoning productivity in the workplace or adding additional training costs? Further, from a learning development perspective, how can one precisely and financially measure the benefit of a reusable learning object (RLO) that saves development time and time-to-market for other training modules and other learners? Of course, online learning is not a panacea or a type of silver bullet, although many mistakenly think of it that way. Bad or unnecessary training of any type, given to those who are not ready to learn for whatever reason, can occur whether in a classroom or online.

TRADITIONAL AND ONLINE LEARNING BENEFITS AND COSTS

While cost justification and cost benefit arguments are made for both traditional and online learning, time-to-market is often an advantage of online learning that cannot be overlooked for its economic and customer value. Children's Healthcare of Atlanta reports an interesting case example. An expensive and patient-inconvenient problem was identified with the completion of a routine lab test, which was being done incorrectly, resulting in lab tests having to be redone—a duplication of costs to the hospital, an inconvenience to the patients, and a source of delay in physicians' diagnostics. Within one month after a brief and inexpensive asynchronous online course was created, all the required staff had completed the training. The procedural error rate for the test dropped to zero, resulting in cost savings in term of the supplies, equipment, and manpower no longer needed to repeat the lab test (Raths, n.d., as cited in Latshaw, 2001).

Additionally, a fundamental truth of online learning is that there is no evidence that traditional learning is superior (Moore & Kearsley, 1996). In many cases, all other things being equal, sustainable, repeatable, and consistent online learning simply makes sense, both financially and from a performance perspective.

A complete list of every financial aspect to consider is very difficult to create, because of the uniqueness of training requirements and the huge range of online solutions. Of course, such a list would quickly be out of date. Table 11.1 identifies some elements of which to be aware as learning professionals focus on their respective environments.

To determine effectiveness of online learning program, Conner (n.d.) recommends measuring the following, at minimum:

Table 11.1 Elements of Cost to be Considered

Classroom elements	Online learning elements
Facilities (building, amortization, rental/lease, utilities, insurance, cleaning, etc.)	Training platform (servers, intranet, software licenses, maintenance, infrastructure, support staff)
Equipment (furniture, PCs, flip charts, boards, overheads displays, training systems/servers, etc.)	PCs, networks, intranets
Supplies (printing, workbooks, refreshments, meals, pens, markers, etc.)	Supplies (CDs, supplemental workbooks)
Administration (registration and tracking systems, invitations, reminders, etc.)	Administration (registration and tracking systems, invitations, reminders, etc.)
Course development (designers, subject matter experts, editors, etc.)	Course development (web development, designers, subject matter experts, editors, etc.)
Course delivery (instructors, facilitators, support staff overhead)	Support (Facilitators or coaches, help desk, customer service)
Learner time away from work (overtime for coverage)	Learner readiness for online learning

- Enrollment—are learners beginning the courses?
- Activity—are learners moving through the courses?
- Completion—what is the rate of completion?
- Scores—how well did learners do on testing?
- Feedback and Surveys—what is the perception of success?

IMPORTANCE OF EVALUATING TRAINING

Table 11.2 lists some important reasons to evaluate training in the workplace. When comparing traditional learning with online learning, Rumble (1997) states that evidence supports that online learning can be more cost efficient, but it is not necessarily the case. For example, if the audience for elaborately designed and developed asynchronous courseware is small, no economies of scale can occur, as when audiences are larger, and the course can last for long periods of time without adjustment or revision. In other words, fixed costs are too large to justify.

One benefit that is generally associated with online learning is that it is time compressed. When looking at the cost of time away from the job and job coverage issues, this time compression is attractive and worthy of factoring into the financial analysis.

ACADEMIC DISTANCE EDUCATION

It has long been thought that distance education can likely be the most cost-efficient means of expanding higher education. Costs of traditional educa-

Table 11.2 Why Evaluate Training?

To validate training as a business tool	Training – one of many actions taken to improve performance and profitability. Proper evaluation is important, in order to compare it against other methods of performance improvement.
To justify the costs incurred in training	Training budgets are cut when money is tight. Only by thorough, quantitative analysis can training departments make the case necessary to resist these cuts.
To help improve the design of training	Continuous improvement provides a better value proposition for the organization. Without formal evaluation, the basis for changes can only be subjective.
To help in selecting training methods	Fortunately, a variety of delivery methods exist: classroom, blended, on the job, self-study, etc. Using comparative evaluation techniques, organizations can make rational.decisions about the methods to employ.

Source: Shepherd (1999). Reprinted with permission of author.

tion are driven by labor costs of instructors. Since labor costs are directly related to the number of students to be educated, the costs increases as the number of students increases. Distance education changes the production function of education by substituting media for instructors, so there are mass production opportunities in many cases (Rumble, 1997). Still, it can be difficult to compare cost efficiency of distance education with that of traditional education. For example, care must be taken that fair comparisons are made in the type of student (full-time vs. part-time), drop out levels, capital costs, fixed costs, recurrent costs, division of labor for course development, accurate student learning hours, etc.

Rumble (n.d.) has developed a tool for the quick analysis of comparing costs between elearning and traditional learning. The tool allows for input of such factors as development time, number of students, teaching resources, course days, administrative costs, and student and teacher daily costs for both e-learning and traditional instruction. Other costs specific to each approach may be entered, such as daily classroom, travel, accommodation costs, and per-course or per-student printed materials for traditional instruction; and network, coaching, and computer equipment costs for e-learning. The major conclusions one reaches by using such a tool are that (1) the high cost of travel and non-productive times can be overcome through online learning, and (2) expensive e-learning development for small groups is not generally cost-efficient.

WILL THE DOGS EAT THE DOG FOOD?

Aside from financial and pedagogical aspects of the traditional versus online learning question, it is important to note that online learning does meet resistance in some cases from the learners themselves; although as time progresses in the digital age, this aversion appears to lessen. Perhaps this resistance can be related to fear of change, to apprehension of the new or unknown, or to self-selection. In speaking of an online degree pursuit, Eugene Rubin has stated there are those that simply have distaste for learning online and simply would not try it (Ramirez, 2003). In business, there has been some success in teaching people how to learn online by offering brief, non-threatening, and yes, even fun, live online learning or blended events to familiarize employees with what it is "all about." Once the time and place benefits are seen by the participant, some employees begin to prefer online learning and become somewhat impatient in a traditional class. Even very sociable learners can make this transition and become evangelists for the convenience benefits of blended and online learning.

VALUE-ON-INVESTMENT IN LEARNING

Organizations will receive the value of online learning because of the aggregated ability 1) to save money (costs savings), 2) to generate enhanced skill and knowledge (which leads to improved job performance and business results), and 3) to provide essential anytime-anywhere access to anyone, all at the speed at which global business now operates and demands (Rosenberg, 2001). Therefore, the value proposition for elearning is:

E-learning cost efficiency + e-learning quality + e-learning service + e-learning speed = e-learning value.

Rosenberg (2001) also addresses the arbitrary but commonplace business goal of converting a specific percentage of a training program to e-learning. This goal can be reached by "playing around" with the numbers (i.e., numbers of training days, numbers of students, numbers of courses, etc.), but a less-focused accounting goal and more-focused value proposition would be to do an assessment of the impact of the e-learning to the business overall (West, 2004). For example, quickly training sales representatives on new product enhancements through convenient e-learning perhaps makes more sense than purchasing off-the-shelf Microsoft PowerPoint training for those who might take the course sometime in the future.

FINANCIAL COMPARISON BETWEEN CLASSROOM AND ONLINE

One often overlooked aspect of using e-learning is the time-to-market aspect of a trained and ready workforce, which online learning can bring about faster. For example, a business is about to shift from Netscape email to Microsoft Outlook email. Here is an example of a cost-benefit

Table 11.3 Option One – 100% Classroom Training

# of employees to be trained	1,200
# of classrooms available	3
# of days of training	1
# of employees in each class	10
# of external contract instructors to be hired	3
Cost per day per instructor	$500
# of elapsed days to train 1,200 employees	1,200 employees ÷ 10 per class = 120 one-day classes ÷ 3 classrooms = 40 elapsed days
Cost for instructors	120 x $500 = $60,000
Cost for employee being away from the workplace	Average annual salary and benefits = $62,400 ÷ 2,080 hours = $30 per hour. $30 per hour x 8 hours x 1,200 employees = $288,000
Total costs to competency in the workplace	$60,000 + $288,000 = $348,000 after 40 elapsed days

analysis, where traditional versus online learning off-the-shelf training is considered.

Note in Table 11.3 that the comparison of instructor time versus student time away from the workplace reinforces the point made by Rosenberg (2001) that the largest expenditure is not in instructor costs, but in lost opportunity costs when students are away from the job. Note also in Table 11.4 that e-learning is typically more efficient, because it can take from 25–60% less time to convey the same amount of information as in a traditional classroom setting.

Table 11.4 Option Two – 100% Online Learning

# of employees to be trained	1,200
# of copies of concurrent elearning training available	Virtually unlimited
# of days of training	4 hours
Cost per employee for training	$150
# of elapsed days to train 1,200 employees	Virtually unlimited, but realistically could occur in 10 days
Cost for training cost for instructors	$100 x 1,200 = $120,000
Cost for employee being away from the workplace	Average annual salary and benefits = $62,400 ÷ 2,080 hours = $30 per hour. $30 per hour x 4 hours x 1,200 employees = $144,000
Total costs to competency in the workplace	$120,000 + $144,000 = $264,000 in 10 elapsed days

The examples in Table 11.3 and Table 11.4 are not meant to be complete, because each situation requires a common sense approach of all the factors impacting the cost-efficiency. For example, a blended element could be considered: A brief kickoff being delivered through desktop web conferencing, using a web conferencing system that requires no travel for instructors or students and no additional expenditure (assuming seat license purchases have already been made and seat time is available). To further extrapolate the benefits of speedier online learning in this example, what is the real benefit to the organization of having a trained and ready workforce in one-fourth the time? Certainly, overall productivity from online learning would be enhanced, whereas the delay in traditional classroom learning could represent real business delays, and therefore costs.

CONCLUSIONS

Summing up ROI regarding training, Jay Cross (2004) states that the DuPont model is totally inappropriate for today; it fails to recognize the value of intangibles, and is mainly backward- rather than forward-looking. New models are emerging to help quantify the costs and benefits of training, such as "time-to-market," and "time-to-competency." Christine Pope, director of e-learning services for SmartForce, teaches customers to take a three-pronged approach to evaluation of training: First look at cost savings (of e-learning results over classroom results), then move to performance improvement (involving supervisory evaluations and financial data beyond training metrics), and finish with competitive advantage or bottom-line results (Raths, 2001). Additionally, there is a growing number of training professionals that think after-the-fact evaluations are entirely the wrong way to go—they are promoting ROI forecasting (Graber, Post, & Erwin, n.d.).

The high costs of online learning and the added versatility of learning management systems to capture data have combined to interest business leaders in forcing training to improve addressing and measuring business results. As training professionals invent new ways to evaluate training, they need to correlate those results to business objectives. Regardless of what is measured or how, the consensus seems to be that what is important is that business values are finally being attached to the corporate learning experience.

REFERENCES

Bassi, L. J., & McMurrer, D. P. (2001). Do firm's investments in education and training pay off? Enterprise networks & servers. Retrieved September 3, 2004, from http://www.unisysworld.com/monthly/2001/07/payoff.shtml.

Berry, J. (2000, November 6). The elearning factor. Retrieved September 4, 2004, from http://www.internetweek.com/indepth/indepth110600.htm.

Conner, M. L. (n.d.). FAQ: How do I measure return on investment (ROI) for my learning program? Retrieved September 3, 2004, from http://www.learnativity.com/roi-learning.html.

Cross, J. (2001). A fresh look at ROI. Learning circuits. Retrieved September 2, 2004, from http://www.work911.com/cgi-bin/links/jump.cgi?ID=2562.

Cross, J. (2004, September 3). Personal communication.

Glover, R. W., Long, D. W., Haas, C. T., & Alemany, C. (1999, March). Return-on-investment (ROI) analysis of education and training in the construction industry. Retrieved September 4, 2004, from http://www.cdc.gov/elcosh/docs/d0100/d000132/d000132.PDF.

Graber, J., Post, G., & Erwin, R. (n.d.). Using ROI forecasting to develop a high-impact, high-volume training curriculum. Retrieved September 15, 2004, from http://www.businessdecisions.com/Docs/ASTDROI Chapter.doc.

Latshaw, G. (2001, July 22). Progress report – eLearning Forum Metrics Committee. Report presented at eLearning Forum Meeting on ROI. Retrieved March 2, 2007, from http://www.elearningforum.com/meetings/2001/july/Gary.pdf.

Moore, M. G., & Kearsley, G. (1996). *Distance education: A systems view.* Belmont, CA: Wadsworth Publishing.

Peters, O. (2000). *Learning and teaching in distance education: Pedagogical analyses and interpretations from an international perspective.* London: Kogan Page.

Ramirez, A. (2003). Interview: Speaking personally—with Eugene Rubin. *The American Journal of Distance Education, 17*(1), 59–69.

Raths, D. (2001, May). Measure of success. *Online Learning, 5*(5), 20–22, & 24. Retrieved September 15, 2004, from http://www.onlinelearningmag.com/onlinelearning/search/search_display.jsp?vnu_content_id=1041605.

Rosenberg, M. J. (2001). *Elearning: Strategies for delivering knowledge in the digital age.* New York: McGraw-Hill.

Rumble, G. (n.d.). *Cost justification model.* Retrieved September 12, 2004, from http://www.skillsriver.com/elearningscript.htm.

Rumble, G. (1997). *The costs and economics of open and distance learning.* London: Kogan Page.

Shepherd, C. (1999, January). *Assessing the ROI of training.* Retrieved June 13, 2007, from http://www.fastrak-consulting.co.uk/tactix/features/tngroi/tngroi01.htm.

Sommer, B. (2002, January). A new kind of business case. *Optimize, 3.* Retrieved September 3, 2004, from http://www.optimizemag.com/article/showArticle.jhtml?articleId=17700652.

Taylor, J. (n.d.). *Measuring return on investment for soft skills training.* Retrieved September 3, 2004, from http://www.work911.com/cgi-bin/links/jump.cgi?ID=5041.

West, W. V. (2004). Value-on-investment and the future of e-learning in the training market. *Educational Technology, 44*(5), 41–45.

12

TRANSFORMING WORKPLACE LEARNING

The Role of Embedded Learning in Creating a Competitive Workforce

Jade Nguyen Strattner

IBM, USA

Diana G. Oblinger

EDUCAUSE, USA

INTRODUCTION

Education is a workforce issue that touches virtually every organization—from business to government, to public and private. Studies show that business results are tied to workforce competency. As a result, more and more companies and government agencies are investing in education and training to help improve their bottom line.

In its earliest days, workplace learning was the interaction between master and apprentice; in the last 25 years, off-site corporate-training retreats and interactive computer simulations have emerged. The evolution of workplace learning has accelerated in the last two decades, paralleling the increasing demands on businesses and workers.

A transformation is under way in today's workplace, where stand-alone training is yielding to more comprehensive learning solutions. In the current environment, access to just-in-time information, advice, and performance support are as central to learning as traditional classrooms were in past generations. The embedded learning experience is based on the recognition that technology offers the opportunity to integrate learning with work to enhance performance in a dynamic, interactive and measurable way.

DRIVERS OF CHANGE

Three powerful forces are causing organizations to rethink what learning means, how it is delivered, and how it is linked to organizational performance.

- The marketplace is increasingly competitive—learning must be redefined to enable organizations to be responsive to the new market environment.
- Evolving work and lifestyle changes are causing workers to place different demands on enterprises; learning must accommodate the needs of workers who span generations.
- Emerging technology is enabling us to access and personalize learning in ways never before possible.

These three forces impact the future of work and learning.

MARKET DRIVERS

The market environment is changing in important ways, somewhat independently of economic cycles. These changes are causing organizations to realize how critical learning is in their ability to compete. Consequently, organizations continue to invest in employee development but, at the same time, they are demanding increased accountability from their learning investments.

Changes in the market environment that are driving transformation in learning include global competition, a knowledge-dependent economy, growth through innovation, and new business models.

Global Competition

Whether measured by flows of goods and services, direct investment, and other capital flows, the transfer of knowledge or technology, or the movement of people—the economies of the world are tied together even more so than in the past. Workers who increasingly interact in a global marketplace and participate in global work teams will require the skills needed to collaborate and interact in diverse cultural and linguistic settings.

Knowledge-dependent Economy

How businesses generate revenue is dramatically changing. Since 1950, U.S. employment in the manufacturing sector has fallen from nearly 40% of total employment to less than 18%, while the service sector has risen from 14% to more than 35% (Moe, 2000). Simultaneously, the demand for skilled jobs has increased from 40% in 1950 to 85% in 2000 (Goman, 2004). As a result, the value of companies is based less on physical capital than on the earning power derived from human capital.

Growth through Innovation

While volatility and the drive for ever-higher productivity are now part of the permanent landscape, it is clear that growth is on the agenda again. IBM's Global CEO study (2004) revealed a remarkable convergence of CEO views around two main themes: Business growth and customer responsiveness. But to grow in the new market environment, the needs of the market must be sensed and appropriately responded to in real-time. In short, to excel, organizations must be able to innovate and adapt on demand. At the heart of the capacity to innovate and adapt is the ability to learn. An organization cannot innovate or transform itself without first learning something new. It is not surprising, then, that 75% of the CEOs surveyed believe that employee education will become a critical success factor over the next few years.

New Business Models

The need for flexibility and innovation is forcing organizations to become more componentized—to break down the overall business into the pieces (or components) that make it up. This allows an organization to stop looking at itself through lenses such as organization, geography, and product or customer segment, and start looking at itself through the lens of what is actually being done. Traditional organizations have been oriented primarily around a hierarchical structure that emphasizes functions or lines of business. Successful enterprises in the new market have business models that are componentized around value rather than function.

The above trends suggest a significant shift in both the kind of work that drives the economy and the kind of workers needed to do that work. The new market environment places a premium on innovation, new business models, and new ways of organizing work. In order to survive and thrive in an increasingly service-led and knowledge-driven economy, individuals and organizations must continually acquire and apply new skills and develop new ways of leveraging information and knowledge.

TECHNOLOGICAL DRIVERS

Technology can be used to improve learning. Not only does technology provide new capabilities, but it can expand existing ones. In addition, computer technology is constantly becoming more powerful and affordable. Consider that by the year 2010, the average 10-year-old will have access to more computational power than existed on the planet in 2001 (Harris, 2003).

Both technology and the activities it enables are critical to creating more powerful learning environments. A number of emerging technologies hold promise for future learning applications, particularly embedded learning.

Broadband

The use of broadband connectivity in the home is increasing. In most developed markets worldwide, broadband reaches one-third or more of all online households with the expectation that nearly one-half of all homes will have broadband by 2010 (IDC, 2005). Broadband makes it possible to provide more realistic applications (e.g., using multimedia or simulations) and reduce response time, making it feasible for individuals to learn at home or the office.

Collaboration

As collaboration emerges as an activity that leads to learning, communication tools like web conferencing, instant messaging (IM), and application sharing are gaining increased importance. In addition, social networking tools make collaboration more effective; they help organizations understand who knows who and how people interact. Beyond identifying the network, presence awareness tools let learners know what experts are available or which queries should be directed to other sources.

Simulation

Simulation techniques—ranging from game-based immersion to text—are growing as the preferred method for developing specific skills. Simulations and games are currently being applied to learning situations in management, the military, healthcare, and other segments.

Intelligent Devices

Tablet based personal computers (PCs), e-books, and sensors that process, display, communicate, and seamlessly interact with each other are providing enhanced delivery capability in learning.

Wireless Technologies

Wireless networks and increased computing capabilities in mobile devices are creating new opportunities for just-in-time learning. As a result, wireless learning applications are becoming more widespread, particularly for field service/mobile workers.

KEY TECHNOLOGY CAPABILITIES THAT ENABLE NEW FORMS OF LEARNING

The increasing power and affordability of computer technology, combined with its adaptability and interactivity, are changing the learning experience dramatically. It is not the technology, per se, that is important; it is the capability it enables. Some of these capabilities are important for convenience and flexibility. Others relate to interactions that lead to learning.

Always-on

Increases in bandwidth, availability of mobile media and global tracking technologies create an "always-on" infrastructure that lets learners access whatever learning they need, whenever they need it.

Interaction and Collaboration

New tools for collaboration, multimedia authoring tools, context recognition, and personalized filters are providing people new ways to interact. New technologies such as virtual reality, voice recognition, shared displays, and text-to-speech conversion are engaging multiple senses in learning. In addition, collaboration technologies can be embedded into workflow and used to facilitate knowledge transfer.

Adaptability

Intelligent devices that sense, process, display, communicate, and interact with people and other devices are enabling the delivery of anytime, anywhere learning. Biotechnology developments such as biometrics, eye-tracking interfaces, and assistive technologies are enabling learning systems to detect and adapt to learners' specific and unique needs and capabilities, such as physical handicaps, learning disabilities, and native languages.

Flexibility

Web-based training and course delivery improves scalability, flexibility, and reusability. As a result, learning can be available 24 × 7 in flexible formats, whether at work or at home.

Integration

Tools, content, and processes can be integrated to deliver a more seamless, useful learner experience. Informal, context-based learning is gaining recognition as the most valuable form of learning. In addition, standards such as SCORM and web services are enabling the widespread adoption of modular and interoperable architectures. This trend is leading to greater integration of point solutions within integrated learning platforms.

Reusability

Content can be shared, modified, and redeployed to meet different needs without requiring recreation. In addition, knowledge can be harvested from communities and experts, and then redeployed through tools such as knowledge management.

DEMOGRAPHIC AND EMPLOYMENT DRIVERS

Embedded learning takes on increasing significance due to many of the demographic and employment changes in government, business, and industry. During the last few decades, there has been a shift in the balance of worker supply and demand. Turnover, new roles, and reskilling are placing additional demands on both employers and employees. In addition, younger workers are demanding a different environment than those who are retiring.

Since workplace learning is not age or situation dependent, demographic characteristics of learners mirror those of our population. Six major forces are driving unprecedented changes in workforce demographics.

Skills Gap

In the United States, the demand for skilled jobs more has increased from 40% in 1950 to 85% in 2000 (Goman, 2004). Not only are greater skills required, but those skills change rapidly. It is estimated that 50% of any employee's skills will become obsolete every 3–5 years (Moe, 2000). In addition, the amount of knowledge workers need to have has exploded; knowledge is growing much faster than our ability to absorb and apply it. Information on the web is doubling every 2.8 years (Shea-Schultz & Fogarty, 2003). At the same time, 38% of a knowledge professional's time is spent looking for information to effectively conduct his or her work, and only 20% of the knowledge available in today's organizations is being leveraged to add value (Albrecht, 2001).

Multi-generational Workforce

Breakthroughs in medicine and healthcare allow people to continue to live longer; consequently many choose to work later in life. Approximately 70% of U.S. workers plan to work into their eligible retirement years or never retire (National Intelligence Council, 2000). This longer work life is also possible due to the advent of knowledge-based work, versus manufacturing, because it requires less physical labor and reduced physical risk. This longer work life is creating a more multi-generational workforce than ever before. Older workers may be struggling to adapt to the Internet, while their younger co-workers can't imagine life without it.

Diversity

Today's workforce is more diverse than at any previous point in history. The measures of diversity go beyond ethnicity to include gender, age, and sexual preference.

Increased Time Pressure

The demands of the current workplace leave employees with very limited time for formalized learning. In today's on-demand, rapidly changing environment, individuals operate with a high level of business urgency and very little time to learn. There is such a rapid churn of the skills and knowledge required to maintain job performance that learning can no longer be provided as a discrete, periodic event.

Blending of Work and Life

Thanks in part to the ubiquity of the Internet, working and living are blending. More employees work from home, whether full-time, flex-time, or simply extending the work day. A range of activities can occur in a multitude of places—office, home, car, or coffee shop. Laptop and Blackberry users are evident in a host of settings. There is a diminishing difference between work and other environments.

Worker Mobility

Voluntary turnover has been accelerating over the past decade. Studies suggest that employees, on average, switch employers every six years (Kransdorff, 1996). Data from 2004 indicates that out of 140 million U.S. workers, 45 million change jobs each year; historically the United States has higher job turnover than other countries, the majority of it being voluntary and targeted at finding a better job (Bosworth, 2004). Another trend, self-employment, appears to be growing. Twenty-six percent of U. S. workers are free agents (Conlin, 2000).

Importance of Education

Due to frequent changes in skill requirements, as well as employee turnover, development and placement may be the key mechanisms by which organizations sustain talent. Career growth and future learning and development opportunities are two of the top three reasons people stay with companies (Wagner, 2000). In fact, workers who have good training and professional development paths average 12% turnover; workers who do not have learning and growth opportunities average 41% turnover (Bontis, 1999).

CONVERGENCE

Although the idea of embedded learning is not new, the ability to implement it today is the result of the convergence of a number of forces. One is the need for applied, just-in-time learning. Never before have companies needed the caliber of skills and expertise that is required for competitive advantage today. Another is our understanding of how people learn. Many of the principles behind embedded learning have now been proven. For example, people learn best when material is presented in a problem-solving context or in the context of how the material will be used. Material presented either theoretically or out of context is rarely remembered and difficult to transfer to new situations. Technology now makes it possible to develop and deliver this type of context-sensitive learning.

As recently as 5 or 10 years ago, it was much more difficult to develop embedded approaches due to the immaturity of technology and IT infrastructure. In the last few years, companies have developed learning infrastructures. Chief learning officers are appearing. Organizations have instructional designers on staff. Learning management systems and learning content management systems make it possible to organize, deliver, and track learning. The convergence of needs, technology, and demographics all make embedded learning an important development for organizations.

EMBEDDED LEARNING

Definition

Our notions of how people learn have evolved over time. We now view learning as something that is constructed, an active process in which the learner develops his or her own understanding by assembling facts, experience, and practice. We also understand that learning is a social process; people learn from others and with others. Learning requires both practice and participation. In fact, becoming part of a community—such as in the workplace—enhances learning and knowing through shared practice.

How people learn has changed with the web. Those who use the Internet frequently have developed a type of multimedia or information literacy. Understanding is not just based on text, but combines images and sounds. At the same time we've seen shifts in how we approach learning, moving from an environment of being told (authority-based learning) to one based on discovery or experiential learning.

Learner behavior indicates that our current delivery mechanism (the course) is out of phase with employee needs. Workers develop many of their skills by modeling the behaviors of co-workers. In fact, 70% of what people know about their jobs comes informally through the people they work with (Loewenstein & Spletzer, 1994). When asked to acquire new skills because their work has changed, 70% of survey respondents wanted more interactions with co-workers, not more classes (Cross, 2005). Further evidence that courses are not the optimal delivery mechanism may be provided by the fact that 75% of workers fail to complete e-learning courses (Kruper, 2002).

Embedded learning inserts learning activities into job tasks, seamlessly integrating relevant information into the workers' workflow making learning highly relevant and available to their work. Learning simply becomes an aspect of the work process being performed.

Rationale

Embedded learning supports the premise that much of the learning that happens in the workplace today happens outside the classroom context. According to the U.S. Department of Commerce, at least 80% of employee learning happens in the workplace (Tough, 1999). For most people, the workplace routinely provides learning experiences. Rather than simply labeling this kind of learning as informal and leaving it to chance, proponents of embedded learning analyze how learning happens organically and define strategies to amplify the learning that naturally occurs within the system.

In many ways, embedded learning is based on the premise that the closer people are to needing to know something to do their jobs, the more motivated they are to learn. If organizations can make critical information available at that moment of need, they create an inherent "teachable moment." A teachable moment is the ideal time to leverage learning without having to remove the learner from work.

To maximize the effectiveness of the teachable moment, we can use technology to make the right information available at the right time, thereby transparently embedding learning into our work. The paradigm then evolves from "learn, then do," to "learn while doing." Content is delivered within the context of a person's role, interests, and current activity, creating dynamic, personalized, role-based workplaces that include access to both formal and ad hoc learning.

EMBEDDED LEARNING AT HONDA

Ray has been a Honda technician for 19 years. He thought the longer he worked, the easier it would become. However, cars are becoming more complex and technology is changing faster and faster. When he services the newer model cars, he sometimes has to walk back to the computer to look up diagrams for wiring or instructions for various parts. He shouldn't complain, because he remembers when he used to have to thumb through pages of a paper manual to find the information he needed. Back and forth, and back and forth, he went between the manual and the car.

Ray could use embedded learning to provide him with critical information he needs right where he is doing the repair. Just think how much time he would save if he had such a learning environment.

Microvision (see www.microvision.com) is actually providing this environment to Honda technicians. The product, *Nomad Expert Technician System*, is compact and wearable. It receives data wirelessly from Honda's online system. It is a "personal heads-up display" that the technician can see through. From the technician's point of view, the display superimposes a diagram right over the actual Honda part being repaired, with step-by-step instructions. Embedding critical information right into work is making a huge difference in productivity. During a field test in California, they found an average increase of 39% in skilled technicians' productivity. One technician claims using Nomad is "similar to having the information in my head." User performance has improved, Honda cars are being "fixed right the first time" and the sponsors are happy. Honda is looking at additional application opportunities.

EMBEDDED LEARNING AT IBM

At IBM, there is a strong movement towards embedded learning through an employee intranet called On Demand Workplace (ODW). ODW provides access to both formal and informal learning in a dynamic and personalized way, offering tools such as performance support, collaboration, and expertise location. Thus, learning is available to employees when they need it most. IBM's ODW provides another powerful proof of concept for embedded learning.

IBM's ODW is the primary vehicle for providing business-critical information to employees. An IBM learning transformation "white paper" (IBM Learning Solutions, 2004) notes that ODW has become the primary trusted source for employee information, with an average of 2.4 million pages of company-related content viewed by IBM employees per business day. In addition to providing up-to-the-minute organizational and industry news, the intranet home page provides customized information to employees based on their job roles, responsibilities, and areas of interest.

Case: Matt and ODW

We can see how learning can be embedded in the workplace of an IBM salesperson named Matt. Matt's ODW has three main tabs: Home, Work, and Career and Life. The Home tab provides Matt with company, competitor, and news updates in one place. The Work tab integrates information, learning, expertise, application functionality, and data around workflow. The Career and Life tab provides Matt real time access to personalized career planning, human resources (HR), and learning resources.

It is in the Work Tab that the concept of embedded learning comes to life. There, Matt is able to access a personalized view of revenue, pipeline, and current clients and deals. Based on Matt's profile, the system "pushes" relevant resources to him. Here we see industry client and solutions news that have been retrieved and sorted, based on Matt's unique needs. The system can further refine resources by using information that Matt provides. The Data Collector frames a search based at the intersection of both profile and task, so that the real time results are more precise. Finally, based on the work that Matt is currently engaged in, ODW finds industry, work process, product, or client experts who may be helpful, providing him real time access to expertise. This is distinct from traditional collaboration tools, which are usually initiated by the user via a company directory search or cycle of phone calls. Instead, the system is tracking to task and role, and is surfacing resources which map to the task and role, providing focused real-time access to resources that may be able to help.

BENEFITS OF EMBEDDED LEARNING TO INDIVIDUALS

There are a number of benefits that embedded learning brings to individuals. Those benefits range from improved flexibility to improved workplace competence.

- *Flexibility.* Embedded learning is inherently flexible; it can be done on the job, any place, at any time, allowing workers to continue meeting multiple demands for their time.
- *Relevance.* Embedded learning allows us to shift the presentation of material from a "just in case" mode, to one where material is relevant to what the learner needs and is presented in a real-life context.
- *Time savings.* Because employees no longer need to learn just in case, but can learn "just in time," their time—and the company's—is saved. Rather than taking courses that require being away from work, they are able to integrate learning into their daily activities.
- *Skill enhancement.* Through embedded learning, employees are able to acquire new skills. Although those skills are directly related to their work activities, they may also extrapolate to other environments.
- *Job advancement.* Greater skill and better job performance, due to embedded learning, can result in job advancement, merit pay increases and greater job satisfaction.

BENEFITS TO ORGANIZATIONS

Faced with an increasingly competitive and global market environment and changing workforce demographics, more and more organizations are revisiting workplace solutions that deliver higher levels of worker efficiency and effectiveness. They are looking for ways to generate more value, not just output, per employee. Embedded learning can have high payback for organizations, particularly in environments where the workflow is formalized and where workers need to maintain their knowledge of rapidly changing products, procedures, or standards. Surfacing quality-learning activities on the job enables workers to repeatedly and easily use updated information in context. There are several specific benefits of embedded learning to organizations.

Improved Productivity

Workers in the United States spend 15–30% of their workday looking for the right information to do their job. That amounts to billions of dollars in productivity loss as workers sort through data to hunt down information. To make matters worse, recent studies show that workers are unsuccessful at finding the information as much as 50% of the time. The problem is expected to get worse, given that information is now doubling about every three years (study cited earlier). Embedded learning can profoundly impact productivity by enabling workers to access just-in-time information that is tailored for the individual's role, task, access device, and available time.

Organizational Learning

More sophisticated embedded learning environments enable two-way information sharing. In these environments, learners become both producers and consumers of information. As they access just-in-time information, they will also be expected to update organizational data sources with the latest insights from real world market experiences. This way, others within the enterprise can benefit and leverage that understanding, enabling a culture of organizational learning.

Integration Across Value Net

Linkage between strategy and execution won't occur without all members in the supply chain—inside and outside of the enterprise—understanding the strategy. As embedded learning extends to customers, partners, and suppliers, organizations integrate horizontally more efficiently and effectively.

Capacity to Innovate

Embedded learning moves us from "learning before doing" to "learning while doing." In doing so, it saves workers time on the front end of a process, allowing them more time for reflection and analysis. We can better analyze our actions and understand where improvements can be made and where innovation is required. This higher order learning is the differentiator for future organizations.

LIMITATIONS OF EMBEDDED LEARNING

Although there are multiple advantages to embedded learning, it should not be viewed as a substitute for all other learning formats. Embedded learning is an excellent choice for learning related to specific work tasks. However, other types of learning are important in creating well-rounded, innovative, and competitive employees. The limitations of embedded learning, as we have discussed it, include the scope of learning opportunities, types of learning environments, and the learning orientation of workers.

Scope

The focus of embedded learning is workplace related. As a result, the scope of the learning opportunities is limited. It is unlikely that individuals will find significant opportunities for personal growth or civic understanding through embedded learning. The scope of learning is also prescribed by the position, the task and the perspective of a specific company.

Type of Learning Environment

Well-rounded learners have honed their skills in a variety of learning environments—face-to-face, online, workplace, lecture, and problem-solving. Embedded learning is focused on the workplace and is delivered via technology. Although this is an effective learning environment, it is not the only one to which learners should be exposed. The same can be said of the type of expertise gained. Embedded environments are good for developing skills and delivering content. However, it is a more difficult environment in which to convey attitudes, confront beliefs, or develop complex interpersonal skills.

Learning to Learn

In a complex, rapidly changing environment, companies are looking for employees who have learned how to learn. The ability to constantly acquire new skills, perspectives, and knowledge are important to innovation and competitiveness. Embedded learning enables workers to learn effectively, but it is not the best tool for instilling the desire or ability to learn on one's own. Employees should identify gaps in knowledge and construct their own learning paths, sorting through what information is valid, assessing their own strengths and weaknesses, and developing an educational plan. This meta-cognitive approach goes beyond what embedded learning can deliver.

CONSIDERATIONS

Although embedded learning shows tremendous promise, it represents a significant change for most organizations. Prior to moving into an embedded learning program, organizations should examine a series of questions, ranging from whether learning is strategic to their organization, to whether they have the right management and governance structure.

Reinvent the Role of Learning

One of the first questions to ask is whether learning is considered strategic to the organization. Beyond stating that learning is strategic, more important measures include how much the organization invests in learning, to whom it is available, how it is rewarded, and so on.

Change the Learning Paradigm

The first step to successfully navigating this change to a more pervasive learning environment is to understand the difference between learning and training. Successful learning functions must stretch beyond the realm of formal training to focus on enabling productivity through more informal, embedded methods.

Target Investments

You don't have to embed learning into every business process. Focus on those areas that will yield the greatest business impact, but also those that are the most ready for change. Embedded learning is particularly effective in environments where the workflow is formalized and where workers need to maintain their knowledge of rapidly changing products, procedures, or standards. By proving success in initial areas, you can establish a foundation for more pervasive change.

Reorganize Governance and Management

For many organizations, embedded learning will require a change in their governance and management system. Learning professionals in these organizations will need to take on a new role. They are no longer just creators of content or planners and implementors of training events, but also facilitators of human capital and performance management, engaging in complex processes that are deeply embedded in the organization.

CONCLUSION

Embedded learning represents an important evolution in how we conceptualize and deliver learning. Rather than simply using technology to automate age-old learning methods or digitize existing content, embedded learning integrates a new learning design with technology to deliver improvements in workplace learning.

The need for embedded learning is significant. With changes in workforce demographics, competitive pressures, and the need to constantly innovate, traditional training and education models alone are not sufficiently flexible or effective. Embedded learning provides organizations with a new tool that integrates learning into work processes and links to organizational priorities.

Shifting to an embedded learning environment is a complex task. Awareness of this new modality is the first step. However, implementing embedded learning will require more than purchasing a software system; it requires a change in the organization's learning paradigm.

While embedded learning holds great promise, it is not a panacea. Embedded learning is a targeted form of training. In a rapidly changing environment, workers need training as well as education. However, in an on-demand world where innovation, speed, and execution are critical, embedded learning enables organizations to gain a competitive edge that brings value to the organization and the individual.

REFERENCES

Albrecht, K. (2001, February). The true information survival skills: Internet age requires different thinking and behavior. *Training & Development, 55*(2), 24–30.

Bontis, N. (1999). Managing organisational knowledge by diagnosing intellectual capital: Framing and advancing the state of the field. *International Journal of Technology Management, 18*(5/6/78), 433–462.

Conlin, M. (2000, August 28). And now, the just-in-time employee. *Businessweek Online.* Retrieved August 15, 2005, from http://www.businessweek.com/2000/00_35/b3696044.htm.

Cross, J. (2005). *Informing learning—the other 80 percent.* Retrieved August 15, 2005, from http://www.leader-values.com/Content/detailPrint.asp?ContentDetailID=135.

Goman, C. K. (2004, May). The forces of change. *Link&Learn.* Retrieved August 15, 2005, from http://www.linkageinc.com/company/news_events/link_learn_enewsletter/archive/2004/05_04_forces_change_goman.aspx.

Harris, J. (2003). *The learning paradox.* Oxford: Capstone Books.

IBM Global CEO Survey (2004). IBM. Retrieved August 15, 2005, from http://www-1.ibm.com/services/ondemand/business/ global_ceo_study_2004.html.

IBM Learning Solutions (2004, June). *IBM learning transformation story.* Retrieved August 15, 2005, from http://www-304.ibm.com/jct03001c/ services/learning/solutions/pdfs/learning_transformation.pdf.

IDC (2005). *IDC predicts 46% of Western European households will have broadband by 2009.* Retrieved August 15, 2005, from http://idc.com/getdoc.jsp?containerId=pr2005_07_22_123254.

Kransdorff, A. (1996). Succession planning in a fast-changing world. *Management Decision, 34*(2), 30–34.

Kruper, J. (2002, March). Putting the learner front and center: Using user-centered design principles to build better e-learning products. *The eLearning Developers' Journal,* 8–11. Retrieved August 15, 2005, from http://www.unext.com/UNext_news/front_and_center.pdf.

Loewenstein, M.A., & Spletzer, J. R. (1994, June). *Informal training: A review of existing data and some new evidence* (Working Paper 254). Washington, DC: U. S. Department of Labor, Bureau of Labor Statistics. Retrieved August 15, 2005, from http://www.bls.gov/ore/pdf/ec940090.pdf.

Moe, M. (2000, May 23). The knowledge web: Part 1—fuel for the New Economy. Merrill Lynch. Knowledge Enterprises Group. Retrieved August 15, 2005, from http://www.internettime.com/itimegroup/MOE1.PDF.

National Intelligence Council (2000). *Global trends 2015: A dialogue about the future with non-governmental experts*. Washington, DC: Author.

Shea-Schultz, H., & Fogarty, J. (2003, January 8). Online learning today: 7 strategies that work. *LTI Newsline*. Retrieved August 15, 2005, from http://www.elearningmag.com/ltimagazine/article/articleDetail.jsp?id=42799.

Tough, A. (1999). *Reflections on the study of adult learning* (WALL Working Paper No. 8). Retrieved March 13, 2007, from https://tspace.library.utoronto.ca/bitstream/1807/2722/ 2/08reflections.pdf.

Wagner, S. (2000, August). Retention: Finders, keepers. *Training & Development, 54*(8), 64. Retrieved August 15, 2005, from http://www.findarticles.com/p/articles/mi_m4467/is_8_54/ai_64705632.

13

OPEN BASIC EDUCATION

Organizational Structures, Costs, and Benefits

Palitha Edirisingha

University of Leicester, United Kingdom

INTRODUCTION

Providing basic education for all citizens is a priority for most world leaders. Open basic education programs have often been geared towards this end, through a variety of learning methods and technologies, taking education to the doorsteps of those who missed formal schooling. This chapter takes a critical look at the development of various forms of open basic education (OBE) programs in many parts of the globe. First, it proposes a systematic way of categorizing OBE programs, to help the policy maker identify organizational structures suitable for local needs. It then examines the costs and economics of OBE programs. Third, the chapter assesses the outcomes that can be achieved through OBE programs. Finally, it draws implications for the policy maker. The chapter draws widely on both the literature and empirical evidence collected by the author from a series of case studies on OBE programs in South Africa, India, Botswana, Thailand, and Canary Islands.

OPEN AND DISTANCE LEARNING METHODS—
ORGANIZATIONAL STRUCTURES

Open and distance learning methods have been used as alternatives to increase access to basic education in both developed and developing countries. A review of relevant literature reflects the diverse range of organizational structures and practice currently available. This diversity also means that different authors tend to categorize organizational structures differently. Yates and Tilson (2000, pp. 9–10) discuss seven models and approaches: Educational television, radio learning groups, forums and campaigns, schools broadcasting, radiophonic schools, open schools, multi-channel systems, and basic education schemes. Their typology is based on the main technologies and methods used to deliver the content. Yates (2000, p. 230), looking at the same organizational structures, provides a different classification with eight types of organizational structures: ETV/Teleschools, Asian open schools, Study-centres model, New African open schools, Schools of the Air, Radio-based models, Multi-channel learning, and Basic education training programs. This classification is based on geographical location and technology used. Perraton and Creed (2000, p. 5) recognize five kinds of initiatives: Alternative secondary institutions, programs for raising school quality, adult education and extension work, teacher education, and the work of open universities in relation to basic education. The audiences served, and the nature of the content provided, form the basis for their classification. In addition, they identify examples of using computers in schools and the development of specialized agencies promoting open basic education. Focusing on health education, Pridmore and Nduba (2000, pp. 193–197) discuss seven types of organizational structures: Radio schools, educational television, mass campaigns, open schools, interactive radio instruction, radio and television dramas, and social marketing. This classification is also based on the technology used to deliver the content and facilitate the learning experience.

Unlike the open and distance learning institutions providing higher education, OBE programs use an array of methods, technologies, and institutional and governance structures—a possible reason for the confusing systems of classification. This means that the policy maker, confronted with this complex picture of OBE models, has the difficult task of recognizing the salient features of organizational structures that are best suited for his or her economic, social, political, and cultural context. This chapter aims to address this issue by suggesting a framework to serve as a tool for the policy maker and the practitioner, to identify organizational structures suitable for their local needs.

ORGANIZATIONAL STRUCTURES FOR OPEN BASIC EDUCATION—TOWARDS A CLASSIFICATION

The proposed classification of OBE structures is based on four main inter-related criteria: The audience served, curriculum/content offered, the location of provision, and the technologies and methods used. The following analysis enables us to build a framework illuminating the diversity of practice and the cost-benefits of each type of organizational structure.

The Audience

The audience for OBE is of primary importance; its characteristics should determine the technologies and methods used. For example, young children require methods that incorporate considerable amount of face-to-face teaching. The audience consists of three main groups: Children, adults, and mixed audiences of children and adults. The definitions of these categories vary according to legal and cultural aspects of a particular context. However, for this analysis, children are classified as those at normal schooling age, while adults are considered as those who have moved into societal responsibilities, but were unable to go to formal schools when they were children (Dodds & Edirisingha, 2000). The third group, mixed audiences of both children and adults, becomes important in contexts where a distinction between adults and children does not apply.

Curriculum and the Content

Three sub-categories emerge from the literature and our case studies.

School-Type Curriculum   These OBE programs offer the same subject content offered in formal schools, such as mathematics, sciences, and languages. Upon successful completion, learners receive certificates that are similar to those gained from the formal system.

Alternative Curriculum for School Equivalency, Vocational, and Life Skills   An alternative curriculum includes life- and economic-related skills, such as farming and other income generation activities; improvement of family and community such as health, nutrition, home economics, and family planning; and training for leadership, community work, extension, and health work. These programs may also include subjects similar to those offered in formal schools, enabling the learners to gain qualifications comparable with those offered by the conventional system.

An Alternative Curriculum for Vocational and Life-Skills   The content is not usually comparable with that of a formal system. School equivalency is not a concern. The subject matter is specific to particular subgroups in the local population such as illiterate adults, women, girls, farmers, craftsmen, and unemployed youth.

THE LOCATION OF EDUCATION PROVISION

The location offers two options: In-school and out-of-school. In-school programs supplement the formal school curriculum and raise the quality of instruction in schools. The out-of-school programs, on the other hand, aim to expand the access to education. In doing so, they may provide either a school-type curriculum or an alternative curriculum, catering to different audiences. The audience for an alternative curriculum is mostly adults, overlooked by the formal system, seeking knowledge and skills in a variety of areas including literacy and numeracy.

The Classification Scheme

Based on above criteria, the OBE organizational structures can be put in two main categories: In-school and out-of-school. Table 13.1 summarizes the classification scheme based on audience, curriculum, teaching methods, and technological media, and provides examples from literature review and our case studies.

In-School Programs

The first block in Table 13.1, the in-school category, provides three examples: Interactive Radio Instruction (IRI) in South Africa, Information and Communication Technologies (ICT) in classrooms in Botswana, and ICT for teacher training in Botswana. Generally, in-school programs are for improving the quality of existing teaching and learning in schools; for example, by bringing new education resources into the classroom, by overcoming the shortage of trained teachers, and by training the existing teaching force.

The IRI approach, pioneered in 1974 in Nicaragua by Stanford University in the United States, is a well-documented and a well-researched educational intervention in developing countries (Agency for International Development [AID], n.d; Bosch, 1997). The IRI program in South Africa was started in 1992 by Open Learning Systems Education Trust (OLSET), a nongovernmental organization. The program aims to overcome the shortage of English teachers; it provides daily one-half-hour English lessons for black South African primary schools, reaching more than 500,000 children. It also has a large-scale teacher development program.

Two other in-school programs, ICT in schools and ICT for teacher training in Botswana, represent a newly emerging category of programs in developing countries. They use ICT in two ways: By bringing new resources into schools, and by facilitating teacher training at a distance. Both programs in Botswana were implemented by the nation's Ministry of Education (MOE). The teacher training program was a fixed-term project, which ran from 1996–99 and trained 40 teachers, while the ICT for in-school program was piloted in 11 junior secondary schools from 1997. Per-

Table 13.1 A Framework to Classify Open Basic Education Programmes

	Programme	Country	Date started	Status and governance	Audience	Curriculum	Teaching media and methods
In-school programmes — School curriculum	Interactive Radio Instructions (IRI)	South Africa	1992	Non Governmental Organisation	Primary school children	Formal, primary, English as a second language	Daily half-hour radio, classroom activities with the teacher, print material, posters
	ICT in schools	Botswana	1997	Ministry of Education	Junior secondary children	Junior secondary school curriculum	Email, Internet, group work, teacher interventions
	ICT for teacher training	Botswana	1997-1999	Ministry of Education	Junior secondary teachers, college lecturers, in-service officers	Teacher's professional development	2 face-to-face sessions (each time 2-weeks long, 4 times a year), email
Out-of-school programmes — School-type curriculum	Telesecundaria[1]	Mexico	1966	Ministry of Education	Primary school leavers	Formal: Junior Secondary (7th – 9th grades)	Television programmes, print, and classroom sessions
	Supervised Study Centres[2]	Zambia, Zimbabwe, Malawi	Zambia: 1974 Zimbabwe: 1960 Malawi: 1965	Ministry of Education	Primary school leavers and secondary school 'dropouts'	Formal: Junior Secondary and Senior Secondary	Printed, some radio, daily 3-hour supervised study at local centres, tutor marked assignments
	Open Schools[3]	Indonesia	1984, after 5-year pilot	Ministry of Education	Primary school leavers	Formal: Junior Secondary	Printed study material, and face-to-face study

(continued)

Table 13.1 Continued

Programme	Country	Date started	Status and governance	Audience	Curriculum	Teaching media and methods
Botswana College of Open Learning (BOCODOL)	Botswana	1999, following DNFE in 1978 and Botswana Extension College in 1973	Parastatal within the MOE	Primary school levers	Formal: Junior Secondary, Senior Secondary	Printed study material and face-to-face study
National Open School (NOS)	India	1989, following a ten-year pilot project	Autonomous within the Ministry of Human Resources Development	14+ years	Alternative/equivalent to primary, junior and senior secondary, and Non-formal: vocational and life-related	Printed study material and face-to-face study (weekly tutorials)
Department of Non Formal Education (DNFE)	Thailand	1979, following non-formal education since 1938	Independent department within the Ministry of Education	14+ years	Alternative/equivalent to formal primary, junior and senior secondary, and Non-formal: vocational and life-related	Printed study material, radio and television programmes, weekly tutorials
Radiophonic Schools	Columbia, Latin America, America, Canary Islands	1947 1963	Church-based organisations, NGOs	No age limit 14+ year	Alternative/equivalent and Non-formal: literacy, numeracy, combined with life-related skills	Radio programmes, print materials supported by 'auxiliars' in radio schools

Alternative curriculum for school equivalency and/or vocational and life-skills

Alternative curriculum for vocational and life-skills

Programme	Country	Date started	Status and governance	Audience	Curriculum	Teaching media and methods
Adult Basic Education Programmes in DNFE	Botswana	1977, following Botswana Extension College in 1973	Ministry of Education	Adults	Literacy, numeracy	Print, face-to-face sessions
Functional Educational Project for Rural Areas (FEPRA)[4]	Pakistan	1982	Allama Iqbal Open University	Rural women	Literacy, income generation, improvement in family and community	Printed material, face-to-face sessions
The African Institute for Economic and Social Development (INADES-formation)[5]	7 West African countries, Kenya, and Tanzania	1962	Jesuits	Rural people, farmers, women, agriculture extension workers	Farm practices, women's participation in development, soil conservation, irrigation, civic education	Correspondence lessons, radio broadcasting, face-to-face sessions
African Medical and Research Foundation (AMREF)[6]	Kenya	1980	Non Governmental Organisation (AMREF)	Health and extension workers	Health	Print, audio cassettes, weekly radio

Sources: [1]Durán (2001); [2]Perraton (1982); [3]Sadiman (1994); [4]Warr (1992); [5]Perraton (2000); [6]Perraton (2000); Other organisations, author research.

raton and Creed (2000) report the progress of initiatives that come under this category in many parts of the world.

Out-of-School Programs

The second major category of OBE programs, out-of-school, aims to expand access to basic education. The audience includes children, adolescents, adults, and mixed audiences. Table 13.1 shows examples of three categories under out-of-school programs.

Out-of-school, School-Type Curriculum The OBE programs providing a school-type curriculum deliver the same subject content as those offered in formal schools, leading to certificates that are either the same as or comparable with those gained from a formal system. Table 13.1 shows four examples, of which three are based on the review of literature: Telesecundaria (Durán, 2001), Supervised Study Centres (Perraton, 1982), and Open Schools in Indonesia (Sadiman, 1994). The review of Botswana College of Open and Distance Learning (BOCODOL) is based on our case study. Telesecundaria is the oldest among the four, established in 1966, and BOCODOL is the latest, started in 1999 as a restructuring of the Department of Non Formal Education (DNFE) in Botswana. The first three programs are located within the Ministry of Education (MOE) of the country, while the latter is a parastatal organization with links to the MOE. Enrollments in these programs are limited to those with relevant academic qualifications. Except in Telesecundaria, the methods and media used are mainly face-to-face, supported by print. In Telesecundaria, the learners study from television programs, supported by teacher-led activities. All four programs lead to school equivalency through a curriculum similar to that of the formal system.

Out-of-School, Alternative Curriculum for School Equivalency and/or Life-Related Skills The third block in Table 13.1 presents three OBE programs under this category. They are National Open School (NOS, India), DNFE (Thailand), and Radiophonic schools (Canary Islands). The oldest program among the three models in Table 13.1 is the Radiophonic schools, started in Colombia in 1947 and later expanded to Central and Latin America. The program in the Canary Islands was started in 1963, and the DNFE in Thailand was started in 1979, following various non-formal initiatives in place since 1938. The Indian NOS was started in 1989, following a 10-year pilot program. Programs under this category enable learners to gain vocational and life-related skills; they may also enable the learners to gain school-equivalency qualifications.

This category of programs differs from school-type curriculum category in a number of ways. These programs enjoy considerable autonomy, which influenced their development (Edirisingha, 2001). NOS is an autonomous body within the relevant ministry, while the DNFE in Thailand is an independent department within the MOE. Radiophonic schools system, spread in Latin America and Canary Islands, is a church-based organization. The audiences in the three programs are mixed, without an upper age limit for learners, although there is a minimum age of 14 years. The content is a mixture of what is normally taught in schools and non-formal subject matter—an alternative curriculum. All three models offer a wide range of learning opportunities, from functional literacy to senior secondary level. Learning methods consist of face-to-face tutorials coupled with radio programs and printed material.

Out-of-School, Alternative Curriculum for Vocational and Life-Related Skills The fourth block in Table 13.1 includes examples of four programs offering an alternative curriculum for vocational and life-skills. These consist of one case study (Adult Basic Education Programs of DNFE in Botswana), and three programs reviewed from literature: Functional Education Project for Rural Areas (FEPRA) in Pakistan (Warr, 1992), INADES-Formation in West Africa (Perraton, 2000), and African Medical and Research Foundation (AMREF) in Kenya (Perraton, 2000). The INADES-Formation was established in 1962, DNFE Botswana in 1977, and the FEPRA in 1982. These organizational structures cater to particular subgroups in the local population such as illiterate adults, women, girls, farmers, craftspeople, and unemployed youth. The content is specific to the learners, and may not be comparable with that of the formal system, and learning may not lead to certificates.

The objective of Botswana DNFE is literacy skills, but other programs have wider objectives. The FEPRA (Pakistan) was initiated as a program for rural people, including women, for a variety of income-generation activities and improvement of family and community welfare (agriculture, health, nutrition, home economics, family planning, and community development). The INADES-Formation provides farmers, agricultural extension personnel, and women with training on farming practices, development, and civic education. With its headquarters in the Ivory Coast, the program operates in seven francophone countries, and in Kenya and Tanzania. The AMREF provides training programs for extension agents and health workers. The methods and media used in these programs combine face-to-face study with audio-visual material, printed text, and radio broadcasts.

In conclusion, this section classified OBE organizational structures based on four main criteria: Audience, content/curriculum, location, and media and methods. The framework evolved would be useful for the policy maker to identify and to develop suitable organizational structures that are best suited to particular local contexts. The following section compares cost advantages and disadvantages of these organizational structures.

COST ADVANTAGES AND DISADVANTAGES

Cost of providing education can be measured in a number of ways. Four main measures used in the current analysis of organizational structures are: Cost per learner, cost per graduate, economies of scale, and cost recovery. Table 13.2 provides a comparison of cost per learner and cost per graduate in five case studies of OBE programs, with those in the formal sector.

The in-school programs, discussed previously, are an additional component in an education system. Their costs are also additional to existing costs, making it difficult to make straight comparison of costs. The policy maker needs to assess the cost of these programs against outcomes, and arrive at decisions that would best suit the needs and conditions of the particular context.

In the case of out-of-school programs that we have examined (in India, Thailand and Canary Islands), in each program, OBE costs are lower than the costs of conventional alternatives. The costs per learner in the OBE programs are always lower than the comparative figures of the formal school.

The next comparison is the cost per graduate between OBE programs and the conventional alternative. In the cases of Thailand and the Canary Islands, the cost per successful student looks as if it should be lower than the cost per completer within the formal system. In these two countries, the costs per learner are very modest compared with the costs per learner in formal schools. The case of India is different, at the current level of cost per successful completer. The NOS can be competitive, if it could raise its completion rates to the kinds of levels Thailand is achieving, and assuming a 75% completion rate in regular schools. Bearing in mind the difficulties and poor educational background of these learners, the programs demonstrate that there is an economic case to be made for this kind of OBE approaches.

In most educational systems, the cost per graduate can be expected to be higher than the cost per learner. A big gap between these two, however, implies large non-completion rates. The learners may have poor educational backgrounds and, as adults, they usually have social and economic commitments that hamper their studies, leading to increased dropouts and lower graduation rates. While this is the reality, a large gap between the cost per learner and the cost per completer implies an inefficiency of the system.

The third kind of cost analysis is the potential for economies of scale. Table 13.3 shows the enrollment and cost per learner figures for South African IRI, Indian NOS, and Thailand DNFE. These programs demonstrate that there is potential for reducing the cost per learner over the years by reaching economies of scale. This is good news for the educators who work with shrinking funds for education. A long-term plan would enable lowering the costs.

Table 13.2 A Comparison of Cost per Learner in OBE Programmes and the Formal Systems

The country	ODL programme		Formal Primary	Formal Secondary	GNP per capita
	Cost per learner	Cost per graduate	Cost per learner	Cost per learner	
South Africa	Interactive Radio Instructions (IRI) $2	Not relevant	$479	Not relevant	$3,160
Botswana	ICT in schools $27	Not relevant	Not relevant	$1,170	$3,020
	Botswana College of Open and Distance Learning (BOCODOL) $470	Not available	Not relevant	$1,170	
	Department of Non Formal Education (DNFE) $169	Not available	$323	Not relevant	
India	National Open School (NOS) $10	$92	$40	$44	$340
Thailand	Department of Non Formal Education (DNFE) $25	$66	$449	$333	$2,740
Canary Islands	Radio Emisora Cultural Canaria (Radio ECCA) $63	Not available	$2 128	$3,046	$13,500

Sources: Author's research. The cost per learner has been calculated US$ values at 1998

The fourth and the last cost analysis is the potential for cost recovery. A common challenge for the program planner is generating funds for their programs. Irrespective of the sources of funds—whether from foreign resources or from the national government—managers of OBE programs operate within financial limitations. One way to generate funds is to charge student fees, and plan to recover some, or most of the costs, as demonstrated by NOS in India.

Figure 13.1 illustrates the case of NOS where most of the recurrent costs are recovered through the fees charged to the learners. NOS demonstrates that, by increasing enrollments, an OBE organizational structure can recover all of its recurrent costs from students' fees alone. As the figure shows, NOS reached financial self-sustainability in terms of its recurrent cost recovery by 1997–98. This financial sustainability was achieved by increasing enrollments, thereby increasing the income generated from student fees, and by receiving government support as grants throughout its 20-year period.

When the Open School was started in India as a pilot in 1979, the annual enrollment was a mere 1,672 (National Open School [NOS], 1991).

Table 13.3 Economies of Scale

| Program | IRI, South Africa | | NOS, India | | DNFE, Thailand | |
Year	Enrollment	Cost/learner	Enrollment	Cost/learner	Enrollment (thousands)	Cost/learner
1990/91	N/A	N/A	40,884	52.40	1,049	46.54
1991/92	N/A	N/A	34,781	50.29	1,300	44.99
1992/93	14,249	32.90	53,567	34.61	1,554	45.94
1993/94	28,498	33.90	62,283	28.32	2,486	31.72
1994/95	30,000	N/A	64,496	46.27	3,569	23.89
1995/96	41,018	7.80	75,433	46.06	3,592	32.21
1996/97	227,302	3.23	93,703	36.64	3,228	32.69
1997/98	308,806	2.07	112,214	34.39	2,548	25.47

Sources: Author's research. The cost per learner has been calculated US$ values at 1998

Enrollments increased to more than 130,000 within 20 years. The course fees have been kept at an affordable level, which, according to the NOS management, has enabled the increase in enrollments. Fees are as follows: For the Foundation course, Indian Rs 200 ($4.60); for the Secondary course, Indian Rs 800 ($18.40); and for the Senior Secondary course, Indian Rs 925 ($21.28). Learners from disadvantaged categories receive concessions.

Radio ECCA in the Canary Islands, too, charges student fees, recovering 70% of its costs from student fees. The fees are affordable to the learners, according to the Radio ECCA management. Currently, the learners at the basic education level pay about $23 per year. The conclusion is that the ODL programs have the potential to achieve financial self-sustainability,

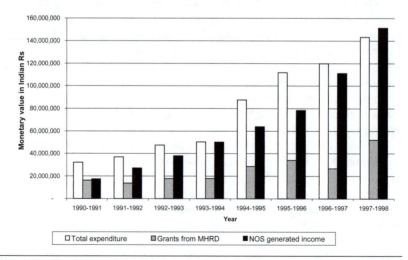

Figure 13.1 Cost Recovery at the NOS, India. *Source*: Author's Research.

at least partially over the years. External funding during the initial period helps the program to establish its roots.

The idea of charging fees from learners at the basic education level, however, poses an ethical question: Why should the learners who attempt their only learning opportunity through an OBE system be required to pay fees, while their counterparts in the conventional school receive their education free? India and the Canary Islands justify their actions on the grounds of affordability, while Thailand and Botswana do not charge their students at the functional literacy levels. In Thailand, however, learners at secondary levels pay for their studies.

On the issue of cost advantages and disadvantages, we can conclude that the programs of basic education that we have examined provide evidence of cost advantages in relation to "cost per learner," "cost per completer" (compared with regular schools), "economies of scale," and "potential for cost recovery." On the negative side, however, where data are available, there is a large gap between the cost per learner and the cost per graduate in the OBE programs. A large gap implies a large proportion of drop-outs and low graduation rates.

Although it is helpful to compare the cost of providing basic education in relation to a conventional alternative, such comparison needs to be treated with caution. Many programs providing basic education at a distance may not have a conventional alternative. Such a comparison can also be unfair, since the learners who study in an OBE program may come from different social and economic backgrounds to those in the conventional system. Some categories of learners may only be reached through ODL methods and media.

EVIDENCE OF OUTCOMES

Decisions on whether to invest in OBE as an add-on, and/or as an alternative, need to be informed by an understanding of the potential outcomes from various organizational structures. We have used five measures of outcomes: Enrollment and completion rates, contribution to increasing equity, the quality of teaching and learning, teachers' professional development, and internal efficiency in schools.

Table 13.4 presents the first measure of outcomes: Enrollment and completion rates. It compares, where possible, the completion rates of the ODL programs that we have studied, with the comparative figures of the conventional alternative.

In Table 13.4, the enrollment figures for OBE programs are presented as either the annual enrollments or the total in-roll, depending on the availability of data. These figures are compared with the total in-roll in the formal equivalent.

Table 13.4 Comparison of Enrollments in the OBE and Formal Systems

OBE system	Enrollment	Completion rate	Formal alternative	Enrollment	Completion/ Progression rate
IRI, South Africa	543,805 (total)	Not relevant	Primary	8,159,430 (in 1996)	Not relevant
ICT for teacher training, Botswana	40 teachers (total)	90%	Secondary teachers	641 untrained (in 1996)	Not available
BOCODOL, Botswana	1,641 (annual)	Not available	Secondary	111,134 (in 1995)	Not available
NOS, India	130 000 (annual) 400,000 (total)	26% junior secondary 23% senior secondary	Secondary	68,872,393 (in 1996)	70% junior secondary 76% senior secondary
DNFE, Thailand	2,547,664 (total)	64% functional literacy 40% primary 26% lower secondary 23% upper secondary	Primary Lower secondary Upper secondary	5,892,000 (in 1998) 2,424,300 in 1998) 1,695,400 (in 1998)	89.2% primary to secondary 86.9% junior secondary to upper secondary Not available
Radio ECCA, Canary Islands	13,207 (total)	Not available	Not applicable	Not applicable	Not applicable
DNFE, Botswana	6,121 (total)	Not available	Primary	318,629 (in 1996)	90% progression to junior secondary

Sources: Author's research

The table shows that some programs reach large numbers of learners, at least in absolute numbers, such as the South African IRI, the Indian NOS, and the Thailand DNFE. The ICT programs in classrooms in Botswana were on a pilot basis so the coverage had been purposely limited. Enrollments in Radio ECCA need to take into account the fact that the country was reaching about 96% literacy, and that the program was focusing on a small portion of learners who did not have access to basic education, among a total population of only 1.4 million in Canary Islands. The program was started in 1964 when the illiteracy rate was about 25%, and the program was reaching about 20,000 learners after the first five years.

In terms of completion rates, the OBE programs show lower graduation rates than their formal alternatives. Examples are the case of NOS in India and DNFE in Thailand. The pass rates in 1998 in secondary and senior secondary levels at NOS were 26% and 23%, respectively. Figures for the formal system were 70% and 76% for the year 1994 (Gaba, 1997). In Thailand, DNFE completion rates for the year 1998 were 64% in functional literacy, 40% for primary, 26% for lower secondary, and 23% for upper secondary. A possible reason for higher pass rates for functional literacy is that the course is taught face-to-face.

Comparisons of completion rates between OBE and formal systems need to be approached with caution. This is a difficult task, because, as evident from Table 13.4, only Indian NOS and Thailand DNFE provide figures for completion rates. Other programs do not keep figures on completion rates. In BOCODOL, for example, learners took the common government examination as private candidates, and their results were not fed into the BOCODOL administrative system. Comparisons also need to take into account the characteristics, backgrounds, and needs of learners studying at a distance (Murphy, 1992). According to educators at DNFE Botswana, for example, their adult learners do not always take examinations, so the completion rates do not necessarily reflect positive or negative outcomes. Some adults may only study a part of a course. They often have family and other social commitments, making it more difficult to allocate adequate time for learning, compared with students in a formal system.

Enrollments and completion rates in numerical figures alone do not provide a complete picture of outcomes reached from ODL programs. A mere comparison of the absolute numbers enrolled in the two systems would show that the OBE programs enroll only a small percentage compared with enrollment in the conventional system. The NOS in India, for example, enrolls only 0.58% of learners, compared with the total enrollments in the formal sector. A closer look at who benefits from OBE programs, however, reveals that these programs provide learning opportunities for sections of the population excluded from the formal sector. Nath, Sylva, and Grimes (1999), for example, illustrate how rural communities in Bangladesh are benefited from OBE programs.

The second outcome measure, therefore, is the contribution to increasing equity. The gender ratio, access to older populations, access to marginalized groups, and improving the performance of rural schools are some of the indicators that were used to measure the equity of educational provision. Table 13.5 compares how the researched programs contribute to equity in terms of these indicators.

The programs that we have examined show that they contribute to increasing the equity in a number of ways. These programs attract learners from both male and female audiences equally. The two in-school programs, IRI in South Africa and ICT in classrooms in Botswana, however, are exceptions; they are add-ons to existing school programs, so do not affect the gender equity. Nevertheless, these programs are aimed at increasing the quality of learning in poorly-resourced schools and, therefore, are contributing to increased equity in rural schools. This is particularly the case with the IRI program in South Africa.

Four of the out-of-school OBE programs in Table 13.5 (BOCODOL in Botswana, DNFE in Thailand, Radio ECCA in Canary Islands, and DNFE in Botswana) enroll more females than males. In these countries, the gender composition is more or less balanced in the formal system. The exception is the Indian NOS, where the gender proportion is biased towards males, which is the case in the conventional system, too. While we cannot attribute a reason for the higher enrollments from female learners in the four programs mentioned, it is worth noting that the majority of teachers or facilitators in these three programs are females. Enrolling more female facilitators might have an effect on redressing gender inequality. The out-of-school programs in Botswana, Thailand, and the Canary Islands demonstrate that the methods can sometimes attract a different audience, and do sometimes redress the gender balance.

The investigated programs also provide learning opportunities to certain sections of the community without basic education: Older populations, the geographically isolated, the physically disabled, and the culturally and socially marginalized. As Table 13.5 shows, four programs provide education opportunities to a significantly higher proportion of learners who are above the normal secondary school-attending age: 90% in India, 80% in Thailand, 99% in Canary Islands, and 91% in Botswana. Data available from NOS India and DNFE Thailand show that these two programs enroll learners from marginalized sections of the country, 33% and 47.9%, respectively. Socially marginalized groups include those belonging to disadvantaged tribes and castes, minority ethnic groups, prisoners, and disabled.

We have some evidence on the other three outcome measures in relation to the in-school programs: The quality of teaching and learning, teachers' professional development, and internal efficiency in schools. The in-school programs are mainly aimed at improving the quality of teaching

Table 13.5 Comparison of Contribution to Equity in the ODL and Conventional Systems

	ODL system					Conventional alternative	
	% Male	% Female	% above secondary schooling age	% marginalized		% Male	% Female
IRI, South Africa	50.4	49.6	Not applicable	Not applicable	Primary	Not applicable	Not applicable
ICT in classrooms, Botswana	46.8	53.2	Not applicable	Not applicable	Secondary	Not comparable	Not comparable
ICT for Teacher training, Botswana	n.a	n.a.	Not applicable	Not applicable	Secondary teachers	57	43 (1995)
BOCODOL, Botswana	31.4	68.6	Not available	Not available	Secondary	46.8	53.2 (1996)
NOS, India	62.7	37.3	90	33	Secondary	60.7	39.3 (1996)
DNFE, Thailand	47.3	52.7	80	47.9	Primary		
Secondary	51	49			Secondary		
Radio ECCA, Canary Islands	21.9	78.1	99	Not available	Primary and secondary	51	49
DNFE, Botswana	33.4	66.6	91	Not available	Primary	50.4	46.6

Source: Author's research

Notes: The age limit taken into account in calculating the percentage above secondary school age in the four out-of-school programmes vary as follows (according to the data availability): NOS in India, above 16 years; DNFE in Thailand, above 14 years; Radio ECCA in Canary Islands, above 16 years; and DNFE in Botswana, above 15 years. DNFE age category is for those who study at the functional literacy level. Canary Islands age category is for those who study at the basic education level.

and learning in schools. The IRI program in particular has been successful in increasing learning gains. This is the case with the program that we
have examined in South Africa, as well as the other IRI programs in the
developing world. IRI approach, since its inception in 1974 in Nicaragua,
has been intensively evaluated, both formatively and summarily, using a
range of quantitative and qualitative methods (Leigh & Cash, 1999). The
South African program also has been subject to a number of evaluations
reported in Potter and Leigh (1995) and Leigh (1995). The results show a
significant increase in the test scores of the students who learned from
radio programs, in some cases, a 20% increase for IRI learners compared to
a control group. The improvements in test scores have been higher for the
learners in rural schools than for those in the urban schools. The greatest
learning gain differentials, 21%, were demonstrated in farm schools where
infrastructure such as buildings, instructional materials, and skilled or
even unskilled teachers were weakest (Leigh & Cash, 1999).

In terms of teacher's professional development, two of our case studies are relevant: The IRI in South Africa and ICT for teacher training in
Botswana. The South African IRI has a special built-in teacher training
component. The OLSET, the NGO that implements the IRI program, has a
cadre of staff called teacher-coordinators, who help the teachers in the use
of the program. They visit schools regularly and conduct training workshops for the teachers. Evidence suggests that the regular exposure to the
daily English lessons and support of the coordinators help the teachers to
become better in both language and general teaching skills. English is the
second language for these teachers, who often do not have formal teacher
training qualifications. The other case study, the three-year teacher training program in Botswana, shows that ICT has the potential for successful teacher training at a distance. The program, which ran from 1996–99,
combined face-to-face teaching with self-study, facilitated by email communication between the learners and the tutors in the United Kingdom.

In the case of the IRI approach, there is some evidence that the children
who attend IRI lessons enjoy the learning experience, and are therefore
more likely to attend school (Leigh & Cash, 1999). Although we haven't
investigated this further, we can infer that more attendance at school and
increased learning gains would contribute to increasing the internal efficiency in schools.

The ICT-in-school program that we have discussed in Table 13.5 was
not examined for evidence of outcomes in terms of learning gains and
contributions to internal efficiency. ICT is a new approach in developing
country rural schools, promoted by both international donor agencies and
those with commercial interests. Interviews with managers and educators
in Botswana revealed that they were facing a difficult task in integrating
the new ICT into school curriculum. Our case study unraveled an array
of issues, from the top level (e.g., country's connection to the Internet),

down to the individual school level (e.g., costs and unreliability of Internet connectivity; see Edirisingha, 2001). There is a lack of understanding of, among others, the technical and financial implications of ICT, and pedagogical guidelines for successful use in classrooms, some of which have been well documented by Cuban (1986, 2001).

CONCLUDING REMARKS AND IMPLICATIONS FOR POLICY

This chapter was concerned with alternative methods of providing basic education, which, as Hopper (2000) points out, are yet to be given due attention, both by international communities and national governments in the fight against illiteracy in developing countries. Authorities on basic education have been demonstrating the value of non formal methods since the latter part of the 20th Century (see Coombs & Ahmed, 1974; Ahmed & Coombs, 1975; Young, Perraton, Jenkins, & Dodds, 1980; Perraton, 2000; and Yates & Bradley, 2000). With a view to strengthen the argument, this chapter covered three main themes: OBE organizational structures, their development in different parts of the world, and their costs and outcomes.

The chapter proposed a systematic way of looking at OBE organizational structures based on four criteria: The audience served, curriculum/content offered, the location of provision, and the technologies and methods used. The purpose was to help the policy maker understand the range of options available to offer different curricula and content to a diversity of learners, and to make decisions on how these organizational structures can be best used within different political and cultural contexts. In-school programs can improve the quality of instruction of existing provision, while the out-of-school programs can increase the access to basic education to adults, children, and a mixture of audiences. The chapter then assessed various governing mechanisms available, the range of curricula offered to a diversity of audiences, and the various media and methods used.

The cost-benefit analysis, presented in the chapter based on empirical evidence from a number of OBE programs, leads us to conclude that these programs have the potential to achieve financial self-sustainability, at least partially, over time, provided that the external funds help the program to establish during the initial period. On the issue of cost advantages and disadvantages, we can conclude that the OBE programs can achieve cost advantages in relation to cost per learner and cost per completer (compared with regular programs), economies of scale, and potential for cost recovery. There is also a large gap between the cost per learner and the cost per graduate in the OBE programs. A large gap implies a large proportion of drop-outs and low graduation rates.

The chapter also provided evidence of outcomes, in terms of enrollment rates, completion rates, contribution to increasing equity, learning gains, teachers' professional development, and internal efficiency in schools. Most of the outcomes were positive. Many out-of-school programs show evidence of large enrollments, although completion rates are lower than those in the formal system. In terms of contribution to increasing equity, the out-of-school programs demonstrate that they can redress gender imbalances in basic education. These programs also provide educational opportunities for the excluded sections of the population—socially, geographically, economically—as well as for those who are older than school-going age. Increasing learning gains, helping with teachers' capacity development, and improving school attendance are three outcomes observed in in-school programs. The IRI approach seems particularly successful in all three measures, while the ICT in schools approach is still to show evidence.

It is important to note that many OBE structures do not have a conventional alternative; therefore, a comparison can be unrealistic. Equally important to note is that, for some category of learners, OBE programs may offer the only opportunities to learn.

The message for the policy maker is a clear and a simple one. As the above analysis shows, there exist OBE programs with technologies and teaching and learning methods that have stood the test of time. Policy makers and the practitioners can be reassured that:

> Even with the old-fashioned techniques of print, cassettes, flipchart, and radio, results have been achieved in varied settings for literate and non-literate people, which confirm that methodology is not a problem. The combination of group study with prepared materials works in practice as predicted in theory. A developed body of expertise, reported in the literature, means that we know how to do it, and how to do it more effectively than we used to. (Perraton, 2000, p. 31)

What is now needed is the political will of governments, both as direct providers and international funders, and policy makers, to make use of OBE methods to increase and expand the access to basic education.

REFERENCES

Agency for International Development [AID] (n.d.). *Interactive radio instruction: Confronting crisis in basic education.* Newton, MA: Author, and Education Development Center.

Ahmed, M., & Coombs, P. H. (Eds.) (1975). *Education for rural development: Case studies for planners.* New York: Praeger.

Bosch, A. (1997). *Education and Technology Technical Notes Series, Vol. 1, No. 1, Interactive radio instruction: Twenty-three years of improving educational quality.* Washington, DC: World Bank.

Coombs, P. H., & Ahmed, M. (1974). *Attacking rural poverty: How non-formal education can help.* London: John Hopkins University Press.

Cuban, L. (1986). *Teachers and machines: The classroom uses of technology since 1920.* New York: Teachers College Press.

Cuban, L. (2001). *Oversold and underused: Computers in the classroom.* Cambridge, MA: Harvard University Press.

Dodds, T., & Edirisingha, P. (2000). Organisational and delivery structures. In J. Bradley & C. Yates (Eds.), *Basic education at a distance: World review of distance education and open learning* (Vol. 2., pp. 87–109). London: RoutledgeFalmer, and Vancouver: Commonwealth of Learning.

Durán, J. (2001). The Mexican Telesecundaria: Diversification, internationalization, change, and update. *Open Learning, 16*(2), 169–177.

Edirisingha, P. (2001). *Basic education at a distance: Costs, outcomes, and sustainability.* (Final Report of a two-year Basic Education research project.) Cambridge, UK: International Research Foundation for Open Learning.

Gaba, A. K. (1997). Open schooling in India: Development and effectiveness. *Open Learning, 12*(3), 43–49.

Hopper, W. (2000). Nonformal education, distance education and the restructuring of schooling: Challenges for a new basic education policy. *International Review of Education, 46*(1/2), 5–30.

Leigh, S. (1995). *Changing times in South Africa: Remodelling interactive learning.* Washington, DC: Educational Development Center.

Leigh, S., & Cash, F. (1999). Effectiveness and methodology of IRI. In A. Dock & J. Helwig (Eds.), *Education and Technology Notes Series: Vol. 4, No. 1. Interactive radio instruction: Impact, sustainability and future directions* (pp. 27–35). Washington, DC: World Bank.

Murphy, P. (1992). Effectiveness of full-time second-level distance education in three African countries. In P. Murphy & A. Zhiri (Eds.), *Distance education in Anglophone Africa: Experience with secondary education and teacher training.* Washington, DC: The World Bank.

Nath, S. R., Sylva, K., & Grimes, J. (1999). Raising basic education levels in rural Bangladesh: The impact of a non-formal education program. *International Review of Education, 45*(1), 5–26.

National Open School (1991). *A decade of open learning: Decennial report 1980–1990* [Internal Report]. New Delhi: National Open School.

Perraton, H. (Ed.) (1982). *Alternative routes to formal education: distance teaching for school equivalency.* Baltimore, MD: John Hopkins University Press.

Perraton, H. (2000). *Open and distance learning in the developing world.* London: Routledge.

Perraton, H., & Creed, C. (2000). Applying new technologies and cost-effective delivery system sin basic education [Thematic Study]. In UNESCO (Ed.), *Education for All 2000 assessment.* Paris: UNESCO. Retrieved March 19, 2007, from http://www.unesco.org/education/efa/efa_2000_assess.

Potter, C., & Leigh, S. (1995). *English in Action in South Africa 1992–1993: A formative evaluation* [Internal Document]. Johannesburg: OLSET.

Pridmore, P., & Nduba, S. (2000). The power of open and distance learning in basic education for health and the environment. In C. Yates & J. Bradley (Eds.), *Basic education at a distance* (pp. 192–204). London: Routledge Falmer.

Sadiman, A. S. (1994). The Indonesian Open Junior Secondary Schools. In M. Mukhopadhyay & S. Phillips (Eds.), *Open schooling: Selected experiences* (pp. 91–102). Vancouver: The Commonwealth of Learning.

Warr, D. (1992). *Distance teaching in the village*. Cambridge, UK: International Extension College.

Yates, C. (2000). Outcomes: What have we learned. In C. Yates & J. Bradley (Eds.), *Basic education at a distance* (pp. 229–247). London: Routledge Falmer.

Yates, C., & Bradley, J. (2000). *Basic education at a distance*. London: Routledge Falmer.

Yates, C., & Tilson, T. (2000). Basic education at a distance: An introduction. In C. Yates & J. Bradley (Eds.), *Basic education at a distance* (pp. 3–26). London: Routledge Falmer.

Young, M., Perraton, H., Jenkins, J., & Dodds, T. (1980). *Distance teaching for the third world: The lion and the clockwork mouse*. London: Routledge.

14

FROM BAOBAB TO BONSAI

Revisiting Methodological Issues in the Costs and Economics of Distance Education and Distributed e-Learning

Thomas Hülsmann

University of Oldenburg, Germany

INTRODUCTION

The title indicates the historical dimension, which comprises the development of distance education to include e-learning. Consequently, the chapter is written in two main sections. The first (Distance Education) characterizes traditional (Fordist) distance education and describes the methodology, which co-evolved with the corresponding institutional developments. My main reference papers for this period are Wagner (1972) and Jamison & Klees (1975). They illustrate that the strengths of Fordist distance education lie in its potential cost-efficiency and the potentially high quality of teaching material. The lack of student/teacher interactivity is considered as its main weakness.

The second section (E-Learning) gauges the impact of the Information Communications Technologies (ICT)[1] revolution on distance education. ICT, in principle, aims to improve the quality of teaching material even further, but, even more importantly, it allows us to facilitate responsive teacher/student (and peer) interactivity at a distance. This strength of e-learning, however, comes at a price: The increasing *variable cost per student* threatens to erode the cost-efficiency advantage of Fordist distance education. The focus here is on distributed e-learning with Jewett (2000a, 2000b) as the main reference paper.

The third section is exploratory in nature and looks at the options to recover some of the efficiencies lost in the transition from distance education to e-learning. Two options are considered: (1) better content management to facilitate re-use of resources; and (2) exploiting the synergies of cooperation.

DISTANCE EDUCATION

Distance teaching may have a long history, but it has moved towards educational mainstream only in the 1960s and 1970s, which have been considered as the "golden age of education" (Papadopoulos, 1994). Due to a virtuous circle of expanding demand powered by demographic and economic growth, cold war systems' competition, and, last but not least, a new theoretical conceptualization of the role of education for economic growth, a historically unprecedented expansion of the education sector took place (Coombs, 1985).[2]

Especially the shifting economic perception of education is of interest here, since it reflects that at the same time when *distance education* established itself as a new subdisipline of education, *economics of education* established itself as a new subdiscipline of economics. The central tenets of this new subdiscipline are comprised in the *human capital theory*, which argues that individuals invest in themselves by acquiring new skills and knowledge, and that the aggregate impact of such investments would lead to economic growth. Seeing education as investment rather than consumption indicates the new interest of economists,[3] and means that economists apply their standard concepts and methodologies to examine education. What will be discussed in the following as "methodologies to researching the costs and economics of distance education" is little more than an application of concepts and approaches of the *economics of education* to *distance education*.

Definition and Theory

The "minimalist" definition of distance education is "education at a distance;" that is, a process of teaching and learning where teacher and learner are geographically separated most of the time. This limiting condition had important implications for the organization of the teaching and learning process itself. A more detailed definition of distance education is presented in Table 14.1. While traditional education in schools and univer-

Table 14.1 Definition of Distance Education

Distance education is:

1. the quasi-permanent separation of teacher and learner throughout the length of the learning process
2. the use of technical media—print, audio, video or computer—to unite teacher and learner and carry the content of the course
3. the influence of an educational organization both in the planning and preparation of learning materials and in the provision of student support services
4. the provision of two-way communication so that the student may benefit from or even initiate dialogue.

Source: Keegan (1990)

sities allowed a seamless movement from content presentation to dialogue, and back, distance education had to separate these traditionally intricately interleafed processes. Moreover, given the then limited means to communicate at a distance (little more than correspondence by "snail mail"), the onus of the teaching learning process had to be shifted from dialogue to the development and design of teaching materials, or, to put it differently, from external interactivity (teacher–student and peer interactivity) to internal interactivity (student content interactivity) (Hülsmann, 2000).[4]

What do we mean by *internal interactivity*? Given the lack of responsiveness of distance education, it was of utmost importance to design the teaching material as a "tutorial in print" to compensate for poor teacher/student communication in two respects: (1) the material had to be written in a clear and accessible manner to pre-empt questions arising from inconsistencies or sloppy arguments; and (2) *in-text questions* and *in-text activities* had to be included to guide the way the student could interrogate the text.[5] This way of designing interactivity into the teaching material led to a specific instructional design quality associated with distance education, a result of which working through distance teaching materials is an experience quite different from "just reading through" a textbook.

The necessities arising from the condition of geographical distance produced institutional responses which, beyond all differences in detail, were similar in a number of substantial aspects. Otto Peters, after having completed a major international survey of institutions teaching at a distance in the late 1960s, listed, among others, the following characteristics: Rational planning, division of labor, use of technology, and standardization. It was Peters who coined the formula of *distance education as the most industrialized form of education* (Peters, 1967, cited in Keegan, 1994). While this statement created some brouhaha in pedagogical circles, it was much in step with the powerful agenda of international agencies like the World Bank and the OECD, where human capital theory has been adopted.[6] An industrialized form of education must have attracted all those who called for cost-effectiveness in education.[7]

Two events have contributed importantly to the shaping of a methodology of distance education: (1) the founding of the British Open University and (2) a number of major instructional technology projects funded by the World Bank.

Costing the Open University

Soon after the foundation of the British Open University (OU) a number of research papers were published in order to find out if the new distance teaching model lived up to its promises of cost-efficiency (Laidlaw & Layard, 1974; Lumdsen & Ritchie, 1975; Mace, 1978; Rumble, 1976; Orivel, 1987; Wagner 1972, 1977). We select here Wagner (1972) in order to illustrate some of the methodological issues.

Wagner started describing the OU teaching system by putting special emphasis on the use of "impersonal media." The methodological framework was that of *cost-efficiency analysis* (CEA).[8] Cost-efficiency is a concept which relates *costs of inputs* to *outputs*. Cost-efficiency analysis compares intervention strategies by relating the size of output to the costs of inputs necessary to produce these outputs. *Other things being equal,* the one strategy is to be preferred which produces the highest output at lowest costs.

Applying this approach to universities, Wagner had to identify the output, both of the conventional university system and of the Open University. He considered research and teaching as main outputs of any university. The teaching output can be measured in *number of students* taught or in *number of graduates*. It soon became obvious that, in order to make a fair comparison between the two teaching systems, a number of adjustments had to be made: (1) adjustments to account for difference in research output; (2) adjustment for types of students, including adjusting for the difference between part-time and full-time students; and (3) a final adjustment to make cost figures comparable.

To begin with the last adjustment: The figures for the conventional universities, which dated back to 1968–69, were increased by 22% to convert them into 1971 prices to account for the 22% cost rise at conventional universities during this period. Cost data for the OU were also deflated to 1971 prices. (Wagner, 1972, p.164)

The adjustment for different research outputs was done in the following way: First, in a backflush costing approach (Rumble, 1997, p. 59), Wagner calculated first the total unadjusted *recurrent costs* in both systems. He got for the conventional universities (CU; p. 168):

(14.1.1) $$TC_{CU} = £\,284\,748\,000$$

and for the Open University (OU; Rumble, 1997, p. 168):

(14.1.2) $$TC_{OU} = £\,9\,177\,000$$

In a next step, Wagner accounted for the difference in research requirements (Rumble, 1997, p. 168, footnote 6). Officially the research requirements at conventional universities absorb 35% of faculty time, while at the OU time set aside for research was then 10% of faculty time. Adjustment was done in the following manner:

(14.1.3)

$$TC_{CU} = £\,284\,748\,000 - (£\,284\,748\,000 * 35\%) = £\,284\,748\,000 - £\,9\,9\,661\,800 = £\,185\,086\,200$$

(14.1.4)

$$TC_{OU} = £\,9\,177\,000 - (£\,9\,177\,000 * 10\%) = £\,9\,177\,000 - £\,917\,700 = £\,8\,259\,300$$

The cost-efficiency ratio Wagner calculated is the *average cost per student*. However student populations differ in a number of respects. While, at the time, the OU taught only undergraduate courses, the course offerings at conventional universities are more diversified and require more resources, including faculty time. Moreover, the OU taught only part-time students, while the conventional universities taught mainly full-time students. The weighing for the conventional system is detailed in Table 14.2. Given that one part-time student was rated as two full-time students, the notional numbers in Table 14.2 are N = 232 137 for the conventional, and N = 18 250 in the OU system.

Hence, the average recurrent costs are as follows (Rumble, 1997, p. 170, footnote 7):

(14.1.5)

$$AC_{CU} = \frac{£\,185\,086\,200}{281\,927} = £\,657$$

(14.1.6)

$$AC_{OU} = \frac{£\,8\,259\,300}{18\,250} = £\,453$$

Table 14.2 Adjusting for Type of Students

	Weight	Actual number	Weighted number
Full-time			
Undergraduates	x 1.0	173,510	173,510
Postgraduates			
Education	x 1.0	6,841	6,841
Arts	x 2.0	12,248	24,496
Science	x 3.0	18,695	56,085
Part-time			
Undergraduates	x 0.5	4,616	2,308
Postgraduates			
Education	x 0.5	2,684	1,342
Arts	x 1.0	5,943	5,943
Science	x 1.5	7,601	11,402
Total		232,138	281,927

Source: Adapted from Wagner (1972, p. 171, Table IV)

In order to adjust for the difference in drop-outs, Wagner first set to determine the total and average cost equation as a function of N. In order to do this, he would need to understand the *cost-structure* of the different teaching systems. By cost-structure we mean the relative composition of the fixed and variable costs in the total cost equation. For the OU, Wagner observed the prominent use of "impersonal media," which was leading to a high ratio of fixed-to-variable costs.

> This high ratio of fixed-to-variable costs is in contrast to conventional universities, where the largest single item in recurrent expenditure—academic salaries—is directly linked to the number of students. (Wagner, 1972, p. 165)

This made him conclude that in the conventional university system there are practically no fixed costs (e.g., for the development of teaching material) for direct teaching, and that it is possible to write the respective total costs as function of number of students as follows:

(14.1.7) $TC_{CU}(N) = £ 657* N$

N being the number of students, while £ 657 = V represents the *variable cost per student.*

Due to the prominent use of "impersonal media," Wagner is able to decompose the unadjusted total costs of the OU in a fixed and a variable cost component (cf. Wagner, 1972, p. 168, Table II):

(14.1.8) $TC_{OU}(36\,500) = £\,6\,945\,000 + £\,2\,232\,000$

Elsewhere in the paper (p.166) Wagner identifies the "direct student costs" (i.e. *variable cost per student* at the OU) as $V_{OU} = £ 61$. This allows one to decompose $TC_{OU}(36\,500) = £\,8\,259\,300$ into fixed and variable cost components which takes the adjustment for research into account.[9] Knowing the number of students (N = 36 500) and the variable cost per student, we can write the variable component as: $V_{OU}*N = £\,61*36\,500 = £\,2\,226\,500$. Given that the general form of the total cost equation reads $TC = F + V*N$, and knowing both, TC and V*N, we can determine the fixed part as $F_{OU} = TC_{OU} - V_{OU}*N = £\,8\,259\,300 - £\,2\,232\,000 = £\,6\,032\,800$. This allows us to write:

(14.1.9) $TC_{OU}(36\,500) = £\,6\,032\,800 + £\,61 * 36\,500$

Hence, in analogy to (14.1.7), we can write the total recurrent costs at the OU as a function of student numbers in the following way:

(14.1.10) $TC_{OU}(N) = £\,6\,032\,800 + £\,61 * N$

Equations (14.1.7) and (14.1.10) allow deriving the average cost functions by dividing the total costs by the respective number of students. For the conventional teaching system we get:

(14.1.11) $\quad AC_{CU}(N) = \dfrac{TC_{CU}(N)}{N} = \dfrac{N * £657}{N} \Rightarrow AC_{CU}(N) = £657$

Note that this means that average costs in the conventional system do not depend on number of students. This signals that the conventional system has no potential for scale economies. This is different for the OU system. Here we get:

(14.1.12) $\quad AC_{OU}(N) = \dfrac{TC_{OU}(N)}{N} \Rightarrow AC_{OU}(N) = \dfrac{£6\,032\,800}{N} + £61$

The first graph in Figure 14.1 refers to the total cost functions (14.1.7) and (14.1.10), while the second graph depicts equations (14.1.11) and (14.1.12). Total cost equations are linear functions with different gradients.[10]

In order to adjust for the expected different level of drop-outs, Wagner first determined the cost per graduate at conventional universities, then calculated the OU drop-out rate, for which the cost per graduates in both systems would be equal. Cost per graduate in the conventional system amounted to between £4,000 and £4,500 (Wagner, 1972, p.176). Hence, in the optimal case, we can assume:

(14.1.13) $\quad\quad\quad AC(graduate)_{CU} = £\,4,000$

In order to determine the OU drop-out rate, for which cost per graduate at the OU equals the cost per graduate in the conventional system, Wagner assumes that the OU system is with 37, 500 students in a *steady state*. The total recurrent cost of the system in steady state is therefore:

(14.1.14) $\quad TC_{OU}(37,500) = £\,61 * 37\,500 + £\,6\,032\,800 = £\,8\,320\,300$

At the same time the OU has an annual intake of about 15,000 students. With a 100% retention rate (denoted below as y %),[11] this would mean that "no student is lost," and the same number graduate as come new into the system. In this fictitious case, we would say that the retention rate is 100% and would calculate:

(14.1.15) $\quad AC(graduate)_{OU} = \dfrac{£8\,320\,300}{15\,000 * 100\%} = £555$

In order to find the OU drop-out rate, for which the cost per graduate in the conventional system is equal to the cost per cost per graduate in the OU system, we need to solve the following equation:

(14.1.16) $\quad \dfrac{£8\,320\,300}{15\,000 * y\,\%} = £\,4000 \Rightarrow \dfrac{£8\,320\,300}{15\,000 * £\,4000} = y\,\% \Rightarrow \dfrac{832\,030\,000}{60\,000\,000} = 14$

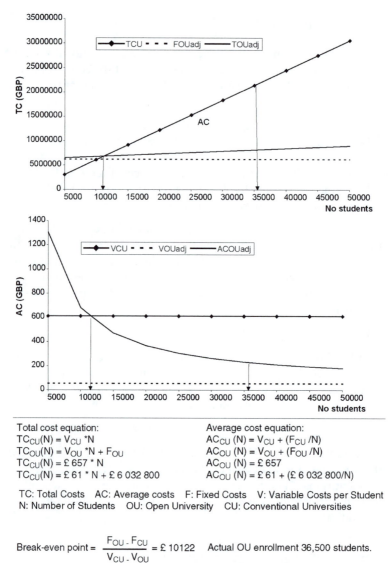

Total cost equation:
$TC_{CU}(N) = V_{CU} * N$
$TC_{OU}(N) = V_{OU} * N + F_{OU}$
$TC_{CU}(N) = £ 657 * N$
$TC_{CU}(N) = £ 61 * N + £ 6 032 800$

Average cost equation:
$AC_{CU}(N) = V_{CU} + (F_{CU}/N)$
$AC_{OU}(N) = V_{OU} + (F_{OU}/N)$
$AC_{OU}(N) = £ 657$
$AC_{OU}(N) = £ 61 + (£ 6 032 800/N)$

TC: Total Costs   AC: Average costs   F: Fixed Costs   V: Variable Costs per Student
N: Number of Students   OU: Open University   CU: Conventional Universities

Break-even point = $\dfrac{F_{OU} - F_{CU}}{V_{CU} - V_{OU}}$ = £ 10122   Actual OU enrollment 36,500 students.

Figure 14.1 Definition of distance education. Source: Based on Wagner (1972)

This means that the OU system would lose its cost-efficiency advantage only if the retention rate is lower than 14 %, or if the drop-out rate would be larger than 86 %.

Hence the OU system differs from the conventional teaching system by its composition of fixed and variable costs. While in the conventional system there is a strong linkage between total direct costs and number of students in the system, the linkage in distance education is less strong. It is possible to expand the system with slower rising costs.

Costing Teaching with Media

Besides the studies, which were costing the OU, another set of research studies became quite influential in the formation of the methodology of costing distance education. They were commissioned in the 1970s and 1980s by the World Bank and UNESCO and included Jamison, Suppes, & Wells (1974); Carnoy & Levin (1975); Wells (1976); Eicher (1977, 1980); Klees & Wells (1977); Eicher & Orivel (1980); UNESCO (1977, 1980, 1982); Perraton (1982); Jamison (1982, 1987); and Bates (1995). These studies focused more directly than the OU studies on the cost of instructional media. Given the high capital investments such instructional technology projects required, much attention had to be given to the question of capital costs. This section will focus on this aspect, since it is a central part of the cost-analysis of distance education.

What are costs? There are two aspects worth discussing: (1) *costs as opportunity costs*; and (2) *costs as consumption of value*. Bowman (1966) distinguishes between "costs as something put in" and "costs as something forgone." Walsh (1970) reviews the historical usage of the term leading to the second option, which defines costs as *opportunity costs*: "The cost of any action is what is forgone...as a result of taking that action" (Livesey, 1993, p. 46). Such a conceptualization of costs can complicate matters, since it would mean, for example, that the cost of setting up an instructional radio project may include the forgone income of a fertilizer plant, which was not built due to the available capital being already tied up in the instructional radio project (cf., Jamison & Klees, 1975, p. 339). While including the whole set of alternatives into one's cost consideration makes sense, when it comes to rank alternative investment choices, it is not always a practicable option. However, there are opportunity costs which can be taken into account, and which can be incorporated into the methodology: The *opportunity costs on forgone interest*.

Since capital costs are by definition the costs of items whose value is *not* consumed within a given financial year, it is only the capital costs for which interest forgone has to be calculated. This leads to the second point: *Costs as consumption of value*. Who consumes which part of the value of the capital cost item (e.g., a radio transmitter, a computer, or course material)? The question is how to convert the upfront expenditure on an item, which is not consumed within one financial period, into annual costs which can be charged to those consuming the value. To simplify matters, we assume that during its lifetime, the value derived from the respective capital investment is the same (the use value of a satellite dish is not dependent on its age as long as it functions). Hence the problem can formulated

Table 14.3 Two Distinctions

Costs	capital	recurrent*
fixed	fixed and capital, e.g. buying a new server	fixed and recurrent, e.g. manager's salary
variable	variable and capital, e.g. science kits	variable and recurrent, e.g. production and mailing of course material

Notes: Other authors (e.g., Rumble, 1997) differentiate between capital and operating costs.

*Operating costs then are subdivided as recurrent and non-recurrent operating costs.

like this: How can we convert an upfront capital cost into an equal stream of annual costs? The conventional depreciation by dividing the upfront investment by the expected useful lifetime, translates to one way of doing this, but obviously takes no account of forgone interest. Given the formidable level of capital costs incurred in instructional technology projects, ignoring interest is likely to severely underestimate costs. See Table 14.3 which distinguishes capital and recurring costs.

At this point, readers are generally provided with an *annualization factor* (cf., equation 14.2.1), by which the planner has to multiply its upfront investment sum to get an annual cost, which incorporates the forgone interest.

(14.2.1) $$a(n,r) = \frac{r * (1+r)^n}{(1+r)^n - 1}$$

where *n* stands for number of years and *r* for interest rate.

Example: Upfront investment US\$ 2,000; lifetime of capital good four years (n = 4); and the interest rate r = 7.5%. In this case a(n,r) = 0.2986 and the annual rate US\$597.

The following may help to make sense of the otherwise rather opaque looking formula. Assuming that the consumed value in the future years is equal, we can denote the respective monetary by *A*. The monetary value of a sum depends on the time you get it. Assuming the logic of interest, a sum *A* received in the ith year can be A/(1 + r). Consequently the upfront investment is to be understood as the *present value (PV)* of the annuity *A* and will amount to the following sum:

(14.2.2) $$PV = \sum_{i=1}^{n} \frac{A}{(1+r)^i}$$

This makes sense: The present value of a fixed amount *A*, which will be received over a given number of years, is the sum of *A*s weighed by the interest forgone, which depends on the year in which *A* is received.

Since *A* is a fixed amount and does not depend on *i*, we can write:

(14.2.3) $$PV = \sum_{i=1}^{n} \frac{A}{(1+r)^i} = A * \sum_{i=1}^{n} \frac{1}{(1+r)^i}$$

At this point, the mathematician will identify in the second factor on the right a *geometrical series*. Such a series can be written in its closed form as shown on the right side of equation (14.2.4) (for the proof cf. Appendix 14.1):

(14.2.4) $$\sum_{i=1}^{n} \frac{1}{(1+r)^i} = \frac{(1+r)^n - 1}{(1+r)^n * r}$$

We note that the right hand expression of equation (14.2.4) is the *inverse* of the right hand expression of equation (14.2.1). This allows us to re-write equation (14.2.3) as:

(14.2.5) $$PV = \sum_{i=1}^{n} \frac{A}{(1+r)^i} = A * \frac{(1+r)^n - 1}{(1+r)^n * r} = \frac{A}{a(n,r)} \Rightarrow$$
$$A = PV * a(n,r)$$

Given that *PV* represents our upfront expenditure, we can calculate *A* by deciding on *n* and estimating *r*. It turns out that the function *PV* is the standard Excel function *PMT*.[12] The *annualized investment* (as opposed to the upfront investment) is consequently calculated by adding together all the annual installments. While for simple depreciation, the sum of the depreciation rates reconstitutes the original invested sum, adding up the annualized rates over the respective years amounts to an often considerably higher sum. This difference signals to what extent simple depreciation would underestimate "real" costs.

This can be illustrated by referring to Jamison and Klees' report on costs of *instructional radio* (IR) in Thailand, Mexico, and Indonesia, and *instructional television* (ITV) in Colombia, American Samoa, Mexico, and Ivory Cost (Jamison & Klees, 1975). The costs are reported in Table 14.4.

Again, comparisons require adjustments. Monetary adjustments are made by converting all figures into U.S. dollars using the U.S. Gross National Product deflator to bring them to the common baseline of US$ 1972. The costs considered in all cases include program production costs, central administration, and transmission and reception costs. A common lifetime of 25 years for all capital investments was used. A *sensitivity analysis of the capital costs* was conducted by annualizing them for the rates $r = 0\,\%$, $r = 7.5\,\%$, $r = 15\,\%$. Figure 14.2 visualizes the considerable effect of varying interest rates. If an interest rate of $r = 15\%$ is to be expected, the project would need about 80 000 viewers/listeners more to bring average costs down to the level of AC calculated on the basis of $r = 0\%$, and about 50 000, when calculated on the basis of $r = 7.5\%$ (cf. Figure 14.2).

Table 14.4 Cost of Instructional Television (ITV) and Instructional Radio (IR)

Project	Year	N	h	F	V	AC	AC/V	AC/h
Instructional Radio (IR)								
Thailand	1967	800,000	25	$100,400	$0.221	$0.35	1.57	0.014
Mexico	1973	2,800	233	$37,700	$0.110	$13.57	123.40	0.058
Indonesia	1971	1,200,000	100	$1,202,400	$0.320	$1.32	4.13	0.013
Instructional Television (ITV)								
Colombia	1965	275,000	50.25	$624,000	$0.859	$3.13	3.64	0.062
American Samoa	1972	8,100	145	$1,268,000	$1.859	$158.40	85.21	1.092
Mexico	1972	29,000	360	$598,000	$2.859	$23.48	8.21	0.065
Ivory Cost	1970	745,000	180	$2,454,000	$3.859	$7.15	1.85	0.040

Source: Based on Tables IV and V in Jamison & Klees (1975, pp. 356–357).

Notes: N denotes the number of listeners/viewers; h the number of IR/ITV hours produced; F, V, AC, as usual denote *fixed costs, variable cost per student* and *average cost per student* respectively. The quotient AC/V denotes the level, to which the potential for scale economies is exhausted. AC/h (written as "Student -Hr.Cost") denotes the *average cost per student per hour of radio or television,* and is calculated by dividing the total input costs by N*h, i.e. TC/(N*h) = (TC/N)*(1/h) = AC/h. The figures reported in the table are in US $ '72 and fixed capital costs are annualized at r = 7.5%. Remember that AC cannot fall below V. Hence the nearer to one, the more scale economies are exhausted.

Note also the type of output measures used (i.e., *viewing or listening hours*). This parameter multiplies the number of listeners reached with the number of learning hours produced. These indicators allow calculating cost-efficiency measures (such as *average cost per student per learning hour* or AC/h). Obviously, AC/h is a highly context sensitive measure and, as such, of limited informational value for the planner. To include as a further measure, AC/V, which measures the extent to which the potential of scale economies has already been exhausted, might be seen as trying to compensate for the high context sensitivity of the *cost per student per learning hour measure* (AC/h, see Table 14.5).

The absence of *cost-effectiveness* measures in the strict sense[13] should be noted. The idea of cost-effectiveness analysis to relate input costs to outcome-based indicators measuring the effectiveness of learning has been largely abandoned in favor of simple-to-collect *performance measures* (number of students/listeners/viewers, number of graduates, number of lessons produced). One reason for this notable absence of genuine cost-effectiveness measures was the reluctance of economists to tread the minefield of measuring and comparing learning outcomes in a way attributable to a specific intervention (e.g., teaching strategy, medium used). The second reason was the *hypothesis of media equivalence,* which suggests that planners could be relaxed about media choice since there is little demonstrable impact of it on learning effectiveness.[14] If used professionally, learning outcomes would not vary significantly with media choice. Under the

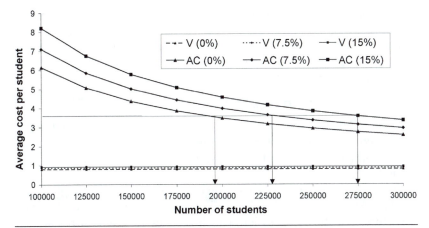

Figure 14.2 Effects of interest rates on cost per student. *Source*: Based on Jamison & Klees (1975, pp. 356–357)

assumption that you can teach effectively in any medium used appropriately, the cost per learning hour could be treated as a proxy measure for cost-effectiveness.

However, the high context sensitivity of measures like AC/h greatly reduces their informational value for planners and decision makers. This is why Hülsmann (2000) suggests focusing on media specific *fixed costs of development per student learning hour* (cost/SLH). He was able to identify different orders of magnitude for the costs/SLH for the various media. In fact, he suggested characterizing the various media by a pair of figures: (1) *fixed costs of development per student learning hour*; and (2) a *variable cost per student* per suitable unit of distribution (which may be for printing and mailing costs for a set of study guides, or for cassette media replication and mailing of cassettes). The respective pair of figures would allow modeling the costs of media. This suggests abandoning the *Procrustean bed* of cost-effectiveness analysis,[15] and instead to use cost-analysis *to keep cost implications of instructional design decisions visible.* Educators should decide

Table 14.5 Cost per SLH

Medium	Cost per student learning hour (in 1998 US$)	Ratio to print costs
Print	825	1
Radio	24,750 to 44,550	x 50
Television	148,500 to 206,250	x 150 to x 180
Audio	280,050	x 36
Video	29,700 to 138,600	x 36 to x 170
CD-ROM	33,000	x 40

Source: Based on Perraton & Moses (2004, p. 149) and Hülsmann (2000, pp. 17–19).

about their instructional design choices close to the context (which would enable them to take into account *learner profile, content characteristics,* and *media capabilities*). Modeling the costs would provide quick feedbacks to the planners and instructional designers if the educationally preferred option is affordable.

Fordist Distance Education: SWOT Analysis

The methodology to analyze the costs and economics of distance education developed in the context of the emergence of economics of education, and the formation of distance teaching universities and instructional media projects.

The *strengths* of distance education comprises the possibly high quality of teaching material on one side, and on the other side the peculiar cost-structure of distance education, which reduces average cost per student through scale-economies. Both cost-efficiency and the flexibility of distance education extended the options of access to education in general, and higher education in particular.

Two *caveats* should be added here. First, bringing down the *average cost per student* does not mean bringing down total costs. In fact, total costs will rise (albeit less quickly than in conventional system). Moreover, to establish a system which harvests scale economies in the pursuit of lower average cost per student does not come cheap, and may not be affordable for resource poor countries (Butcher & Roberts, 2004, p. 242).

Second, while Perraton's *Costing Cube* (Figure 14.3; based on Perraton, 2000) clearly identifies the route to go in order to increase cost-efficiencies,

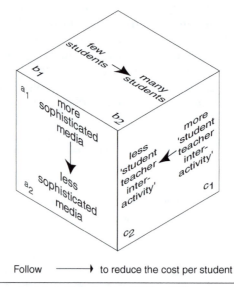

Follow ——▶ to reduce the cost per student

Figure 14.3 Costing cube. Adapted from Perraton (2000, p. 137)

it needs to be added that the parameters F, V, and N are not independent from each other and cannot be set at will by the planner. Obviously, it would be best to limit direct student/tutor interaction (a central element of student support and generally contributing to V) and/or go for less glamorous media to lower fixed costs F. However, this may backfire since it may reduce the attractiveness of the program leading to declining enrollment rates N, which, in turn, might prevent the institution from fully harvesting the scale economies, leading possibly to unexpectedly high average costs.

The main *weakness* of this type of distance education is nothing but the other side of the coin of its major strength—its cost-efficiency. While the possibility for student/teacher interaction has been made part of the very definition of distance education (to distinguish it from learning through media, like reading books and listening to the radio), it has never been generally accepted as a full substitute for the dialogue possible in conventional settings, not least because of the lack of responsiveness of traditional communication media (Rumble, 2001).[16]

A further weakness of dedicated distance teaching institutions is the trade-off between *scale* and *scope* (*course load*, i.e., the number of courses an institution offers). Any attempt to substantially diversify course offerings means eroding the scale economies on which cost-efficiency is based[17] (the effect is visualized in Figure 14.4: An institution increases course offerings from 58 to 87. While *scale economies* continue to bring average costs down, the effects operate on a higher level depending on the level of course offerings).

Like strengths and weaknesses, *opportunities* and *threads* seem to be like Siamese twins. The opportunities for distance education lie in its inherent flexibility, which became increasingly attractive in the wake of

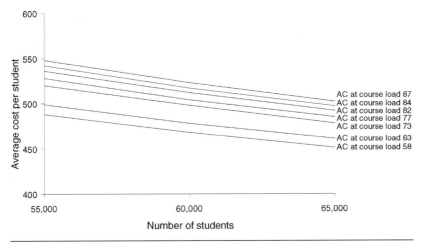

Figure 14.4 Course offerings and cost per student. *Source*: Based on data in UNESCO. (2002, p. 74) Data are projected unit costs per student at the OUUK (cost figures in in GBP).

the *knowledge society*. The sequence of studying and working was substituted by a more complex pattern of training and working and part-time studying (Jarvis, 1983). But while the market for flexible learning certainly expanded, new competitors entered the field, and those who needed flexible and part-time modes of studying ceased to remain a captive market for dedicated distance institutions.

As early as 1994, Greville Rumble reflected on the *vulnerability* of distance teaching institutions, observing that, increasingly, conventional universities entered the market (Rumble, 1994). In Britain, the drive to increase *internal efficiencies* in conventional universities (i.e., increasing the throughput of students without proportional increase in funding) led to experimentation with resource-based teaching.[18] While it may well be that within the conventional system, the quality of the student support for out-of-campus students and the quality of the resource material is not of the standard which dedicated distance teaching institutions are able to offer, the *perceived* quality and the identical degree—which camouflages the mode of study—attracts students. Moreover, given the high diversity of course offerings in conventional universities and improvements of authoring tools (especially in an increasingly digital environment), conventional universities would not encounter the same trade-off between scale and scope as the distance teaching universities experience.

Rumble's diagnosis does not suggest that the conventional university, which develops into a dual mode one, offers the better quality or is more cost-efficient. What makes dedicated institutions so vulnerable is the *piranha effect*: The aggregate effect of mushrooming competition (most universities nowadays run some distance teaching courses),[19] which eats into the formerly captive market of distance learners, thus eroding the much needed scale economies.

The ICT revolution has even amplified this vulnerability, since it further facilitates the entry of competitors to the distance learner market, and it drives up variable cost per student—at least if the new ICT capabilities of communicating at a distance is to be fully exploited.

E-LEARNING

We use the term e-learning to refer to ICT-based teaching and learning.[20] Sometimes the term distributed e-learning is used to refer to forms of e-learning, which comply with the *minimalist definition of distance education*: A form of education where teacher and students are separated for most of the time. In order not to overload terminology here, the term e-learning is generally used to refer to e-learning as part of distance education.[21]

Types of E-learning

ICT-based education means exploiting the capabilities of *information* and *communication* technologies for teaching and learning. E-learning can develop distinctively different formats, depending which aspect of ICT is emphasized.[22] If primarily the programming and information processing capabilities are used, as it is the case with CBTs/WBTs, interactivity between teacher and student (*external interactivity*) is largely substituted by automated interactivity (*internal interactivity*). It is very clear that the digital format enhances internal interactivity enormously. Options include: (1) remedial mathematics—students can work through an unlimited set of exercises, getting immediate feedback (e.g., Jewett, 2000c); (2) language training—many e-books now include interactive training of vocabulary, grammar checks, and even pronunciation controls; (3) virtual science labs—dissecting a virtual frog or rat can at least be a very useful and less costly substitution for the real thing (cf. http://www-itg.lbl.gov/ITG. hm.pg.docs/dissect/info.html); (iv) remote control experiments in physics or engineering[23] (cf. Whalley, 1998); (v) simulations (e.g., complex climate simulations); (vi) software agents may offer threads of related discussions from the course archive ("Uncle Bulgaria," cf. Masterton, 1998); and (vii) simulated discussion along the line of Weizenbaum's ELIZA experiment (cf. Weizenbaum, 1976).

The development and design of such automated interactive elements, which "takes the human out of the loop" (cf. Wiley, 2003, p. 21), may help a lot in some cases, but eventually has its limitations on both the cost and the effectiveness sides. On the effectiveness side, Turoff (1997) argued that tasks which can really be automated lose the right to their place in higher education.[24] Other authors, like Weizenbaum (1976) and Dreyfus (2004), see principle limitations in automating more complex communication processes.

On the cost side such software development can be very expensive. While the bad message is that costs can spiral out of control, the good message is that the cost-structure follows the Fordist model and promises scale economies. We call this way of using ICT the *type-i mode* since it exploits the information processing and programming capabilities of ICT.

The possibly more interesting avenue opened by ICT may be derived from its capabilities to facilitate and sustain communication at a distance. Communication, *external interactivity* (or interactivity between teacher and student and peer interactivity), has been the *Achilles Heel* of distance education; a handicap, distance education has sought to circumvent and compensate through unbundling teacher functions into content development and instructional design on the one hand side, and auxiliary measures of student support on the other.[25] In spite of wide recognition for the distance education specific instructional design formats, it has been repeatedly questioned, if such a format can be considered as a full substitute for the traditional face-to-face discussion in seminars and classes. (Rumble 2001a, p. 3). We call this way of using ICT the *type-c mode* since it exploits the capabilities of ICT to sustain communication at a distance.

There are essentially two *type-c* sub variants of exploiting the ICT capabilities for e-learning: The *synchronous* and the *asynchronous* option. The synchronous option, to some extent, introduced a *schism* within the distance education "church." Leading theoreticians like Peters ostracized videoconferencing as not belonging to the family of distance education (Peters cited in Bernath & Rubin 1999, p. 162). In fact, while asynchronous forms of distance education compensate its pedagogical deficiencies—such as lack of responsive interactivity by developing distinctive pedagogical strength[26]—videoconferencing is promoted mainly for pragmatic reasons. It is clearly seen as inferior to a face-to-face seminar or discussion, since the technology limits spontaneous communication[27] and generally does not exploit fully the capability of televised lectures (i.e., the respective asynchronous format).

It is important to recognize that the type-c capabilities of ICT-based distance education are not just additional capabilities to further enhance what distance education can do. In some sense, they call into question the very rationale of distance education as we know it.

Distance education has been organized around a deficit. Distance education's incapability for effective student/teacher communication was this birth handicap. It forced a migration from *external interactivity* to *internal interactivity*, which in turn led to the very two things for which distance education has been praised: (1) the high quality of its course material, and (2) its cost-effectiveness. The "miracle" of Daniel's triangle (Figure 14.5; Daniel, 2001) lies in the fact that (1) and (2) are compatible via the underlying mechanism of scale economies.

This connection is the reason why the new communication capabilities are not an add-on, which would eliminate the remaining deficiency of distance education to make it finally perfect. On the contrary, it calls

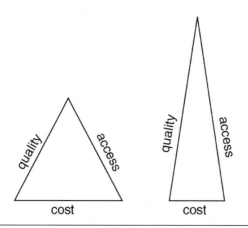

Figure 14.5 Daniel's Iron Triangles. Source: Author's rendition based on Daniel (2001).

into question the need to migrate from external to internal interactivity ("Why design dialogue into text when you can embed text into dialogue?"). Unfortunately, it is just this migration out of external interactivity which is at the heart of the cost-efficiency of distance education. The migration out of external interactivity reduces V, while the migration into internal inter-activity assures quality, possibly at high costs, but at high fixed costs (F). This means that by way of scale economies, these high costs are compatible with low average costs per student.

Now since you can communicate at a distance, you need to decide if you want to. The question of "if you want to," has to be answered in full awareness of the consequences of this option, that is, giving up the central selling point of distance education, its cost-effectiveness.[28] However, the distinction between these two modes of e-learning (*type-i* and *type-c*) denotes opposite poles on a continuous scale rather than isolated alternative options. Especially since the availability of learning management systems (LMS), a seamless integration of the two types is possible. A learning management system (such as *Lotus LearningSpace, Blackboard,* or *WebCT*) allows us to embed all sorts of type-i items like film clips, audio files, simulations, and multiple choice questions, and combine them with the use of type-c applications like with asynchronous (threaded discussion) or synchronous (text or voice chat) forms of communication.

The extent to which type-i or type-c components are used does not so much depend on the limitations of the LMS, but on the *learning scenario* the course designers opt for (Baumgartner & Bergner, 2004). The definition of learning scenarios has consequences in terms of costs, since it includes decisions about the sophistication level of the embedded media, as well as of the level of communication. It is possible to use the same LMS to implement learning scenarios of totally different cost-structures.

Distributed E-learning

Jewett's conceptualization of distributed instruction echoes the definition by Keegan cited earlier that "information technology rather than the post office serves as the delivery and communication media for the courses" (Jewett, 2000a, p. 38). It reflects the situation many university and colleges find themselves in. ICT infrastructure is ubiquitous and its cost can be largely treated as "sunk costs," while faculty and staff costs move into the fore. This is the situation for which Jewett (2000b) developed a framework, which is based on the experience of the *Technology Costing Methodology* (TCM) project, promoted by the *Western Cooperative for Educational Tele-communication* (WCET).

For this context Jewett (2000b) proposes a framework (see Table 14.6) that at first sight appears to differ significantly from the established approach, since there is little explicit use of the traditional distinctions

Table 14.6 Distributed Technology

1.	Instructional materials are prepared (developed and maintained) by teams of faculty.
2.	Materials are presented (distributed) to students via IT media, and students accomplish coursework at times and places (which may be remote from a campus) convenient for them.
3.	Some (if not all) student interaction occurs via IT media with faculty who are not necessarily the same as those who prepared the materials originally.
4.	Student performance on course assignments and examinations is evaluated and grades are assigned by faculty who are, again, not necessarily those who prepared the course materials.

Source: Jewett (2000a, p. 38). *Dollars, Distance, and Online Education: The New Economics of College Teaching and Learning.* Martin J. Finkelstein, Carol Frances, Frank I. Jewett and Bernhard W. Scholz (Editors). Copyright © 2000 by The American Council on Education and The Oryx Press. Reproduced with permission of Greenwood Publishing Group, Inc., Westport, CT.

between fixed vs. variable, and capital vs. recurrent costs. Instead Jewett focuses on *labor productivity.*

Costs to produce something can be represented by the following total cost equation:

(14.3.1) $$TC = w * L + Rest$$

where *w* represents *labor cost per unit*; L, *amount of labor* and *Rest,* all other expenses. The average costs we get by dividing the total costs by the quantity of output Q.

$$AC = \frac{TC}{Q} = \frac{w * L}{Q} \quad \frac{Rest}{Q} = \frac{w * L}{Q} + \frac{Rest}{Q} \Rightarrow$$

(14.3.2) $$AC = \frac{w}{Q/L} + \frac{Rest}{Q}$$

Note that the term Q/L represents *labor productivity.* Other things being equal, you can bring down AC by decreasing labor costs (w), or by increasing productivity (Q/L).

Jewett then sets out to demonstrate that online learning can increase labor productivity by reducing duplication of work typical for traditional teaching, through "unbundling" the teaching function. His standard situation is the traditional college, where the number of faculty positions required depends on enrollment level[29]. Jewett shows that, under certain assumptions, you need less staff under *distributed technology,* as opposed to *classroom technology.* The faculty position requirements "under classroom technology" (FPc) can be calculated as enrollment (N), divided by the average section enrolment (G), which gives the number of classes or sections to be taught. This number has to be divided by the workload of a full-time staff position (measured in terms of number of classes or sections, here denoted as k). We can write:

$$FPc = \frac{N}{k * G} \Rightarrow$$

(14.3.3)

$$FPc(N) = \left(\frac{1}{k * G}\right) * N$$

Example: For G = 25, k = 8, we get the following function:

(14.3.3a)

$$FPc = \frac{N}{8 * 25} = \frac{1}{200} * N \Rightarrow$$

$$FPc(N) = 0.005 * N$$

Shifting from *classroom technology* to what Jewett calls *distributed technology* means unbundling the various teaching tasks, which include: p1 = developing content; p2 = instructional design for presentation; and p3 = direct student related workload, including discussion and assessment. The figures pi, i ε {1,2,3}, are percentages denoting the relative weight the different tasks have in preparing a course such that 0 < p1 + p2 + p3 ≤ 1. Analyzing the different tasks, we find that only p3 varies with the output parameter N. This means that p1 + p2 eventually will contribute to fixed costs and only p3 to the (semi-) variable costs. Hence the FP function under distributed technology can be written like this:

(14.3.4)

$$FPd = \frac{p1 + p2}{k} + \frac{p3}{k} * \frac{N}{G}$$

Example: For G= 25, k = 8 and assuming that all three teaching functions require equal amounts of time, we get.

(14.3.4a)

$$FPd = \frac{\frac{1}{3} + \frac{1}{3}}{8} + \frac{\frac{1}{3}}{8 * 25} * N \Rightarrow$$

$$FPd(N) = 0.08333 + 0.00166 * N$$

Differentiating (14.3.3) and (14.3.4), we already see that under distributed technology the number of faculty positions required increases less steeply than under classroom technology. This means that by eliminating the duplication of work typical for the classroom technology—which is due to the fact that in principle each section is prepared anew—under distributed technology faculty time is freed for the teaching tasks.

(14.3.5)

$$FPc(N) = \frac{1}{k * G} * N \Rightarrow$$

$$\frac{dFPc}{dN} = \frac{1}{k * G}$$

(14.3.6)

$$FPd(N) = \frac{p1 + p2}{k} + \frac{p3}{k * G} * N \Rightarrow$$

$$\frac{dFPd}{dN} = \frac{p3}{k * G}$$

Since both FPc and FPd are linear functions, both derivatives are constant, depending only on the parameters faculty workload (k), section/class size (G) and the percentage of workload going into direct student teacher interaction (p3), but not on N. Using the figures from the above examples we get for (14.3.5):

$1/(8*25) = 1/200 = 0.005$ and for (14.3.6) $(1/3)/(8*25) = 0.00166$.

We can now infer the direct teaching related costs (DC) under both technologies by multiplying the amount of labor (faculty positions required) by the costs of labor (faculty salaries). Under classroom technology this is:

(14.3.7) $$TCc(N) = FPc * w = \frac{N}{k * G} * w$$

The respective average costs are described in (14.3.8). The denominators in the second line describe the labor productivity under this technology.

$$ACc(N) = \frac{TCc}{N} = \frac{FPc * w}{N} \Rightarrow$$

(14.3.8) $$ACc(N) = \frac{w}{N/FPc} = \frac{w}{SFRc} = \frac{w}{k * G}$$

The average cost per student depends only on three parameters: Faculty salary (w), faculty work load (in terms of numbers of classes), and class size. There are no scale economies.

For the description of direct costs under the distributed technology, Jewett's arguments are again slightly simplified here. Combining equation (14.3.1) and the classical total cost equation, which describes total costs as the sum of fixed and variable costs ($TC = V*N + F$), we subsume the part of (14.3.4), which contributes to the fixed costs, under F and rewrite the remaining term as p3*Fc. This allows us to write the direct costs under distributed technology as:

(14.3.9) $$TCd(N) = (FPc * p3) * w + F$$

and the respective average direct costs as:

$$AC = \frac{TCd}{N} = \frac{(FPc * p3) * w + F}{N} \Rightarrow$$

(14.3.10) $$AC = \frac{w}{N/(FPc * p3)} + \frac{F}{N} \Rightarrow$$

$$AC = \frac{w}{SFRd} + \frac{F}{N}$$

The student/faculty ratio under distributed technology is $N/FPc * p3$ as opposed to N/FPc under classroom technology. This means that labor productivity under distributed technology has increased. The limit towards

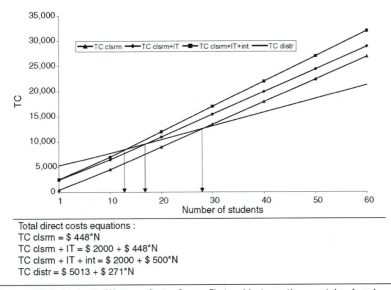

Total direct costs equations :
TC clsrm = $ 448*N
TC clsrm + IT = $ 2000 + $ 448*N
TC clsrm + IT + int = $ 2000 + $ 500*N
TC distr = $ 5013 + $ 271*N

Figure 14.6 Technology's Effects on Costs. *Source:* First and last equations are taken from Jewett (2003); the second and the third equations are filled in to illustrate Jewett's arguments in Jewett (2000a).

which AC can fall, therefore, is determined by the same parameters as the average cost under classroom technology: The faculty salary, the faculty workload, class size, and—this makes the difference—p3 which represents a measure for the remaining linkage between volume of activity and costs. To the extent p3 approaches 100% (meaning p1 + p2 approaching 0%), the productivity of the distributed technology falls back to classroom level. The smaller p3 becomes the higher the productivity under the distributed technology.

Figure 14.6 demonstrates that making use of especially the information processing capabilities of e-learning (i.e., *type-i* in the above developed terminology) only adds to the fixed costs, leading to an upward parallel translation of the total cost graph costs under classroom technology. If, in addition, the communication capabilities of ICT are used (*type-c*) then, in addition to the upward parallel translation, the gradient becomes steeper, indicating that also variable costs increase. Only if substitution effects are realized, leading to lower variable costs per student, total direct costs rise less steeply with volume of activities than in all the other cases. This, according to Jewett, can be achieved through distributed technology.

Figures like the ones cited from Jewett are by and large consistent with development costs reported for other web courses. Boettcher (2000; 2004, October 31), who distinguishes between web, web-centric, and web-enhanced courses, reports the cost figures shown in Table 14.7.

Table 14.7 Costs of Different Types of Web Courses

	%	Base	Rate	No. Hours	Faculty cost per hr	Total faculty costs
Web	1	45	10	450	$ 50	$ 22500
Web centric	0,5	23	10	230	$ 50	$ 11500
Web enhanced	0,25	11	10	110	$ 50	$ 5500

Source: Adapted from Boettcher (2000, p. 191), with the modified rate (10 hrs instead of 18 hrs) for moving content to the Web proposed by Boettcher (2004). Boettcher refers to the following standard context: 3 credit course stands for 45 hours of teaching plus additional 2*45 hours of directed study; hence the 3 credit course amounts to 135 SLH. Benchmarks for calculating faculty costs assume an annual salary of $ 68 000 (= 1360 hours * $ 50). A course extends over which amounts to a teaching load 136 hrs (17 weeks * 8 hrs =136 hrs); the assumption seems to be that a faculty member teaches 5 courses per annum which would amount to 50% of the annual workload, the other 50% being research and contribution to administration.

The figures Hülsmann reports for OMDE courses of specifications (see Table 14.8), similar to those of Boettcher and Jewett (three credit courses, though the OMDE courses require 150 instead of 136 student learning hours), are of the same order of magnitude, except that they are web courses rather than web-enhanced courses. They could be characterized as a typical type-c application (i.e., exploiting the communicative capabilities of ICT), characterized by rather low development costs and comparatively high variable costs.

While, in essence, the argument by which Jewett demonstrates the cost-effectiveness advantage of distributed technology is the same as for more traditional (Fordist) distance education, it is worth comparing the equations in Figure 14.6 and Tables 14.7 and 14.8, with total cost equations characterizing courses of the British Open University or the Norwegian NKS (Hülsmann, 2000, p. 147; GBP deflated to 2004 U.S. dollars):

TC = $ 1 213 600 + $ 164*N   TC = $ 140 000 + $ 224*N

Viewing the numbers, it becomes obvious that while there is a formal analogy between distributed technology and Fordist distance education, they play in two very different leagues. This can be best seen by comparing scale economies evoked in both cases. The potential for scale econo-

Table 14.8 OMDE Course Costs

Courses	F	V	Total costs	F/V
OMDE 601	$15,700	$292	TC = $15,700 + $292*N	54
OMDE 605	$6,600	$173	TC = $ 6,600 + $173*N	38
OMDE 606	$8,433	$281	TC = $ 8,433 + $281*N	30
OMDE 624	$6,773	$226	TC = $ 6,773 + $226*N	30

Source: Adapted from Hülsmann (2003)

mies can be measured by the quotient F/V. Jewett's distributed technology scores with $5,013 / $217 = 18 while the OU course $1,213,600 / $164= 7,400 and the NKS course $140,000/$224 = 625. Obviously we do not compare like with like here, since learning hours, credits, and enrollment numbers are completely different.

The Jewett (and TCM) framework of costing was specifically developed for a situation which may emerge as the standard situation for distance learning in higher education. In this context, the main cost driver which makes a difference is faculty cost, since ICT infrastructure becomes standard and availability of computers for students is widespread. The question is: To what extent is ICT employed to increase faculty productivity?

The argument Jewett uses to demonstrate the productivity advantage of distributed technology is essentially the same as the arguments Wagner and others have used to demonstrate the cost-efficiency advantage of Fordist distance education. In both cases, the key to increased efficiency is "unbundling" teaching function into content development and design on one side, and direct student related workloads on the other. As in Fordist distance education, efficiency gains depend on the extent to which the *onus* of teaching can be shifted away from external interactivity, towards content production; or in costing terms, to costs which do not vary with the number of students. In Jewett's analysis, the elimination of redundancies due to "re-inventing the wheel" for each course frees faculty time for direct student related work, thus increasing productivity under distributed technology.

While the formal similarity of both arguments produces a certain *déjà vu* experience for the distance educator, the difference of scale economies indicates that both types of distance education play in leagues as different as *baobab* and *bonsai*.[30]

In fact, the basic reason for the difference between baobab and bonsai is obvious and due to the type-c capabilities available in distributed e-learning.[31] It is not only that it drives V up; it also takes out the pressure to go for a large N—and that for two reasons. First, the need to migrate from internal to external interactivity eases due to the availability of communication capabilities at a distance. This, in turn, reduces the willingness to large course development investments ("Why design dialogue into text if you can embed text into dialogue?"), which in turn takes out the pressure to go for a large N, which otherwise would be a necessary condition to have reasonable AC.

Second, where external interactivity is given a major role, the perception of the role of scale changes. Systems may be still *scaleable*,[32] but the *scale economies* which can be achieved are of bonsai format (because F is generally lower, and V is generally higher than in Fordist distance education).

This form of education is not anymore an educational format *sua specie* (Peters, as cited in Keegan, 1994), but might be located quite near to conventional education, as we know it. There may be, however, ways to recover at least parts of the lost efficiencies of traditional distance education.

E-learning: SWOT Analysis

The *strengths* of e-learning certainly include its flexibility and the potential quality in design, combined with responsive student/teacher and peer communication.The main *weakness*, in comparison with traditional distance education, lies in a loss in cost-efficiency. That even minimal scale economies are unlikely to be exploited, is due to the fact that e-learning applications are often grafted onto organizational settings and role definitions of traditional face-to-face teaching. To introduce a consistent e-learning policy institution-wide may meet faculty resistance.[33]

The *opportunities* lie in exploiting the strengths while minimizing the resultant loss of efficiency. The last section (Recovering Lost Efficiencies) will comment on that. The *threats* lie in the possibility of higher costs, which may mean that, ironically, "distance education—through the adoption of on-line learning—prices itself out of the market" (Rumble, 2004b, p. 48). Moreover, e-learning may lose in quality, since the low scale of e-learning operations may no longer justify high quality media production.[34] This may result in not fully exploiting available instructional capabilities.

RECOVERING LOST EFFICIENCIES

To exploit the full capabilities of e-learning (*type-i* and *type-c*) will certainly drive costs upwards. At the same time, markets diversify and mass demand for standardized homogeneous products of distance education providers has ended (both, because of the *piranha effect* and because of genuine diversification of demand). All this suggests that the Fordist model of distance education has lost momentum.[35] On the other hand, more and more learners appreciate the flexibility and convenience of e-learning which, in spite of added costs, has come to stay.

How to recover at least parts of the lost efficiencies in this context? Here, two options are considered: (1) exploiting synergies of cooperation, and (2) re-purposing developed content in the form of re-usable learning objects.

Business Models of Cooperation

Given that captive markets for distance learners are a thing of the past, and given the typical context of conventional institutions "going dual-mode," planners cannot base their planning on large enrollments (i.e., large N).[36] But high course development investments (implying high fixed costs, F) can only be legitimized on the basis of large N. Hence the planner sails between Scylla and Charybdis: Not investing in course development leaves him open to the charge of "chained media." Fully exploiting media capabilities may, in the words of Rumble, price the product out of the market.

The question is, "How can we, in spite of limited markets and demands for customized products, get a large N, which is the precondition to operate scale economies?" The answer is: By cooperation.

Remember that distance education as a system is characterized by a division of labor, which is reflected in different system components, such as course development and student support (to name but the two most important). While all these components are required, it is by no means a logical necessity that they are to be hosted in the same institution. Especially, the e-learning environment facilitates such cooperation.

> Technology and e-business approaches make it possible for integrated processes of open and distance education to be disintegrated into their constituent parts: curriculum development; content development; learner acquisition and support; learning delivery; assessment and advising; articulation; and credentialing. These processes can then be managed by different organizations. (Rumble & Latchem, 2004, p. 134)

Table 14.9 is a selection of good reasons for cooperation. The first one of them indicates that cooperation may contribute to the above mentioned problem: How to bring back scale into a system characterized by limited local markets and specialized demand.

Bernath and Hülsmann (2004) have demonstrated how a small institution like the Center for Distance Education at the Carl von Ossietzky University Oldenburg can exploit the synergies of alliances and partnerships. They described a number of such models of co-operation in which ZEF supplied different system components at mutual benefits.

Table 14.9 Reasons for Cooperation

Consortia, partnerships, strategic alliances etc. are formed by educational, training and corporate providers for a variety of reasons, but principally to:

- share costs or spread these over a larger number of students;
- share courses, resources and academic and commercial experience and expertise;
- attract funding opportunities (particularly in the European Union which makes inter-institutional collaboration a condition of funding);
- be fast to market or cope with major market demand by joint course development and optimising complementary strengths, as shown by Open Learning Australia in its earlier years of operation;
- capitalize on partners' knowledge of, and reputations in, local markets;
- accommodate other countries' governmental requirements for local institution involvement as a condition of entry;
- ensure adequate provision of local services such as marketing, counselling, admissions, registration, and examination invigilation;
- de-bundle learning materials, tutorial support and course assessment to provide expanded market opportunities;
- achieve a franchise arrangement.

Source: Selected from Rumble & Latchem (2004, p.128)

1. The *Branch Model*: ZEF co-operates with the FernUniversität in Hagen (the main distance teaching university in Germany) to provide educational counselling and tutorial services to their students in the North Western regions of Germany. For the state of Lower Saxony this is a low cost option, since local students are qualified at marginal costs. At the same time, this arrangement contributes to the efficiency of the FernUniversität Hagen.

2. The *Subcontractor Model*: ZEF co-operates with the University of Maryland University College (UMUC) to develop and teach online courses within the Master of Distance Education (MDE), jointly offered by UMUC and Oldenburg University.

3. The *Shared Ownership Model*: ZEF co-operates with three centres for distance education at other universities in Lower Saxony to operate a technical infrastructure for online distance education (via online). This again is an efficient way of capacity building, which allows the participating centres to offer services to their own universities as well as selling services to outside clients.

4. The *Franchise Model*: ZEF has developed course material for professional development in nursing which has been franchised to other universities. In this case ZEF operates as a curriculum developer and content provider. The cost-efficiency depends on scale economies, which can only be achieved in such broad alliances. (Bernath & Hülsmann, 2004, pp. 485–486)

Michael Moore even regards such "network systems" as "the emerging organizational paradigm" and writes:

In the *strategic alliance*, participants in a network contribute technological and managerial expertise and capital and share the costs of developing new technologies, spreading the financial risks of entering new markets. Although quite common in the manufacturing industry, in distance education so far, strategic alliances have not made much headway in collaborative design and delivery of the products, that is, courses and programs. Rather, they have been directed towards cooperative marketing of their existing courses.

However, in the distance education field, it is not only the strategic alliance but also the *vertical disaggregation* form of network that is likely to be of greater interest in the future. Vertical disaggregation is the process developed in the manufacturing industry to deal with shortening product life cycles, by which large firms outsource the production of various components of the product to smaller suppliers. As in manufacturing, in the knowledge industries too it looks as if vertical disaggregation will become the means of reducing product life cycles and improving efficiency and quality. What that means in distance education is outsourcing some of design and a lot of the product development of course materials. It means devolving learner support services to local points of contact and specialized services. It means drawing in instructor resources from wherever they may be located rather than solely on the faculty on campus. (Moore, 2003, p. 4; emphasis added)

A factor which undoubtedly will contribute further to the feasibility of such networking is *Learning Object Modeling* (LOM).

Learning Objects

One way of increasing N is lengthening the shelf life of a course. However, given the shortening *half lives* of knowledge this may not be tolerated by the customer.

However, instead of amortizing course development costs *horizontally* along the life time of a course, we could think of amortizing "re-usable items" of a course *vertically* across different courses within and beyond the institution. Such a reusable item is often referred to as learning object, which Mason & Rehake define as "a digitized entity which can be used, reused or referenced during technology supported learning" (Rehake & Mason, 2003, p. 21). Examples can be complex climate simulations or short Java applets to illustrate characteristics of trigonometric functions.

Obviously, in order to make use of such "nuggets," documentation and archiving management has to be improved. *Exportability* from one learning management system to another or *searchability* requires the introduction and compliance to standards and an appropriate level of *granulization*. SCORM (*Shareable Content Object Reference Model*) is such a learning object management model.

Table 14.10 summarizes various strategic lines of development for the protagonists of learning objects, which vary in the degree to which they are "designed to remove the humans from the loop" (Wiley, 2003). One line of development sees learning objects like Lego blocks which, optimally, could be assembled by an automatic agent according to user specifications.

Table 14.10 Using Learning Objects

	Lego blocks	Brick and mortars	Learning communities
Primary goal	Make learning as scalable, economically viable and effective as possible	Make learning as scalable, economically viable and effective as possible	Make learning as scalable, economically viable and effective as possible
Primary means of achieving goal	*Automation*: Design to remove humans from the loop	*Productive tool*: Design to make teachers more productive	*Collaboration*: Design to bring humans into the loop

Source: Adapted from Wiley (2003, Table 1, p. 21).

Another option is the "brick and mortar" model, where learning objects are like resources for the teacher to conceptualize and to integrate in his/her course. In this model, a human teacher remains in the loop, but is provided with tools to enhance his/her productivity. In a final variant, the learning objects idea is combined with the idea of the learning community. Learning objects are managed, used, and even created by the learning community. The use of learning objects may facilitate considerably the process of recovering lost efficiencies through cooperation.

NOTES

1. *Information and communication technologies* (ICTs) are here understood as comprising digital information processing and communication.
2. Coombs speaks about "the greatest world-wide educational expansion in all human history an expansion fueled by hopes and expectations that followed the end of World War II" (1985, p. 3). The trend still continues today: "In both developed and developing countries there is a growing demand for access to education. For example, in the United States the number of undergraduate students was expected to rise by 1 million by 2005; in the U.K. the governments has set a target that one-half of all school leavers will enter higher education by 2010 (DfES, 2001); while in China the expectation is 5 million extra students over the next three years (MOE, 2001)" (Littlejohn, 2003, p.1).
3. As a leading OECD researcher put it: "education is too important too leave it in the hand of pedagogues" (Papandopoulos, 1994, p. 45).
4. The classification of interactivity in brackets is due to Moore and Kearsley (1996, pp. 128–132).
5. It is important to see that the best text is not always the one which "leaves no question open," but that part of good teaching is to point out further ways of interrogating the issue at hand.
6. This may put into perspective the (somewhat tongue-in-cheek) self-description of Peters as "dare devil" (cf. Bernath & Rubin, 1999, p. 143).
7. In fact, distance education attracted educators from the left as well as the right of the political spectrum. The left was interested because of the association of distance education with open learning, which aimed at breaking the mold of traditional elite education (e.g., Open University) by increasing access for non traditional learners. The right was attracted by the implicit promises to increase efficiencies and lower costs.
8. We generally refer to *cost-efficiency* rather than *cost-effectiveness analysis*, though distinctions are somewhat blurred. Cost-efficiency is an input/output measure, while cost-effectiveness relates the costs of inputs to the degree a set goal has been achieved. Cost-efficiency measures are generally based on simply-to-get *performance indicators* (e.g., number of students), but may include assessment related measures like *cost per graduate* (Rumble, 1997).
9. Here we successively include all adjustments made, which leads to a slightly different presentation. Wagner (1972, 1974), while calculating the adjustments in the footnotes, at times continued with the unadjusted figures.

10. Differentiating the two total cost functions, we get the respective marginal costs:

$$\frac{dTC_{CU}(N)}{dN} = \pounds 657 \text{ and } \frac{dTC_{OU}(N)}{dN} = \frac{d(\pounds 6\,032\,800 + \pounds 61 * N)}{N} = \frac{d(\pounds 6\,032\,800)}{N} + \frac{d(\pounds 61 * N)}{N} \Rightarrow \frac{dTC_{OU}(N)}{dN} = \pounds 61.$$

With respect to the *total cost functions* these figures represent the gradients of the straight lines of the TC graphs. With respect to the *average cost function*, they are visualized by straight horizontal lines. In case of the OU system, *variable cost per student* (V) is represented by the asymptotic line, towards which the *average cost per student* (AC) function falls (but beyond which it cannot fall!). In case of the conventional system *average costs per student* and *variable cost per student* coincide.

11. Retention rate = 100% - drop-out rate

12. PMT stands for *payment on a loan*. The standard interpretation is that you take a loan from a bank to be repaid in fixed monthly or annual installments. In this sense, we can interpret an educational investment as a loan on behalf of the users, who will have to repay in terms of their tuition fees during the life time of the course.

13. Based on measures of effectiveness, as percentage to which a set goal is reached (Rumble, 1997, p. 161).

14. For example, Perraton: "We can state the theory of media equivalence baldly: communication media do not differ in their educational effectiveness" (1987, p. 4).

15. *Cost-effectiveness* analysis means here relating costs to the percentage, in which learning objectives have been achieved. In this (rather narrow) sense of cost-effectiveness, analysis *cost per graduate* is not a cost-effectiveness measure.

16. "The argument that it (traditional distance education, T.H.) provides opportunities for 'guided didactic conversation' is clearly unconvincing" (Rumble 2001a, p. 3).

17. Unless the institution is able to compensate eroding scale effects by even higher overall enrollments.

18. Cf. Rumble (2004a, p. 20): "Those who still rest their case for the efficiency of distance education on the comparative cost studies of the 1970s and 1980s need to bear in mind that … the post-1980s massification of traditional higher education and its re-engineering as a result of the development of dual-mode strategies and flexible learning methods suggest that it is time to re-evaluate the relative efficiency of single-mode distance education against the alternative options available."

19. A recent survey on online education in the United States for the years 2002 and 2003 observes: "Among public institutions, the numbers are even more compelling, with 97% offering at least one online or blended course and 49% offering an online degree program" (Allen & Seaman, 2003, p. 2).

20. The Registration Brochure for the Third Pan-Commonwealth Forum on Open Learning at Dundin, New Zealand 4–8 July 2004 (www.col.org/pcf3) defines *online and e-learning* as "terms that have emerged to describe the application of information and communication technologies (ICTs) to enhance distance education, implement open learning policies, make learning activities more flexible and enable those learning activities to be distributed among many learning venues."

21. That we add in the following the attribute 'distributed' acknowledges the indebtedness of the respective section to Jewett. Jewett himself introduces his discussion of terminology with a reference to the Beatles: "Her name was McGill, she

called herself Lil, but everyone knew her as Nancy" (from "Rocky Raccoon," the Beatles, 1966; cited in Jewett, 2000a).

22. The following distinctions between type-c and type-i modes of ICT-based distance education are based on Rumble (2001b, p.75)

23. From the perspective of the user interface, it becomes indistinguishable if you operate a real experiment in remote control or a simulated experiment.

24. "If a topic can be taught by software and there is no need for human communication, then it is no longer worthy of a university course, but is what we have commonly come to view as training and the acquisition of skills" (Turoff, 1997).

25. This seems to be unjust for institutions which strongly emphasize learner support. However, there is little doubt where the prestige is invested. This is reflected in Mills' differentiation of learner support and academic teaching. Learner support, he defines, "… is the totality of the provision by an institution to support the learner, other than generic teaching materials produced by instructional designers/course producers. To be absolutely clear, where learning materials are produced for numbers of students …, this is regarded as the academic teaching and is considered to be outside the framework of learner support" (Mills, 2003, p. 104).

26. For a discussion of the pedagogical strengths of asynchronous discussion cf. Hülsmann (2003); the cost structure of videoconferencing has been analyzed in Hülsmann (2000). The trade-off between communication (external interactivity) and scale economics is obvious.

27. Voice activated videoconferencing has difficulty in dealing with "negative waiting times" in spontaneous discussions.

28. Traditional distance educators clearly spotted the problem as the following titles indicated: Ainsworth (2000) complained about "The unbearable cost of interaction," and Thalheimer (2002) demanded straightforwardly: "Stop Aiming for Interactivity!" Rumble (2004, p. 49) observed: "It will be ironic if distance education—through the adoption of on-line learning—prices itself out of the market."

29. Jewett's argument is slightly more complicated, since the output is *credits earned* rather than *student numbers*. Jewett also introduces a quality controlling parameter ALO (average learning outcome): "The ALO quality index converts student credit units (course credit units times enrollments) from a measure of instructional activity to a proxy of learning outcomes that are produced" (Jewett, 2000b, p. 102). In order not to overload the terminology, we have simplified his argument while keeping the gist visible.

30. However, even minor substitution effects are practically difficult to realize in the traditional setting. Boettcher, for instance reports: "Most of the materials produced are being used solely by the individual who produced them, and not by other faculty. This fact suggests that the 'bundled' instructional teaching approach, where a single faculty member is responsible for all the aspects of a course, is moving from the campus classroom to the Web environment" (Boettcher, 2000, p. 192).

31. Including on-campus face-to-face interaction since the situation is exactly the one of a college or university which "goes dual mode," in the sense of Rumble (1994).

32. … and still leading to happiness in the sense of Dickens' Mr. Micawber: "Annual income twenty pounds, annual expenditure nineteen and six, result happiness. Annual income twenty pounds, annual expenditure twenty pounds ought and six, result misery." (I owe this important reference to G. Rumble.)

33. Schiller (1999) reports that faculty has refused participation in an Instructional Enhancement Initiative "on grounds that the university might try to claim ownership of any of the course materials they posted on the network" (p. 192); Rumble, citing Noble, refers to the "spectre of faculty resistance" (Rumble 2004b, p. 133); this is also reflected in a survey online education in the USA for 2002 and 2003. While students and institutions clearly accepted online education, academic leaders at 40% of the institutions would not "accept the value and legitimacy of online education" (Allen & Seaman, 2003, p. 2).
34. This is partly due to the different institutional settings. Conventional institutions are unlikely to have the same media production capabilities as, for instance, the Open University had due to its cooperation with the BBC.
35. The failure of the U.S. Open University may be seen as a point in case; even if different explanations have been a short look at the founding dated of dedicated open universities confirms such a lost of momentum.
36. One way of increasing enrollments is extending the shelf life of a course; given the shortened half life of knowledge, this option may not be acceptable for the market.

REFERENCES

Allen, I. E., & Seaman, J. (2003, September). Sizing the opportunity: The quality and extent of online education in the United States, 2002 and 2003. The Sloan Consortium (Sloan-C). Retrieved November, 15, 2004, from http://www.sloan-c.org/resources/sizing_opportunity.pdf.

Ainsworth, D. (2000, September 11–13). The unbearable cost of interaction. Paper presented at the International Conference sponsored by the University of South Australia in conjunction with the International

Council for Open and Distance Education (ICDE), University of South Australia, Adelaide, Australia.

Bates, A. W. (1995). *Technology, open learning and distance education*. London: Routledge.

Baumgartner, P., & Bergner, I. (2004, 4–6 March). Categorization of virtual learning activities. In U. Bernath, & A. Szücs (Eds.). *Supporting the learner in distance education and e-learning: The Third EDEN Research Workshop and International Conference* (pp. 124–129). Carl von Ossietzky University of Oldenburg, Germany: Bibliotheks- und Informationssystem der Universität Oldenburg.

Boettcher, J. V. (2000). How much does it cost to put a course online? It all depends. In M. J. Finkelstein, C. Frances, F. I. Jewett, & B. W. Scholz (Eds.), *Dollars, distance, and online education: The new economics of college teaching and learning* (pp. 172–198). Phoenix, AZ: American Council of Education, Oryx Press.

Boettcher, J. V. (2004, October 31). Online course development: What does it cost? *Campus Technology*. Retrieved October 31, 2004, from http://www.campus-technology.com/article.asp?id=9676.

Bowman, M. J. (1966). The costing of human resource development. In E. A. G. Robinson & J. E. Vaizey (Eds.). *The economics of education*. New York: St. Markus Press.

Bernath, U., & Hulsmann, T. (2004). Low cost/high outcome approaches in open, distance and e-learning. In U. Bernath & A. Szcus (Eds.), *Supporting the learner in distance education and e-Learning: Proceedings of the Third EDEN Research*

Workshop, Oldenburg: Bibliotheks-und-Informationssytem der Universitat Old-enburg, pp. 485–491.

Butcher, N., & Roberts, N. (2004). Costs, effectiveness, efficiency. In H. Perraton & H. Lentell (Eds.), *Policy for open and distance learning*. London: RoutledgeFalmer.

Carnoy, M., & Levin, H. M. (1975). Evaluation of educational media: some issues. *Instructional Science*, 4(3/4), 385–406.

Coombs, P. H. (1985). *The world crisis in education: the view from the eighties*. New York and Oxford: Oxford University Press.

Daniel, J. (2001, January). *Technology and education: Adventures in the eternal triangle*. Paper presented at the LearnTec, Karlsruhe.

Dreyfus, H. L. & Dreyfus S.E. (2004). From Socrates to Expert Systems: The Limits and dangers of calculative rationality. University of California. Retrieved November 15, 2004, from http://ist-socrates.berkeley.edu/~hdreyfus/html/paper_socrates. html.

Eicher, J. C. (1977). Cost-effectiveness studies applied to the use of new educational media; methodological and critical Introduction. In UNESCO (Ed.). *The economics of educational media. Vol. 1: Present state of research and trends* (pp. 11–35). Paris: UNESCO.

Eicher, J.-C. (1980). Some thoughts on the economic analysis of new educational media. In UNESCO (Ed.). *The economics of educational media. Vol. 2 Cost and effectiveness* (pp. 10–21). Paris: UNESCO.

Eicher, J. C., & Orivel, F. (1980). Cost-analysis of primary education by TV in the Ivory Coast. In UNESCO (Ed.). *The economics of educational media. Vol. 2 Cost and effectiveness.* (pp. 105–146). Paris: UNESCO.

Hülsmann, T. (2000). *The costs of open learning: a handbook* (Vol. 2). Oldenburg: Bibliotheks- und Informationssystem der Carl von Ossietzky Universität Oldenburg.

Hülsmann, T. (2003). Texts that talk back—Asynchronous conferencing: a possible form of academic discourse? In U. Bernath & E. Rubin (Eds.). *Reflections on teaching and learning in an online master program—A case study* (Vol. 6, pp. 167–226). Oldenburg: Bibliotheks- und informationssystem der Universität Oldenburg.

Jamison, D. T. (1982). An introduction to the method of cost analysis. In H. Perraton (Ed.), *Alternative routes to formal education: distance teaching for school equivalency*. Washington DC: IBRD/World Bank.

Jamison, D. T. (1987). *Educational media; guidelines for planning and evaluation*. London: Sage Publications.

Jamison, D. T., & Klees, S. J. (1975). *The cost of instructional radio and television for developing countries*. Stanford: Institute for Communications Research.

Jamison, D. T., Suppes, P., & Wells, S. (1974). The effectiveness of alternative instructional media: a survey. *Review of Educational Research, 44*, 1-64.

Jarvis, P. (1983). *Adult and continuing education*. London: Routledge.

Jewett, F. I. (2000a). Conceptual framework and terminology. In M. J. Finkelstein, C. Frances, F. I. Jewett, & B. W. Scholz (Eds.), *Dollars, distance, and online education: The new economics of college teaching and learning* (pp. 35–47). Phoenix, Arizona: American Council of Education, Oryx Press.

Jewett, F. I. (2000b). A framework for the comparative analysis of the costs of classroom instruction vis-à-vis distributed instruction. In M. J. Finkelstein, C. Frances, F. I. Jewett, & B. W. Scholz (Eds.), *Dollars, distance, and online education:*

The new economics of college teaching and learning (pp. 85–122). Phoenix, Arizona: American Council of Education, Oryx Press.

Jewett, F. I. (2000c). Courseware for remedial mathematics: A case study in the benefits and costs of the Mediated Learning System in the California State University. In M. J. Finkelstein, C. Frances, F. I. Jewett, & B. W. Scholz (Eds.), *Dollars, distance, and online education: The new economics of college teaching and learning* (pp. 152–171). Phoenix, AZ: American Council of Education, Oryx Press.

Keegan, D. (Ed.) (1994). *Otto Peters on distance education: The industrialisation of teaching and learning.* London and New York: Routledge.

Klees, S. J., & Wells, S.J. (1977). *Cost Effectiveness and Cost Benefit Analysis for Educational Planning and Evaluation: Methodology and Application to Instructional Technology.* Washington DC: USAID.

Laidlaw, B., & Layard, R. (1974). Traditional versus Open University teachingmethod: a cost comparison. *Higher Education, 3,* 439–468.

Littlejohn, A. (Ed.) (2003). *Reusing online resources.* London and Sterling, VA: Kogan Page.

Livesey, F. (1993). *Dictionary of Economics.* London: Pitman Publishing.

Lumsden, K. G., & Ritchie, R. (1975). The Open University: A survey and economic analysis. *Instructional Science, 4,* 237–291.

Mace, J. (1978). Mythology in the making: is the Open University really cost- effective? *Higher Education, 7*(3), 275–308.

Masterton, S. (1998). The Virtual Participant: a tutor's assistant for electronic conferencing. In M. Eisenstadt & T. Vincent (Eds.), *The Knowledge Web: Learning and Collaborating on the Net* (pp. 249–265). London: KoganPage.

Mills, R. (2003). The centrality of learner support in open and distance learning: A paradigm shift in thinking. In A. Tait & R. Mills (Eds.), *Rethinking learner support in distance education: Change and continuity in an international context* (pp. 102–113). London, New York: RoutledgeFalmer.

Moore, M. G. (2003). Network systems: The emerging organizational paradigm [Editorial]. *The American Journal of Distance Education, 17*(1), 1–5.

Moore, M., & Kearsley, G. (1996). *Distance Education: A Systems View.* Belmont: Wadsworth Publishing.

Orivel, F. (1987). *Costs and effectiveness of distance teaching systems.* Dijon: IREDU.

Papadopoulos, G. S. (1994). *Education 1960– 1990: The OECD perspective.* Paris: OECD.

Perraton, H. (1982). *The cost of distance education.* Cambridge: IEC.

Perraton, H. (1987). *The roles of theory and generalisation in the practice of distance education.* Hagen: Zentrales Institut für Fernstudien (ZIF).

Perraton, H. (2000). *Open and distance learning in the developing world.* London: Routledge.

Perraton, H., & Moses, K. (2004). Technology. In H. Perraton & H. Lentell (Eds.), *Policy for open and distance learning.* London: RoutledgeFalmer.

Peters, O. (1967). Distance education and industrial production: a comparative outline. In D. Keegan (Ed.) (1994), *Otto Peters on distance education. The industrialisation of teaching and learning* (pp. 107–127). London and New York: Routledge.

Rehake, D. R., & Mason, R. (2003). Keeping the learning in learning objects. In A. Littlejohn (Ed.), *Reusing online resources.* London: Kogan Page.

Rumble, G. (1976). *The economics of the open university.* Milton Keynes, UK: OU.

Rumble, G. (1994). The competitive vulnerability of distance teaching universities: A reply. *Open Learning, 9*(3), 47–49.

Rumble, G. (1997). *The costs and economics of open and distance learning.* London: Kogan Page.

Rumble, G. (2001a, 1–5 April). *The costs of providing online student support services.* Paper presented at the 20th World Conference of the International Council for Open and Distance education, Düsseldorf, Germany.

Rumble, G. (2001b). *E-education: Whose benefits, whose costs?* Inaugural Lecture, Wednesday, 28 February 2001.

Rumble, G. (2004a). Introduction. In G. Rumble (Ed.), *Papers and debates on the costs and economics of distance education and online learning* (Vol. 7). Oldenburg: Bibliotheks- und Informationssystem der Carl von Ossietzky Universität Oldenburg.

Rumble, G. (2004b). Technology, distance education, and cost (1999). In G. Rumble (Ed.). *Papers and debates on the costs and economics of distance education and online learning* (Vol. 7, pp. 41–52). Oldenburg: Bibliotheks- und Informationssystem der Carl von Ossietzky Universität Oldenburg.

Rumble, G., & Latchem, C. (2004). Organisational models for distance and open learning. In H. Perraton & H. Lentell (Eds.). *Policy for open and distance learning.* London: Routledge Falmer.

Thalheimer, W. (2002, June, 6). Stop aiming for interactivity. e-learning. Retrieved June 17, 2002, from http://www.elearningmag.com/elearning/ content/content-Detail.jsp?id=21297.

Turoff, M. (1997). Alternative futures for distance learning: The force and the darkside. Retrieved September 28, 2001, from http://eies.njit.edu/~turoff/Papers/darkaln. html.

UNESCO (1977). *The economics of educational media.* Paris: Author.

UNESCO (1980). *The economics of educational media. Vol. 2: Cost and effectiveness.* Paris: Author.

UNESCO (1982). *The economics of educational media Vol. 3 Cost and effectiveness overview and synthesis.* Paris: Author.

Wagner, L. (1972). The economics of the open university. *Higher Education, 1,* 159–183.

Wagner, L. (1977). The economics of the open university revisited. *Higher Education, 6,* 358–381.

Walsh, V. C. (1970). *Introduction to contemporary microeconomics.* New York: McGraw-Hill.

Weizenbaum, J. (1976). *Computer, power and human reason: From judgment to calculation.* W.H. Freeman and Company.

Wells, S. J. (1976). Evaluation criteria and the effectiveness of instructional Technology. *Higher Education, 5,* 253–275.

Whalley, P. (1998). Collaborative learning in networked simulation environments. In M. Eisenstadt & T. Vincent (Eds.), *The knowledge web: Learning and collaborating on the net* (pp. 47–61). London: Kogan Page.

Wiley, D. (2003). The coming collision between automated instruction and social constructivism. In C. M. Gynn & S. R. Acker (Eds.), *Learning objects: Contexts and connections.* Columbus: The Ohio State University.

APPENDIX 14.1

We need to demonstrate that :

$$\sum_{i=1}^{n} \frac{1}{(1+r)^i} = \frac{(1+r)^n - 1}{r*(1+r)^n}$$

Proof :

Let $s_n = \sum_{i=0}^{n} \frac{1}{(1+r)^i}$ which can be expanded as follows :

$$s_n = 1 + \frac{1}{(1+r)} + \frac{1}{(1+r)^2} + \dots + \frac{1}{(1+r)^{n-1}} + \frac{1}{(1+r)^n}$$

Multiplying both sides of the last equation by $\left(\frac{1}{1+r}\right)$ we get :

$$s_n * \left(\frac{1}{1+r}\right) = \frac{1}{(1+r)} + \frac{1}{(1+r)^2} + \dots + \frac{1}{(1+r)^n} + \frac{1}{(1+r)^{n+1}}$$

Substracting $s_n * \left(\frac{1}{1+r}\right)$ from s_n the right hand sides collapse in the following manner :

$$s_n - \left(\frac{1}{1+r}\right) * s_n = 1 - \frac{1}{(1+r)^{n+1}}$$

Now we simplify the left part of the equation :

$$s_n * \left(1 - \frac{1}{1+r}\right) = \frac{(1+r)^{n+1} - 1}{(1+r)^{n+1}} \Rightarrow s_n * \left(\frac{1+r-1}{1+r}\right) = \frac{(1+r)^{n+1} - 1}{(1+r)^{n+1}} \Rightarrow s_n * \left(\frac{r}{1+r}\right) = \frac{(1+r)^{n+1} - 1}{(1+r)^{n+1}}$$

and multiply both sides by $\left(\frac{1+r}{r}\right)$ we get :

$$s_n = \frac{\left[(1+r)^{n+1} - 1\right] * (i+r)}{(1+r)^{n+1} * r} \Rightarrow s_n = \frac{(1+r)^{n+1} - 1}{(1+r)^n * r}$$

By the above definition $\sum_{i=1}^{n} \frac{1}{(1+r)^i} = s_n - 1$

But then we can write :

$$s_n - 1 = \frac{(1+r)^{n+1} - 1}{(1+r)^n * r} - \frac{(1+r)^n * r}{(1+r)^n * r} \Rightarrow s_n - 1 = \frac{(1+r)^{n+1} - 1 - (1+r)^n * r}{(1+r)^n * r} \Rightarrow$$

$$s_n - 1 = \frac{(1+r)^n * (1+r) - 1 - (1+r)^n * r}{(1+r)^n * r} \Rightarrow$$

$$s_n - 1 = \frac{(1+r)^n * [1 + r - r] - 1}{(1+r)^n * r} \Rightarrow s_n - 1 = \frac{(1+r)^n - 1}{(1+r)^n * r} \Rightarrow$$

$$\sum_{i=1}^{n} \frac{1}{(1+r)^i} = \frac{(1+r)^n - 1}{(1+r)^n * r}$$ which completes the proof.

15

IMPLICATIONS FOR PLANNING AND MANAGEMENT OF DISTANCE AND ONLINE LEARNING

William J. Bramble

University of New Mexico

Santosh Panda

Indira Gandhi National Open University

INTRODUCTION

As editors, we worked hard to identify the ideal contributors to this volume. We were not disappointed by the response to our request for authors. The chapter contributors comprise an impressive and expert set of scholars, persons who have experience and expertise gained from their significant participation and research in distance and online learning around the world. When we received the chapter contributions, we were impressed with both the breadth and depth of the content. Our direct focus for the book is on the economics of distance and online learning, but the variety of contexts in which economics can be assessed and the myriad of issues to be considered was in many ways unanticipated.

Let us highlight some of the issues and approaches illustrated in the chapter contributions in terms some of the themes they presented. The reader is referred to the individual chapters of this volume for a more thorough treatment of each theme.

FORM OF THE LEARNING SYSTEM

A first theme relates to the form of a distance or online learning system. For example, Hülsmann pointed out the differences between what may be termed the "Fordist" model for distance learning (named for Henry Ford's approach to mass production of automobiles; see Wagner, 1972; Jamison & Klees, 1975) and the e-learning approach that results from the ICT (information and communication technologies) revolution. Hülsmann distinguishes between two types of e-learning: Type-i, which capitalizes on the technical features of the technology, and type-c, which includes electronic means for high levels of interaction through communications technologies. He quite aptly points out that the largest cost savings, though not necessarily the best instruction, comes from the economy of scale possible with systems that follow the Fordist model. Both of the technology-supported options can enhance learning through technology, but type-c generally requires larger levels of investment.

Other contributors to this volume categorize distance and online learning in different ways. Jung focuses on virtual university education. She follows Van Dusen (1997) in defining a virtual university as "a metaphor for the electronic, teaching, learning and research environment created by the convergence of several relatively new technologies including, but not restricted to, the Internet, World Wide Web, computer mediated communication..." Jung points out that the factors driving fixed and variable costs in virtual universities include such things as the number of students and courses, interactive course features, employment schemes, technology development approaches, types of virtual courses, and student support mechanisms. Some of these factors are common to multiple systems of distance learning, but some are specifically relevant to virtual universities. In his chapter, Curran illustrates the variety of institutional strategies that are possible for distance learning through three archetypical university examples: Integrated, quasi independent, and separated; he also mentions a fourth possibility, consortia. He suggests that successful online learning programs require more active leadership and involvement of administrators and more thorough course and program planning. He notes that the approach can affect institutional mission and ethos.

Inglis points out that the form of a distance learning program relates to its costing. For example, costs differ among single mode providers, dual mode institutions, collaborative ventures, industrial training providers, etc. Many single mode providers are large systems in developing countries that benefit from economies of scale and have a large investment in their systems as constituted. As a consequence, they often lag behind in development. Such systems tend to embrace online learning in the context of their existing systems. Dual mode institutions, on the other hand, have evolved from a long history of campus-based instruction and are now adding the online component to campus-based programs. They often work independently and have brought a good deal of creativity to the process. One avenue they provide is the option for blended learning, in which course development costs can be leveraged from the alternative perspectives of on-campus vs. distance delivered instruction (see Moore, 2005). However, dual made institutions don't usually have the extent of distance education-related infrastructure that single mode institutions have. Collaborative ventures among dual mode institutions have the advantage of increasing inputs and reducing costs to the individual partners. Many such ventures have had large initial funding, but have failed as a result of inadequate business plans.

Inglis mentions that industrial training can be provided in-house or by outside vendors. Economies of scale can sometimes be obtained. Recently there has been an attempt to merge online training with knowledge management. Berge and Donaldson consider distance and online approaches to workplace learning, and stress the emphasis in workplace learning on return on investment or ROI. They noted that business organizations require a return on investment beyond the cost savings of an event or program. On the other hand, academic education is broader and more theoretically based. It generally has less interest in short term effects of learning. Strattner and Oblinger propose that stand-alone training is yielding to more comprehensive learning solutions for workplace learning. They note that this approach is being driven by increased competition, evolving work and lifestyle changes, and emerging technologies. Market drivers are globalization, a knowledge dependent economy, growth through innovation, and new business models. These factors have led to an increase in just-in-time training and embedded training.

The point that emerges from the first theme is that there are a number of forms that distance and online learning can take, and the specific form relates to the pattern of costs and strategies for cost comparisons among systems. As several of the authors mention, when you compare distance and online systems to their traditional counterparts there are differences in costing factors, most notably in the higher variable costs for traditional education (with its emphasis on a teacher for every classroom) and higher fixed costs for systems that involve higher investments in technology and courseware development.

DISTANCE AND ONLINE LEARNING
FROM A GLOBAL PERSPECTIVE

Every morning in Africa, a gazelle wakes up.
It knows it must run faster than the fastest lion or it will be killed.
Every morning a lion wakes up.
It knows it must outrun the slowest gazelle or it will starve to death.

It doesn't matter whether you are a lion or a gazelle.
When the sun comes up, you better start running.

The African proverb (above) is quoted in *The World is Flat* by Friedman (2005, p. 114). It illustrates the nature of increasing global competitiveness and, by implication, the consequent role of education in global economics.

Panda and Gaba focus on the development of distance education in India and other developing countries. They specifically discuss the emergence of mega-universities (institutions serving over 100,000 students) and some of the specific challenges they face (see Daniel, 1996). For cash starved universities all over the world, there are three considerations that Panda and Gaba see as paramount: Gross enrollment ratios, student fees, and the pattern of government and public expenditures. They note that in more developed countries there is an already large investment in education. Developed countries thus have a hesitancy about making additional large investments in mass education. In developing countries, where the established base of higher education is lower, distance education is often more appealing. Panda and Gaba describe differences in the financing of dual-mode vs. large state-sponsored, single-mode universities.

Smith and Bramble discuss the case of distance and online learning in the United States and point out that the largest source of public funding for U.S. universities is found at the state, rather than the national level. They describe how the strong, established base of K–12 and higher education in the United States has resulted from a long political and societal progression of legislation and other events. Smith and Bramble relate that the large installed base of colleges and universities and the strong base of communications and computer technology in the United States affects the form and the cost of the types of distance and online learning that are emerging. Jung suggests that external factors such as public funding policy, quality assurance concerns, and culture affect costs in virtual universities. She notes that public policies determine funding availability to universities for virtual education, but that these factors vary from country to country. Jung mentions that quality control may be easier to achieve in mega universities than in smaller contexts and that the local culture can determine which mode of education is preferred.

Open and distance learning have been used to increase access to higher education in developed and developing countries. Edirisingha explains how this is done through a number of organizational structures. Following on the work of Yates and Tilson (2000), who discuss seven types of models and approaches, Edirisingha proposes a classification system for open and distance learning based on four inter-related criteria: The audience served, curriculum/content offered, the location of provision, and the technologies and methods used. Edirisingha illustrates this classification system with examples of learning systems throughout the world.

To summarize the discussion under this second theme of the book—the context of education—in terms of the country or location in which it is developed, can affect the design and operation of a distance or online system of learning, and such factors will relate to the ultimate costs and funding of the systems.

LEADERSHIP ISSUES AND CONSEQUENCES OF CHANGE

Jung and others posit that information and communication technologies (ICT) have offered new possibilities and encouraged institutions to take advantage of Internet and Web technologies for learning. Curran notes that the growth of online learning is seen in developing countries, the United States, and in Europe, though directly comparable data are not readily available for all cases. Berge and Donaldson, citing the work of Peters (2000), assert that distance education has the power to alter traditional teaching and learning systems structurally and to accelerate the change. Distance and online learning is a dynamic, growing sector according to Edelson and Pittman. This is echoed by the other authors as they discuss the growth of this aspect of education throughout the world. Inglis notes that the last decade has seen a massive shift towards online learning in both distance education institutions and mainstream institutions. He suggests that much of this has resulted from a belief of senior managers that this approach will reduce costs through economy of scale. More recently, managers have realized that costs can also increase and that the main benefit of distance education may be an increase in quality.

Yet as Garrison and Kanuka note, all is not well in "River City." Institutions experience barriers (see Muilenburg & Burge, 2001) in planning and managing systems of distance and online learning and the communications and Internet technologies that support them. Innovations in technology have the potential to change education, but they have often been relegated to the margins and consist largely of adding to existing practices rather than constituting a "Brave New World" of their own. Smith and Bramble note that states provide much of the funding for distance education at public universities in the United States, but state funding formulae are often not favorable in their distribution of fixed and variable costs. Several authors add that the relative amount of funding by states for U.S. public universities has declined over the past decade or so.

Edelson and Pittman note that the development of distance and online learning programs has been encouraged by participating universities in the United States, but again note that they have been largely been at the margins of the institutions. Such programs have been used to generate a profit used to support less lucrative outreach activities. Such systems often become "cash cows"; they are often a small profit-making arm of large taxpayer-supported institutions. Edelson and Pittman also state that post secondary institutions vary widely in their proclivity to embrace online learning. The institutions may offer a few low budget items or market large ticket items such as MBA programs. In discussing myths and perceptions of e-learning, Edelson and Pittman refer to often asserted claims that e-learning will replace traditional learning, will increase democratization by improving quality of learning, and will speed tendencies towards globalization. However, it has not been proven that it will do any of these. Edelson and Pittman do predict that U.S. post-secondary enrollments via online courses continue to rise dramatically, that the U.S. government will provide increased support for education at a distance through financial aid and other means, and that students will become increasingly mobile in terms of selecting the institutions from which they take courses. They predict greater competition in this arena and a shakeout of unsuccessful schools in online learning, altering the landscape of higher education for the better. They feel that e-learning will promote the development of richer multimedia learning environments and will lead to scientific learning which will stress greater efficiency. This may reshape the professorate, perhaps reducing autonomy, shifting power toward institutions and away from faculty.

Interestingly, senior academic leaders appear somewhat unprepared to deal effectively with the changes generated by movement towards distance and online learning. As Garrison and Kanuka point out, leaders need to be prepared to re-examine and position their institutions for new and emerging methodologies, such as blended learning, in which traditional forms of instruction are merged with the new. Strong and creative leadership is needed. A critical challenge is coping with resistance to change. Budget constraints raise difficulties for distance and online learning. A starting point, however, is to provide for program redesign and technical support.

NEW MODELS FOR LEARNING:
OPPORTUNITIES AND CHALLENGES

The contributors to this volume all point out that distance and e-learning, despite having deep roots in earlier forms of distributed learning, constitute new forms of learning. They offer new possibilities for institutions, faculty, and most importantly, students. Jung states that ICT has offered new possibilities and encouraged institutions to take advantage of the Internet and Web technologies for learning. She notes that a new kind of institution, the virtual university, is made possible by these developments and that if such universities are started from scratch, there is the possibility for both broader access and lower overall costs. Berge and Donaldson focus on the capabilities of distance and online learning for workplace learning. They assert that online learning offers a fresh approach with new capabilities over traditional learning that has the power to alter traditional teaching and learning systems structurally and to accelerate the change. Smith and Bramble, among others in this volume, mention that a new role for the professorate of colleges and universities as content specialists may result from developments in distance and online learning.

On the other hand, Garrison and Kanuka note in their chapter that many North American institutions experience barriers in planning and managing communications and Internet technologies. He notes that technology innovations have the potential to change education, but they face challenges in existing universities and often consist of supplements to existing practices. Garrison and Kanuka, and Smith and Bramble in their two chapters discuss some of the revenue and governmental issues facing the budgeting of new programs such as distance and online learning. These issues have tended to hold back development. In describing the application of virtual schooling to the K–12 sector, Clark relates that the public is less sure about the value of the technique, though there tends to be greater enthusiasm for this among students. Again, the funding for this sector is less than might be desired.

Panda and Gaba in their chapter on single-mode universities in the Asian context point out the enormous potential of distance learning in this application. However, they see a dilemma in how to keep quality high and costs low in what is typically a cash-starved environment. Panda and Gaba conclude that funding for distance education in the institutions they review is different from that in conventional institutions and is affected by the stage of growth of a system, its client focus, its ability to generate resources, and the subsidy policy of its respective government. They note that in developing countries, dual-mode campuses are worse off in distance education. In dual mode institutions, distance offerings take a back seat in funding decisions, but in all institutions there is a host of problems to be worked out.

Strattner and Oblinger discuss the development of embedded workplace learning in their chapter. Embedded learning, which inserts learning activities into job tasks, emerges from several forces: (1) the need for just-in-time learning, (2) an understanding about how people learn, and (3) greater technology infrastructure and availability of technology. Through embedded learning, the act of learning becomes an aspect of the work process being performed; information is integrated into the worker's workflow, making it relevant and available to their work. The premise here is that the closer a person is to needing to know something to do his or her job correctly, the more motivated he or she is to learn. This creates new learning environment and an inherent "teachable moment."

The models for learning discussed above are a sample of those discussed in the book. They all encounter challenges in their funding, since they all tend to be "new kids on the block." With each of them come unique considerations in terms of planning for funding and assessing costs.

MODELS FOR STUDYING COSTS

Kearsley (1982) points out that there are a number of models that can be applied when studying the costs and benefits of education and training systems. In their discussion of cost effectiveness in distance education, Moore and Kearsley (1996, p. 71) assert that "the research questions of primary interest to educational administrators are about how to organize resources of people and capital in ways that will produce good results at the lowest cost." They note that there are several perspectives on this issue. One is the belief that telecommunications requires extremely expensive capital investment. A second is the counter argument that technology is less expensive than conventional, labor-intensive methods. A middle position is that most telecommunications systems are expensive, but may be cost-effective in delivering education to hard-to-reach areas or populations, especially when used intensively and extensively with large numbers of students. Moore and Kearsley also cite Kember's (1995) Open Learning Model for adult learners as an alternative pathway in a distance education course. The model includes a cost/benefit decision step for the student, in which students consider the costs and benefits of continuing their study.

So, what did the contributors to this volume have to say? Several of the chapter contributors speak directly to the issue of calculating the costs and related quantities in studying the economics of distance and online learning. They cite the work of earlier authors in looking at the economics of distance and online learning. Some examples are as follows. Jung cites the work of Bartolic-Zlomislic and Brett (1999), who used costing measures such as (1) capital and recurrent costs, (2) production and delivery costs, and (3) fixed and variable costs. The works of Whalen and Wright (1999) divided virtual training costs into fixed capital costs and variable operating costs. Capital costs are such costs as those for the server platform and content development. Operating costs are correlated with the time that students and instructors spend using the course. Jung and others cite the work of Rumble (2003), who suggests different methods of measuring average and total costs. Rumble lists the costs driving distance education as technology choice, course development, organizational structure, the curriculum, and the number of learners.

In his chapter on cost analysis, Hülsmann cites the work of Wagner (1972), who proposed the use of cost efficiency analysis in looking at open learning systems. Cost efficiency analysis relates cost inputs and outputs. The inputs are associated costs of providing the learning, and outputs are normally students taught and graduates. Wagner tried to adjust the cost in traditional institutions by taking the research costs of traditional institutions into account. He looked at average costs per students (dividing the costs by the relevant number of students), accounting for completion rates and differences in completion rates and fixed vs. variable costs. The finding was that traditional institutions experienced higher variable costs (especially the cost of professors) and distance education systems had higher fixed costs (technology and course development). Hülsmann also cites the work of Perraton (1987) in developing a *Costing Cube*. The costing cube shows the relationships among various fixed and variable costs in a system, some of which can or cannot be set by the planner. The costing cube then identifies the route to go in order to increase cost efficiencies. One important consideration is that there are clear trade-offs in the amount of interactivity provided by the system and its cost.

Hulsmann cites the work of Jewett (2000) and the earlier work of Keegan (1990, 1994), which proposes a cost model for distributed e-learning. Jewett's model unbundles the teaching tasks in distributed e-learning, showing that the number of faculty required increases more slowly for e-learning than for classroom teaching as the number of students increases. Hülsmann also cites the work of Rumble (1994), who notes that the economics of distance education systems will work differently at existing institutions vs. distance education universities and may favor institutions with broader programs. Rumble also notes the fear of existing institutions of an eroding student base, for which they will then compete with the distance education institutions.

Some of the proposed perspectives for studying the costs of distance and online learning presented in this volume follow.

FIXED VS. VARIABLE COSTS

Jung, following the work of Bartolic-Zlomislic and Brett (1999) and Whalen and Wright (1999), shows that the costs of distance and online learning can be classified into fixed capital and variable operating costs. Thus a basic model for cost analysis is that the total cost of a system is equal to the fixed costs of the system plus the variable costs multiplied by the number of students the system serves. Fixed costs are capital costs of equipment and content development, while variable costs are the costs associated with the students and instructors as courses are offered.

In discussing the costs of virtual university education, Jung notes that the costs of a virtual education system can be categorized in one of three ways: (1) capital and recurrent costs, (2) production and delivery costs, and (3) fixed and variable costs. Under any of these models, the average cost per student can be calculated. Jung suggests that a more detailed picture of costs is obtained following the approach of Whalen and Wright (1999), who divided the costs into fixed capital costs and variable operating costs. Capital costs represent the server platform and the cost of the content development. The costs for the content development include items such as instructional and multimedia design, production of digital materials, software development, content integration and modification, training, and testing. Operating costs include the costs for the time students and trainers spend using the courses. In general, key costs in virtual education can be divided into fixed costs, variable costs, and learner's opportunity costs (Jung, 2003). Fixed costs drop rapidly as more students are served, because of economies of scale (Puryear, 1999). Variable costs rise with increased numbers of students. Learner's opportunity costs offer another perspective, common to both traditional and online distance learning.

A basic model for distance education (and by extension distance and online learning) is as follows.

Total Costs   = Fixed Costs + Variable Costs
       = Fixed Costs + (Variable Cost per student x Number
         of students)

Average costs per student then are as follows.

Average costs per student   = Total Costs / Number of students
         = (Fixed Costs + Variable Costs) /
           Number of students
         = Fixed Costs/Number of students +
           Variable Costs/Number of students

Average costs can thus be represented as follows.

Average costs per student   = Fixed Costs/Number of students +
           Variable Cost per student

Learners' opportunity costs, which include foregone learner salary during the education period, add another dimension to this if one wishes to determine the attractiveness of a program for students. Opportunity costs could also be assessed for faculty, perhaps based on the work of Wolcott (1995) on faculty incentives and rewards. But, focusing on students, distance education systems have more favorable costs when student numbers are high and the number of courses developed is modest. Expensive approaches to learner interaction or the use of constructivist learning strategies (while perhaps advantageous pedagogically) can increase the variable cost of a system and create less favorable costs for distance learning. Jung asserts that a significant factor in looking at these costs is that traditional universities have the great majority of their expenditures in the areas of instructional costs, student services, academic support, plant operations and facilities, and research (Brown & Gamber, 2002; Chronicle of Higher Education Almanac, 2004), whereas their average expenditure on technology is only about 6% of budget. Virtual universities have shifted a significant portion of instructional costs to course development and have a higher proportionate investment in technology. In his chapter, Inglis discusses the issue of economies of scale in distance learning and the potential trade-off of large scale economies vs. careful attention to quality control.

Hülsmann further develops this methodology. His chapter begins with a consideration of the work of Peters (2000) and Rumble (1994, 2003). Hülsmann begins with a consideration of cost efficiency analysis, building on the work of Wagner (1972, 1977), Laidlaw and Layard (1974), Lumdsen and Ritchie (1975), Rumble (1976), Mace (1978), and Orivel (1987). Cost-efficiency relates costs of inputs to outputs. Cost-efficiency analysis can be used to compare intervention strategies by relating the size of outputs to the costs of inputs necessary to produce these outputs. Other things being equal, the preferred strategy is the one that produces the highest output at lowest costs. Hülsmann notes that in conventional universities, the cost of producing research must be taken into account when one studies the teaching outcomes, whereas in distance universities this is not a major consideration. He also notes (following the work of Wagner (1972) the preponderance of variable costs for professors in conventional universities. Thus there are particularly high variable costs associated with student numbers in conventional universities and consequently less opportunity for economy of scale in these institutions. A cautionary note here is that the greater drop-out rates (see the Simpson chapter) in single-mode distance universities mitigate this disadvantage somewhat and can be taken into account in applying specific models to calculate costs.

In discussing approaches to costing instruction with media, Hülsmann starts with the work of the World Bank and UNESCO in the 1970s and 1980s focusing on capital costs, especially those associated with instructional media. The approaches stress costs labeled as *opportunity costs* and *consumption of value*. This approach also employs the concept of an *annualization factor*, by which the planner has to multiply the upfront investment sum to get an annual cost, which incorporates the forgone interest. The *annualized investment* is then calculated by adding together all the annual installments.

An output measure could be for example *viewing or listening hours*. One can then calculate cost-efficiency measures (such as *average cost per student per learning hour*). This represents a measure of the cost-efficiency of the system, at least in a specific context. This is of course not cost effectiveness, since there is no measure of the success of the students in learning in the model. However, the results of this type of analysis provide information useful to instructional designers concerning alternative designs for learning systems.

SWOT ANALYSIS

The strength of distance education is that it holds the possibility of high quality teaching on the one hand, and the possibility of economies of scale on the other. Two *caveats* are: Bringing down the *average cost per student* does not mean bringing down total costs, and achieving true economy of scale may require a huge investment in a system to serve very large numbers of students. Because of this, distance education systems may not be affordable for resource-poor countries (Butcher & Roberts, 2004). While Perraton's *Costing Cube* (Perraton, 1987) identifies the route to go in order to increase cost-efficiencies, there are complications to the picture. The main *weakness* of interactive forms of distance education is the other side of the coin of its major strength, its cost-efficiency. And, while student/teacher interaction has been made part of the very definition of distance education (to distinguish it from learning through media), distance education interactivity has never been generally accepted as a substitute for the dialogue possible in conventional settings (Otto Peters' comments in Keegan, 1993, about the role of distance education in a postindustrial society notwithstanding). A weakness of dedicated distance teaching institution is the trade-off between *scale* and *scope* (*course load*, i.e., the number of courses an institution offers). Larger numbers of courses offer greater opportunities for student enrollment, but raise course development costs.

RETURN ON INVESTMENT

In their chapters, Berge and Donaldson, and Simpson consider the study of Return on Investment (ROI) to determine the value of distance and online learning. An example of this is ROI study reported by Osiakwan and Wright (2001), in which they assess the profitability points and return on investment figures for a particular distance training system for operating equipment. Berge and Donaldson note that in academic settings, education is broader and more theoretically based. The outcomes of learning are often far downstream, and the focus on immediate effects of learning, while simpler, may be of less ultimate importance. In the business world on the other hand, there is a bottom line to each operation, and training is an important factor in achieving business goals. Training is also important to determining workers' future earnings.

ROI addresses the issue of determining the benefit of training to a business organization. It is a technique developed at the DuPont Corporation to measure benefit vs. cost. It takes the following form.

$$\%ROI = (benefits / costs) \times 100$$

Or for the overall business

$$Net\ Income / Book\ Value\ of\ Assets = ROI$$

ROI works best for physical capital and equipment, but it has potential utility for studying costs in distance and online learning, especially when applied to training. ROI may fall short in assessing human capital, because of three problems with the technique: (1) obtaining accurate measures of full costs, (2) measuring benefits without relying on subjective estimates, and (3) isolating the impact of training on changes in performance. Some criticisms of ROI for measuring training impact are: (1) ROI is a traditional measure based on historical data, (2) since it is backward looking it offers no new insights into how to improve business results for the future, and (3) in educational applications ROI is used primarily for self-justification rather than continuous improvement.

Berge and Donaldson note that training is traditionally a good investment, yielding a variety of benefits. To study ROI they suggest that one could perform a gap analysis (what is vs. what should be), but that this is difficult for most managers. Another technique is to ask the students to set goals for themselves and then assess the benefits they expect to receive. Then managers can assess the value of the training to the company when comparing the expected benefits to future worker compensation. Berge and Donaldson assert that studying online learning through ROI analysis makes sense when one compares this new approach with alternatives. Following the recommendation of Conner (n.d.), the authors recommend measuring, at a minimum: Enrollment, activity, completion, scores, and feedback and surveys. In looking at ROI use in evaluating academic e-learning, the notable change is that of substituting media for instructors, so there are mass production opportunities. The value proposition for e-learning is given as

e-learning value = e-learning cost efficiency + e-learning quality + e-learning service + e-learning speed.

Using this formulation, one can see whether there are efficiency advantages to e-learning as compared with traditional instruction. This is backward looking, however. A better alternative may be to look at cost savings, performance improvement, and competitive advantage.

Simpson's chapter focuses on ROI as a tool to studying the costs and benefits of distance education, focusing in some detail on the experience of the British Open University. He defines ROI as the ratio of the financial benefits of an education to the investment in that education needed to obtain those benefits expressed as a percentage. He considers the study of ROI specifically for full-time students, educational institutions, and government.

Some unique contributions are the consideration of the "resale value" of qualifications, the "willing to pay" concept, and education as a risk investment (especially in view of retention issues). An important feature of Simpson's chapter is the discussion of student retention. He proposes a modification of Seidman's (2005) formula for looking at the retention issue as follows.

$$R = ACC + EId + (E + I + C).PaC + ExS$$

where R = Retention, E = Early, Id = Identification of vulnerable students, I = Intensive, C = Continuous, PaC = Proactive Contact, ACC = Accurate Course Choice, and ExS = External Support.

Conceptualizing retention in this way may allow the identification of factors in its improvement and allow comparisons in retention practices across distance and online systems of various types.

CONCLUSIONS

You can learn a good deal about the study of costs in distance and online learning by reading this volume. Above all, you will see that the economics of distance and online learning is a complex topic in which many models, techniques, and variables interplay.

Some of the many possible lessons to be gained from this volume by educators and administrators in institutions and organizations that use or are considering distance education are as follows:

1. Distance and online learning systems are developed for various purposes, in various types of institutions, and in various cultural and societal contexts. A common purpose is to expand access to post secondary education; this need is met differently through distance education, depending in part on the amount and types of existing educational infrastructure that exist in a country or region.
2. Cost structures vary depending on the type of system and context under study. For example, there are wide differences in cost structures between single mode and dual mode institutions, between Fordist and ICT and online constructivist models, etc.
3. There are international differences in cost structures and issues. Marked differences exist in the form and costs of distance learning systems in developed vs. less developed countries.
4. An analysis of the various costs involved in developing and operating distance and online learning systems can provide valuable information to planners and managers. The traditional comparative notion of distance and online learning vis-à-vis cost and productivity needs to be reconsidered.
5. Costs can be conceptualized from alternative viewpoints, including the managers of the system, the faculty, the students, the institution or consortium in which systems are housed, the national educational system and economy, etc.
6. Costs can be categorized in different ways. A common and useful breakdown for these systems is in terms of fixed and variable costs. A similar breakdown is capital and operating costs. In general, traditional education systems will include greater levels of

variable expenses, while distance institutions will include greater levels of fixed expenditures.

7. The costs of systems involving the significant use of technology are not necessarily lower than those of traditional education, and such systems are not necessarily panaceas for addressing a multitude of economic and societal issues.

8. Distance and online education costs can often be reduced on a per student basis when the number of students becomes very large. Systems need to be careful not to trade off quality in favor of economics of scale, however.

9. Real time interactivity increases the variable costs of distance and online learning, especially where instructor time is required. The reuse of learning objects (20s) in such systems may help to offset increased costs due to higher levels of interactivity.

10. Various approaches can be used for assessing the meaning of costs derived from a study of a system—these include cost comparisons, SWOT analysis, Return on Investment (ROI), etc. A researcher needs to fit the analysis to the information needs of the study.

These are only some of the many interesting perspectives offered in this book. Other points made by authors throughout the chapters may have implications for readers' practice of and decisions regarding online and distance education that we do not foresee. As such, the reader is encouraged to carefully review the content of the volume to more fully gain insight into the theory, experience, and potential issues as presented by the contributing authors.

REFERENCES

Bartolic-Zlomislic, S., & Brett, C. (1999). Assessing the costs and benefits of telelearning: A case study from the Ontario Institute for Studies in Education of the University of Toronto. Retrieved October 28, 2004, from http://research.cstudies.ubc.ca/.

Brown, W. A., & Gamber, C. (2002). Cost containment in higher education: issues and recommendations. *ASHE-ERIC Higher Education Report*, *28*(5). Washington, DC: The George Washington University, Graduate School of Education and Human Development.

Butcher, N., & Roberts, N. (2004). Costs, effectiveness, efficiency. In H. Perraton & H. Lentell (Eds.), *Policy for open and distance learning*. London: RoutledgeFalmer.

Chronicle of Higher Education Almanac. (2004). Finances of colleges and universities, fiscal year 2001. Retrieved November 15, 2004, from http://chronicle.com/prm/weekly/almanac/2004/nation/0103001.htm.

Conner, M. L. (n.d.). FAQ: How do I measure return on investment (ROI) for my learning program? Retrieved September 3, 2004, from http://www.learnativity.com/roi-learning.html.

Daniel, J. (1996). *Mega universities and knowledge media: Technology strategies for higher education.* New York: Kogan Page.

Friedman, T. L. (2005). *The world is flat: A brief history of the twenty-first century.* New York: Farrar, Straus & Giroux.

Jamison, D. T., & Klees, S. J. (1975). *The cost of instructional radio and television for developing countries.* Stanford, CA: Institute for Communications Research.

Jewett, F. I. (2000). Conceptual framework and terminology. In M. J. Finkelstein, C. Frances, F. I. Jewett, & B. W. Scholz (Ed.), *Dollars, distance, and online education: The new economics of college teaching and learning* (pp. 35–47). Phoenix, AZ: American Council of Education, Oryx Press.

Jung, I. S. (2003). A comparative study on the cost-effectiveness of three approaches to ICT teacher training. *Journal of Korean Association of Educational Information and Broadcasting, 9*(2), 39–70.

Kearsley, G. (1982). *Costs, benefits, and productivity in training systems.* Reading, MA: Addison-Wesley.

Keegan, D. (1990). *Foundations of distance education* (2nd ed.). London: Routledge.

Keegan, D. (Ed.) (1993) *Theoretical principles of distance education.* London: Routledge.

Keegan, D. (Ed.) (1994). *Otto Peters on distance education: The industrialisation of teaching and learning.* London/New York: Routledge.

Kember, D. (1995). *Open learning courses for adults.* Englewood Cliffs, NJ: Educational Technology Publications.

Laidlaw, B., & Layard, R. (1974). Traditional versus open university teaching method: A cost comparison. *Higher Education, 3,* 439–468.

Lumsden, K. G., & Ritchie, R. (1975). The open university: A survey and economic analysis. *Instructional Science, 4,* 237-291.

Mace, J. (1978). Mythology in the making: Is the open university really cost-effective? *Higher Education, 7*(3), 275–308.

Moore, M.G. (2005) Editorial: Blended learning. *The American Journal of Distance Education, 19*(3), 129–132.

Moore, M. G., & Kearsley, G. (1996). *Distance education: A systems view.* New York: Wadsworth.

Muilenburg, L., & Berge, Z. L. (2001). Barriers to distance education: A factor-analytic study. *The American Journal of Distance Education, 15*(2), 7–22.

Orivel, F. (1987). *Costs and effectiveness of distance teaching systems.* Dijon, France: IREDU.

Osiakwan, C., & Wright, D. (2001). Distance training for operating equipment: A cost-benefit and return-on-investment analysis. *The American Journal of Distance Education, 15*(1), 69–79.

Perraton, H. (1987). *The roles of theory and generalisation in the practice of distance education.* Hagen, Germany: Zentrales Institut für Fernstudien (ZIF).

Peters, O. (2000). *Learning and teaching in distance education: Pedagogical analyses and interpretation in an international perspective.* London: Kogan Page.

Rumble, G. (1976). *The economics of the open university.* Milton Keynes, UK: OU.

Rumble, G. (1994). The competitive vulnerability of distance teaching universities: A reply. *Open Learning, 9*(3), 47–49.

Rumble, G. (2003). Modeling the costs and economics of distance education. In M. G. Moore & W. G. Anderson (Eds.), *Handbook of distance education* (pp. 703–716). Mahwah, NJ: Erlbaum.

Wagner, L. (1972). The economics of the open university. *Higher Education, 1,* 159–183.

Wagner, L. (1977). The economics of the open university revisited. *Higher Education, 6,* 358–381.

Whalen, T., & Wright, D. (1999). Methodology for cost-benefit analysis of Web-based telelearning: Case study of the Bell Online Institute. *The American Journal of Distance Education, 13*(1), 23–44.

Wolcott, L. L. (1995). Faculty incentives and rewards for distance teaching. In B. S. Duning & V. V. Pittman (Eds.), *Distance education symposium 3: Policy and administration. Selected papers presented at the Third Distance Education Research Symposium* (ACSDE Monograph No. 11). University Park: The Pennsylvania State University.

Yates, C., & Tilson, T. (2000). Basic education at a distance: An introduction. In C. Yates & J. Bradley (Eds.), *Basic education at a distance* (pp. 3–26). London: RoutledgeFalmer.

INDEX

Page numbers in italic refer to figures or tables

287